LONDON PHOTOGRAPHERS
1841-1908

A DIRECTORY OF LONDON PHOTOGRAPHERS 1841-1908

MICHAEL PRITCHARD F.R.P.S.

REVISED AND EXPANDED EDITION

PhotoResearch
WATFORD

© Copyright Michael Pritchard 1986, 1994

British Library Cataloguing-in-Publication Data
A catalogue record for this book is available from the British Library

ISBN 0 9523011 0 5

Printed by
Lithoflow Ltd, 26-36 Wharfdale Road,
Kings Cross, London N1 9RY

Published by
PhotoResearch
38 Sutton Road, Watford, Hertfordshire. WD1 2QF. England
Tel: 0923 468356 • Fax: 0923 468509

Distributed by
ALLM Systems and Marketing
21 Beechcroft Road, Bushey, Hertfordshire. WD2 2JU. England
Tel: 0923 230150 • Fax: 0923 211148

Cover illustrations
The front cover illustration is taken from a carte de visite back and T. Bolas's The
Photographic Studio (Marion & Co., 1895). The back cover is a detail from a carte
de visite back issued by The Imperial Photographic Co. of 44 Baker Street, London.

CONTENTS

INTRODUCTION

The first edition of this directory[1] appeared in 1986 and proved to be very popular with photographic collectors, museums, historians and genealogists. The support of, especially, the Society of Genealogists in ordering the original edition has allowed this second, revised, edition to go ahead.[2]

The original idea behind the directory was to provide a handy reference to the 2500 or so photographers who were active in London between 1841 and 1908. The 1908 cut-off point was chosen as the Post Office directories altered their format at this point. The first edition relied primarily on the *Post Office London Directory*.

This second edition adds some extra information published in other printed sources, notably the contemporary photographic press, newspapers and *carte de visite* backs. Information contained in this edition should be more accurate and precise, although there will always be names lacking because of the nature of the reference material consulted. A new appendix provides a list of names of photographers about whom no other dating information has been found. This information has largely been taken from information printed on photograph backs.

The directory is part of a much wider research project being undertaken by the Royal Photographic Society's Historical Group to document photographers active in Britain to *c*.1910.[3] To date over thirty have been published ranging from some of the largest cities such as Birmingham, Glasgow and Manchester, to small towns such as Abingdon, Eastbourne and Watford. The project is on-going and new places are being added when the research has been completed and funds are available to publish the lists. The group would welcome offers to produce similar listings and has a leaflet giving hints on how to go about the task. A listing of those directories published to date

is given in Appendix 2. The group would welcome both further contributions to the series and financial support to aid publication.

The one area where it was hoped that the first edition of this directory would have stimulated a response was in locating collections of London studio photographs or the archives of London photographic studios. While it is likely that most photographers destroyed their negatives or left them behind when they gave up their business it is remarkable how little has survived. Over the years some collections have ended up in private or company collections, in museum archives and picture libraries and where found these have been noted. These do tend to be more specialist topographical or news photographs/negatives rather than portraits.

Very little information of this type has come forward and the author would welcome notification for publication in a future edition and, in the meantime, for recording in the specialist photographic history journals. Information relating to holdings of photographs, negatives or studio daybooks recording sitters and sitter reference numbers would be especially useful for family history researchers attempting to date family photographs.

LAYOUT

This book consists of two distinct parts. The first part comprises chapters which discuss the use of directories as a research tool and details their particular advantages and disadvantages. This is followed by chapters that discuss the rise of photography generally and, more specifically, in London.

The second part is the directory of photographers giving their main name changes, addresses and dates of occupation at their various addresses. For selected companies a brief history, based on research in the contemporary literature is given. By their nature these firms tend to be the better known of the period. This is concluded with appendices which add further photographers which do not appear as photographers in the *Post Office London Directories* and a list of other directories of early photographers.

HOW TO USE THIS DIRECTORY

It is expected that the main use of this book will be in the dating of *cartes de visite* and family photographs - although the information may form the basis for a geographical/economic study in its own right and as a quick reference for photographic historians.

The directory has largely been compiled from the *Post Office London Directory* and its form follows the conventions, however idiosyncratic, used there. Some of the contractions of words used in the original directories have been expanded to make this book easier to use. Original variations in the names of companies and individuals have been retained, except where there has been an obvious misprint in the Post Office directory. Slight variations in names should be cross-checked against similar entries. All changes in company names, for example the adding of 'Limited' or 'and Company', street name and numbering have been retained as this may help to date more precisely an address appearing on a photograph.

One important point to remember is that the *Post Office London Directory* only covered the central area ie. the postal districts of N, S, W, E, WC, EC. Places which we now consider as 'London' may not be covered here and will require individual search in directories for these outer areas. The coverage of these directories improved throughout the nineteenth century. The Guildhall Library and local history collections in the outer London boroughs have good collections of these directories.

DATING PHOTOGRAPHS

Genealogists and those researching their family history will find this book of particular use as an aid to dating their photographs. The limitation of the source material is noted in the following chapter but this directory should prove useful where other information is limited. In many cases the printed information on a photograph is the only clue to it's date and even an approximate date may assist the family historian in identifying a likely family member.

The numbering of London's postal districts can be of help in providing a rough date for a photograph. In 1856 London, as it then was, was divided into ten postal districts: EC, E, WC, W, N, NW, SE, SW, S and NE, of which the last two were dropped within a few years. In 1917 numbered sub-districts were introduced. The 1s and central districts corresponded to the original divisions with the additional districts from two onwards in alphabetical order (with a few irregularities). For example, the Eastern district became E1 whilst Bethnal Green sub-district became E2 and Bow became E3.

Aside from printed information on a photograph or the mount the image itself may also be of use in ascribing a date. The photographic process can act as a rough means of dating an image or, at least, in setting a lower limit on age.[4] There are several books on dating photographs using costume and these may also prove useful.[5] With both these areas the advice of specialists should be sought.

There are some general dating hints for the non-photographic specialist which may be of use. The principal processes seen as 'photographs' during the period to 1908 are: the daguerreotype, the ambrotype, albumen print and gelatin-silver print. Other processes perhaps with the exception of the tintype are encountered far less often as family photographs.

The daguerreotype is a silvered copper plate with a mirror-like surface and was generally used from 1841 to the early 1850s. The ambrotype is a photographic emulsion on glass and was in use from the early 1850s to the 1890s. These two processes were often mounted in morocco cases, pâpier maché frames or thermo-plastic 'union' cases or as items of jewellery.

The later two processes are paper photographs. The albumen print was introduced in 1850 and was in general use until about 1900 and is usually seen on earlier cartes de visite. The highlights and lighter areas are often creamy-yellow in colour with the darker areas ranging from black to sepia. The gelatin-silver print was introduced around 1880 and is still in use today.

The image can be on a variety of paper bases and it's colour can range from black and white to sepia to a variety of colours depending on whether it was toned or not. It can often exhibit silver oxidisation at the edges. The prints may be loose, mounted on to a variety of cards or mounted and framed.

In addition to these four major processes there are were many, many, others. Some were slight chemical variants on the above while others, such as the carbon print, for example, can be considered a new process. The ferrotype or tintype is perhaps the only other common process found as family photographs. They are generally dark-looking images on tin and were often produced by itinerant photographers at the seaside or at fairs. In general the genealogist is unlikely to meet many of the other processes: they were often expensive at the time or were generally used for more 'artistic' photography.

One point which should be remembered is that then, as now, a photograph could be copied and although the image may use a later process the original could well have been made earlier - experience can often tell if this has been done.

Although this book is largely concerned with professionally taken photographs amateurs were taking photographs from 1839 and were responsible for many of technological advances in the new medium. In general terms it was not until the 1880s with the development of dry plates and rollfilm that amateur photography became easier, and therefore more widely practised.

The first Kodak camera was sold from 1888 and the Brownie camera from 1900. These two products along with similar cameras from other camera manufacturers did more than anything to encourage the spread of amateur snapshots. Most amateur-made prints from this later period will be on gelatin-silver paper or printing-out paper. Professional photofinishing for amateurs did not make much impact before the later 1890s, but the discovery of a print wallet can be a dating clue in its own right.

Rollfilm became accepted for amateur cameras with the 1888 Kodak and Redding's Luzo camera and simple contact prints from negatives were generally all that were produced. Enlargements were only made infrequently and then only from special negatives. Professionals had the facilities to enlarge and reduced their larger plate negatives from the 1860s although generally most professional prints were contact prints from large glass plates that had one or more positions photographed on to it.

The photographic process may help to narrow a date down to a particular period, the address and photographer's details printed on the mount (which is what this book is designed to assist with) may help this further still and the image with its props and sitter's clothing may also help to set upper and lower dates. With luck all of these variables together with what the family historian knows of the expected age and sex of a likely sitter and circumstantial information such as a photograph's location in an album adjacent to a dated *carte* will give a date to a photograph within three to five years of its actual date.

This may not be very precise by some standards but for the family historian, often with very little other information, and with up to 150 years between then and now, it does not seem too unreasonable.

ACKNOWLEDGEMENTS

This book has taken an immense amount of time and many people have provided help.

The initial research was encouraged by Arthur T. Gill Hon.FRPS the first Chairman of the Royal Photographic Society's Historical Group. Dr. Alan Harris, formerly Reader in Geography at the University of Hull, supervised my final year dissertation on which part of the text of both editions was based. Both Arthur Gill and Dr. Harris through their respective writings and own careful research methods have influenced my work and have acted as an ideal to aim for.

On the production side my father, Alan Pritchard of ALLM Systems and Marketing, spent time transferring the original directory from a Wordstar file to one suitable for direct typesetting and page layout using the Xerox Ventura desktop publishing package.

For very specialist books such as this desktop publishing (DTP) provides a low-cost solution and is surely where the future of small-scale publishing lies. *PhotoResearch* hopes to launch further specialist photo-history reference and source books which commercial publishers would not consider handling. A number of projects are already being researched.

The Guildhall Library, library of the Royal Photographic Society and Science Museum Library have all been of use. India Dhargalkar, Head of Photographs at Christie's in London allowed me to use the Photographs Department reference library. George Glastris provided a collection of *cartes* for examination from his own collection. Ian Leith from the National Monuments Record has been particularly helpful in looking through the directory for names represented in the NMR collection and adding material for entries on photographers represented in their collection. Terry Binns provided information on one major collection, Terence Pepper of the National Portrait Gallery allowed me access to the Silvy daybooks, John Kirkham of Barnardos, Ann Sylph of the Zoological Society of London, Mark Haworth-Booth and Sue Percival of the Hulton-Deutsch Collection have all helped.

Collectors and dealers have assisted in adding information to the directory and are proof that photographic collecting remains a friendly area where dealers have a commitment beyond purely commercial considerations. Beryl Vosburgh the owner of Jubilee in Pierrepoint Row, Camden Passage, London, has been an enthusiastic supporter of the directory and has been generous with her own time and in providing access to her personal collection and shop stock. She is a very special person within the photo-history community.

Nick Smith of Victorian Memories, PO Box 65, Henly-on-Thames, Oxon RG9 3PL together with David Hooper of 36 Flag Lane North, Upton Heath Chester CH2 1LE have been of particular help, they deserve special mention for all their support. Both carry stocks of *cartes* for sale and will look out for particular 'wants'.

Those listed below have provided names of photographers since the first edition of this book which are principally incorporated into Appendix 1: Keith I. P. Adamson (who has also generously provided unpublished information on London daguerreotypists from his own meticulous research), David Appleby, C. E. John Aston, A. A. Berrends, P. E. Coker, Jane Collet-White, Marion E. Francis, Roger Jones, E. Grant Longman, Valerie McLeish, Philip Mernick, A. J. Munday, Ian C. Munro, Margaret I. Raven, Dr. R. W. Rimmer, Michael Sandover, Arabella Seymour, J. H. Seymour, Bill Smith, P. A. Sykas and Peter Wright.

DIRECTORIES AND SOURCES

As photographic historians often discover general trade and local directories can often provide the only reference to a photographer or photographic company.

They are not, however, a perfect research tool largely as a result of their compilation and the information contained within them should be used with some caution. If available, contemporary newspaper reports and comment in photographic periodicals can add information and provide snippets of information that can be used to build a wider picture of a firm. Such research is often time-consuming and may not prove very rewarding.[6]

THE EVOLUTION OF THE LONDON DIRECTORY

The first known London directory appeared in 1677 but the origin of the directory as known today originates with the passing of a Parliamentary bill in 1765 requiring streets to be named and houses to be numbered. London with a large population and range of trades was the

An extract from the Post Office London Directory from 1864 (left) and 1902 (right).

area where directory publishers had the greatest potential for selling their product.

The first *Post Office Directory of London* was published in 1799. The 1837 edition was acquired by Frederick Kelly who in 1840, as Kelly and Company, found it expedient to bring the publication into line with its more popular rivals issued by Pigot and Robson. The directory size increased and gained a *Trades* section. The directory was further improved in 1841 by the addition of a street directory.

In 1855 the Kelly directory absorbed its last main competitor Watkin's *Commercial and General London Directory and Court Guide* and became supreme as the Kelly *Post Office London Directory*. The Kelly directories have been used extensively throughout this work. Goss[7] provides an extensive and detailed survey of the London directories and Kelly publications.

DIRECTORY COMPILATION AND PROBLEMS

Norton states: *"A glance at any two directories of the same place for the same year will reveal disconcerting differences"*.[8] These differences limit the usefulness of the directory and are

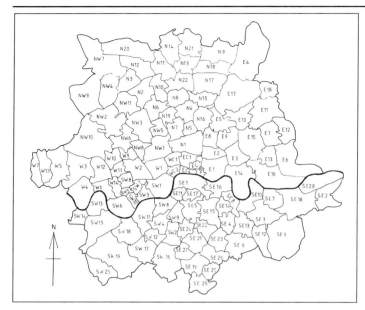

The London postal districts reference map. The introduction of postal codes provides the historian and geographer with a useful research tool (see page 8).

partly the result of the original compilation. Despite this publishers, in order to preserve their reputation, would usually make some attempt to ensure that the material published was reasonably accurate. Those produced by local publishers often have an advantage over those produced by a stranger to the area as the local compiler would have a greater local knowledge. Some of the large publishers such as Kelly, Pigot and White generally made use of local people or experts trained in collecting information.

The actual method of compilation varied and these reflect on the accuracy of the publication. Some information was collected door-to-door by using local people such as booksellers, by agents of the publishers paid by commission, by using other published sources and checking locally, by leaving circulars to be filled up, by advertisements, and by total piracy of previous editions. Generally there was an unwillingness by the public to supply information and methods such as circulars or advertisements frequently produced a poor response. In some cases firms were asked to pay for insertions which also resulted in an incomplete coverage. Other firms saw the

directory entry as a free form of advertising and endeavoured to secure as many listings as possible under different trade headings in order to promote their business.

Although a directory may be 'for' a particular year the actual date of publication and period over which the information was compiled is often difficult to ascertain. Dating may be helped by the inclusion of a date in the preface or in the advertisements usually contained within the directory. The date of publication and any such date contained with the text rarely coincide *"it is obvious that such dates are not exactly applicable to the data in the directory which will have taken a period of time to collect and print"*[8] The variance of the data with the actual situation at a given date will vary depending on the degree of mobility of the population in the area concerned and the time taken in the process of production.

As an example Kelly's *London Post Office Directory* for 1840 contains a preface dated 25 November 1839 and the information was collected in September 1839 and later revised. Generally, the interval between collection and publication seems to have been two to three months. The possibilities of checking the information in one directory by comparison with others of the same date are limited.

The use of directories for historical research provides other problems which are not directly related to the collection of information. Industrial migration and, therefore, locational change may be traced through directory material provided any radical changes in the name of the firms are known.[9] The finding of names of streets is easy but the actual streets may have been destroyed or re-sited. A long road may have evolved from an accretion of lesser roads, terraces and places as, for example, in Commercial Road, Mile End Road and Old Kent Road in London. The principal problem when attempting to relate directory details to maps is that the re-naming of roads has frequently been accompanied by re-numbering. In 1929 and 1955 the re-naming authority for London, the London County Council, published fully annotated lists of street naming orders by number and date with map references, which can assist the researcher.

The first re-naming order made by the Metropolitan Board of Works on the 20 February 1857 gave the name Pentonville Road to the "New Road" from the Angel to Kings Cross. A review of the Hackney directory of 1872 gives an indication of the change occurring in three suburbs of inner London. From a total of 485 streets in which furniture makers were entered 130 were affected by street naming orders, a proportion of over 25%. The same is probably true for photographic studios.

Despite these drawbacks the London Post Office directories are superior to all the general directories in the wealth of information contained and the span of time covered. Their major asset is that they provide a set of consistent and comparable data from photography's beginnings and, although there were undoubtedly errors of omission, there were few of commission. One other reason for the under-representation of photographic studios in directories is that the photographic studio was not the main occupant of a building

and another business is listed instead. Allied to this is the fact that the studio may have been a sideline to a more established business which was listed instead.

As a general guide directories may not record a photographic studio in the edition one year after its establishment and may record it for a year after its eventual demise. Despite their faults directories are an essential tool for the historian. The *Year Book of Photography* for 1888 had an apposite paragraph on Kelly's directories: "*If we are to believe the Professional and Trades' Section of the Ealing, Acton, Hanwell, Gunnersbury, and Chiswick Directory, issued for 1887 and 1888 by Messrs. Kelly and Co., of Great Queen Street, there are only two photographers in the whole of the above- mentioned districts; but we do not believe the Directory. At one time Kelly's Directories were representations of the districts included, and we have known the time when those wishing to get a list of photographers advantageously referred to Kelly's books. If the Directories are to be like that to which we have referred, the sooner we have authoritative official Directories the better. The Postal authorities might easily undertake their production and publication.*"

OTHER SOURCES

The information in the Post Office directories form the basis of this book. But, where available, other sources have been consulted although an exhaustive survey has not been undertaken for this edition.

During the early years of photography up to the 1860s the medium was still new and exciting enough to attract comment in contemporary newspapers and periodicals. The *Times* newspaper, particularly, reported the opening and attendances at the early Beard and Claudet studios and the *Art Journal* reported on developments in photography, both technical and artistic. After this general coverage waned and reports became much less - unless there was a wider news interest.

Photographic periodicals were slow to become established - which is why the early newspaper reports are so important - and it was not until 1853 that the Photographic Society of London was established and commenced publication of its *Photographic Journal*. The *British Journal of Photography* from 1854 and, especially, the *Photographic News* from 1858 are all important sources of reports on developments in photography, visits to studios and for news items regarding studios.

Exhibition catalogues of photographic and more general exhibitions at a national and local level may also be of use.

Patents and design registrations also provide information about photographers in the early years when the division between the manufacturing firms and studios was much less clearly defined than it was to become later in the nineteenth century.[10]

In a few instance company records may have been deposited or acquired by museums or libraries. Where these have been found they are noted in the text. Unfortunately, most seem to have been destroyed and it has only been in the last twenty years that institutions have taken an active interest in acquiring such documentary material.

Occasionally a photographer has published his biography and while the information given may be selective and anecdotal it can often add interest to a research project. John Werge's *The Evolution of Photography* published in 1890 attempts to be a history of photography but its real interest lies in his recollections of meeting some of the photographers and photographic manufacturers from the 1850s onwards.

From the 1920s such photographic biographies became more common from press photographers and those who had a story of wider interest to tell. Such works may not be of very much use to the genealogist but the photographic historian can make use of their material.

THE GROWTH OF EARLY PHOTOGRAPHY

Photography was not a typical innovation. Unlike most new discoveries it did not build upon earlier processes or products already in commercial use. It created a demand for itself which was only limited by commercial restraints and restrictions imposed by those controlling the patents needed to operate the early processes.[11]

THE DAGUERREOTYPE

The first commercially successful photographic process was announced by L. J. M. Daguerre in Paris during August 1839. Within Britain it was in London that the daguerreotype process first established itself and spread out to the provincial towns and cities of the country. Commercial entrepreneurs saw the possibilities to make money, but while Europe and the world were able to use the process freely England was not.[12]

H. de St Croix who had attended Daguerre's first demonstrations started similar shows in London on 13 September 1839. Shortly afterwards Miles Berry obtained an injunction compelling him to cease and charged him with patent infringement. Berry, acting on Daguerre's behalf, had obtained an English patent for the daguerreotype process on 14 August 1839 (number 8194). This action, at odds with Arago's boast to the French Chamber of Deputies that France would present the daguerreotype "free to all the world", had a major effect on the commercial exploitation of the process in England. Berry had, in Daguerre's words "full authority to act as he thinks fit".

Richard Beard purchased the right to use the process for £150 annually and in June of 1841 bought outright Daguerre's patent rights for the process in England. Beard had opened London's first studio on 23 March 1841 on the roof of the Royal Polytechnic Institution in London's Regent Street.

Despite the patent rights Antoine Claudet opened a studio in June 1841 in a glasshouse on the roof of the Royal Adelaide Gallery, just off the Strand in London. Claudet had learnt the process from Daguerre and had purchased a license directly from him to practice it in England. Claudet, rather unfairly, considered Beard a "wideawake speculator".

Thus, London's first two commercial photographic portrait studios opened in 1841. With Beard's control over the granting of licenses to practice the process, the number of studios grew slowly and opened only where Beard wanted them.

RICHARD BEARD 1801-1885

Richard Beard played a major role in determining the location of the early photographic studios and it is appropriate to include a biography. To date little has been discovered about the man and his relation with photography. One paper, on which this section is primarily based[13] has brought some material together, this work adds to that information.

Beard was born on the 22 December, 1801 in Devon. He developed a shrewd business acumen which would be important in his dealings in photography. By early 1833 he moved to London and became a partner in a firm of coal merchants which he soon took over. The first evidence of the expansion of his activities dates from June 1839 when he filed a patent relating to the colour printing of calicoes and other fabrics.

It is not unreasonable to assume that he quickly became aware of the fact that Miles Berry, acting on Daguerre's instructions, had filed a patent for "Obtaining Daguerreotype Portraits, etc". His meeting with an instrument

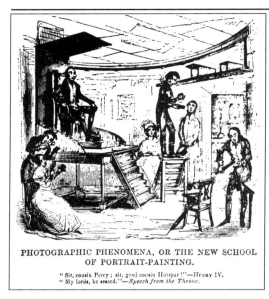

PHOTOGRAPHIC PHENOMENA, OR THE NEW SCHOOL
OF PORTRAIT-PAINTING.

" Sit, cousin Percy ; sit, good cousin Hotspur !"—HENRY IV.
" My lords, be seated."—*Speech from the Throne.*

Figure 1. Richard Beard's London studio in 1842, from a woodcut by George Cruickshank.

maker, William S. Johnson, who had come to find an English buyer for the recently invented Wolcott mirror camera, was important. Beard saw the advantages of this camera and, following an agreement with Johnson, patented it in June 1840. Beard paid £200 and expenses for one half of the invention, the remaining half, with all profits, he purchased for £7000.

Beard wanted to see an early return on his investment and he employed a chemist John F. Goddard to reduce the exposure times needed to produce a daguerreotype in order to make it practicable for human portraiture. Once Goddard had solved this Beard went ahead and opened England's first public photographic studio in the Royal Polytechnic Institution at 309 Regent Street in March 1841. Beard had made a very astute choice for the location of his studio.

The Polytechnic Institution had opened in 1838 and had been established for "the advancement of practical science in connection with agriculture, the arts and manufactures". It

had become the natural meeting place for many of London's inhabitants, visitors and elite.

Following his success Beard realised if he could secure a monopoly he could become very rich. In his first three months of operation his receipts had totalled £3000. He accordingly negotiated two agreements: one with Miles Berry and the other with Daguerre. As a result he became sole patentee of the daguerreotype process in "England, Wales and the town of Berwick-upon-Tweed, and in all Her Majesty's Colonies and Plantations abroad". Beard probably paid about £800 for these rights. Beard opened two other establishments in London: 85 King William Street in the City and 34 Parliament Street in Westminster. At both of these customers had free admittance, whereas if they went to Regent Street they had to pay an entrance fee of one shilling to enter the Institution.

Within three months of opening his own studio Beard was involved in making detailed arrangements to sell licenses authorising the setting up of "Photographic Institutions" in other parts of England. The first provincial studio was opened towards the end of June 1841 in Plymouth. Research originally undertaken for this book uncovered previously unknown Beard studios. Beard assigned licenses for either a specific town or city or on a county-wide basis. By 1842 he had received over £6000 in respect of licenses, in addition, he also exclusively supplied materials and frames for the process.

From 1846 Beard decided against personal involvement in the opening of new studios and instead offered licenses for the London area to independent operators. Competition from other daguerreotype artists (originally granted licenses by Beard) caused Beard to seek out fresh opportunities for his own business which he did by developing new techniques which would give him the edge over his competitors or lead to favourable press reviews. If his ideas were infringed Beard would defend his interests with typical aggressiveness.

Bright, James	
183 Strand	2 December 1845
J. Le Beau	
Hackney Road	12 February 1846
— Joseph	
62 Picadilly	25 April 1846
Redman and Co.	
108 Fleet Street	11 June 1846
Brokenshir	
256 Strand	18 August 1846
— Cubitt	
Edgware Road	21 August 1846
Wynn and Co.	
76 Cornhill	
62 Picadilly	14 September 1846
— Sharp	
Duke Street, London Bridge	12 October 1846
J. Barratt	
222 Regent Street	15 October 1846
H. Paine	
Hopkin's Bdgs, Islington	10 December 1846
W. E. Kilburn	
—	9 February 1847
G. M. Bright	
183 Strand	25 February 1847
A. J. Cocke	
44 Regent Street	30 March 1847
J. H. Croucher & Co.	
22 Ludgate Hill	7 April 1847
J. E. Mayall (Prof. Highschool)	
433 West Strand	18 May 1847
Miss Wigley	
Anderson Street, Chelsea	2 July 1847
108 Fleet Street	11 May 1848
Miss Hamilton	
Frith Street, Soho	29 May 1848
Silvester Laroche	
65 Oxford Street	23 August 1848
Mouque and Colas	
105 Cheapside	10 May 1849
Reeves	
Charing Cross	31 May 1849

Beard defended his patent rights through the courts on a number of occasions culminating in the *Beard v. Egerton* case that lasted between 1845 and 1849. The courts found in Beard's favour, a clear opinion being expressed as to the infringement of the patent and its validity. The case, however, led to Beard's bankruptcy application of 1849 which was granted in 1850. Despite this, Beard continued to operate and set up new establishments with the help of his son Richard Beard junior.

From the mid-1850s Beard's photographic activities within London began to contract. The Royal Polytechnic Institution was vacated by him during 1854, his Westminster premises changed hands and the City establishment moved. The contraction within London was counterbalanced by an expansion which took place in the north-west of England. Partnerships formed by Beard with others in Liverpool and Manchester utilised the new wet-collodion process given freely to the country by Scott Archer.

Beard had left the photographic scene completely by 1860. Richard Beard junior established himself as an india-rubber manufacturer and he left for America at the end of the decade. Beard senior finally set up in business as a "medical galvanist". He eventually retired to Hampstead where he died on the 7 June 1885.

Table 1. London daguerreotypists identified from the pages of the London Times newspaper.

This list prepared by Keith I. P. Adamson details twenty London photographers. Some quickly faded from the scene, others lasted a few years, and some prospered and went on to enjoy long, successful careers in photography.

It includes names not noted by the Post Office London Directory and others with addresses earlier than hitherto recorded - an indication of the problems of the directory as an historical source.

THE CALOTYPE

A second photographic process, W. H. Fox Talbot's calotype process on paper, was less popular than the daguerreotype. It gave a rather course image (although some would claim it more artistic) compared to the very clinical daguerreotype. The calotype was, in fact, the forerunner of modern photography by virtue of the fact that it produced a negative and a positive while the daguerreotype produced only a positive. The calotype's commercial growth was again severely limited, this time by Talbot's tight control over licenses and only one calotype

Table 2. The earliest recorded photographic studios in selected towns and cities.

London	1841
Bath	1841
Brighton	1841
Cheltenham	1841
Liverpool	1841
Nottingham	1841
Plymouth	1841
Southampton	1841
Birmingham	1842
Leeds	1842
Manchester	1842
Oxford	1842
Sheffield	1843
York	1843
Cambridge	1844
Hull	1844
Leicester	1844
Doncaster	1845
Kingston	1854
Rotherham	1854
Cardiff	1855
Peterborough	1856
Norwich	1859
Watford	1859
Abingdon	1863
Beverley	1872
Eastbourne	1877

studio, run by Henry Collen, opened in London. It was located at 29 Somerset Street, Duke Street, from August 1841.

THE RISE OF THE PHOTOGRAPHIC STUDIO

It was not until the introduction of the wet collodion process in 1851 that the number of photographic studios grew significantly. Frederick Scott Archer introduced the process and, importantly, deliberately chose not to patent it. The process was freely available for all to use. Talbot issued injunctions against photographers using the new process, claiming that it infringed his calotype patent. It did not and once this case was settled in the courts against Talbot the number of commercial studios multiplied. The expiration of the daguerreotype patent in 1853 and Talbot's dropping of the renewal of his calotype process patent meant England, for the first time since 1841, was free to practice any process.

From the mid-1850s the only limitation on the setting up of a commercial studio was a demand for the product and the usual economic forces, and the ability to successfully operate the process. The growth of studios seems to have reached a peak by the early 1870s after rapid growth (figure 2). From 1880 it grew only in line with the population and demand. A trend which London clearly illustrates. The rapid growth of studios in London reduced the cost of portraiture dramatically from the early 1850s and encouraged the *carte* mania of the late 1860s. The family portrait album became an essential part of every household.

PHOTOGRAPHY AND DIFFUSION

Photography spread out from London across the country. The movement outwards was neither even nor consistent. Interestingly, from a geographic point of view, a clear spatial

LONDON STUDIOS 1841-1908

No. OF STUDIOS

Figure 2. The growth of the London photographic studio based on entries in the Post Office London directories. Slight initial growth only increased when Richard Beard relaxed his hold over the daguerreotype patent and Scott Archer's wet-collodion process was announced in 1851. Thereafter growth was rapid until it reached a plateau in the late 1860s. It remained steady until the turn of the century.

relationship between Beard's licensees and population levels exists.

Few Beard licensees appear to have operated in a town with a population of less than 30,000 people. The three exceptions to this are Cambridge (24,000), Oxford (24,000) and Southampton (28,000) all of which had large visiting and changing populations which would have provided an extra source of trade. As more licensees come to light it will be possible to define this threshold for Beard licensees more accurately.

Table 2 gives the dates of the first known studio for selected towns and cities.

LONDON AND PHOTOGRAPHY

London was the initial centre of photography in Britain and was the point from which it spread across the country. The spread and growth of photography through time is shown in figure 3. At this level a general trend can be discerned. Photography was initially concentrated in the traditional market core of London in the W1, WC1 and N1 postal districts in 1859. During the period up to 1899 photographic studios continued to concentrate in these areas and spread to neighbouring postal districts including those just south of the river Thames.

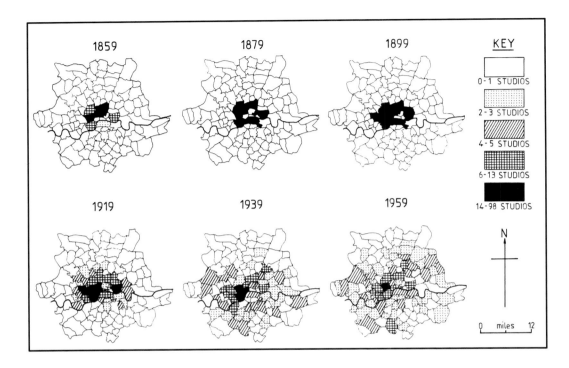

Figure 3. The spread of photographic studios in London 1859-1959. The general pattern is one of initial concentration followed by movement out from the centre, following the rise in population at the edge of the city.

However, by 1919 the pattern had changed significantly. Photographers were still concentrated in the 'West End' of W1, SW1 and WC1 but elsewhere the major concentrations had lessened and there was a spread of photographers further out in to the greater London area. Photographers still remained in the centre of London, but this ring had expanded.

The period up to 1939 and 1959 continued these trends so that by 1959 the only significant concentration of photographers remained in W1 with lesser concentrations in the postal districts surrounding W1.

In addition, compared to earlier years, the area covered by photographers had increased and actually reached the postal districts in the west, south and east at the limits of the London postal area.

The actual streets where the photographic studios concentrated indicate the importance of demand and the public. During the early history of the photographic studio the studios grouped at places where a good crowd could be expected, for example, the Royal Polytechnic Institution and the Adelaide Gallery or on fashionable streets notably Regent street, Oxford street, Piccadilly and certain other streets in the City and Westminster. In 1861 21 out of 153 (14%) studios were listed with addresses in Regent street.

The concentration on these streets and others close by was the result of the need to have a continuous passing trade and to be convenient for those customers that had booked a sitting. The type of person who would want a sitting would be relatively wealthy and would, probably, be visiting other shops in the area. The photographic studio did not generally occupy a shop front on to the street but took over the upper story of the building and the roof. A side entrance on to the main street (usually just a doorway) would allow access to the studio and its reception rooms.

Studios benefited from the proximity of other shops and attractions such as theatres which drew people to the area and helped publicise the studio. Personal recommendation between friends would help business which the studio could capitalise on if it was located in an area frequented by the customer's friends.

Essentially the studios in the central London area were demand orientated. They were located where there were the greatest number of people or, at least, where there existed a number of people over a certain threshold. It is unlikely that a conscious decision was made - the area seemed "natural" and appeared to satisfy certain criteria relating to numbers. There is no sign that corner sites were occupied in preference to middle sections of streets as might result from a conscious decision.

This concentration around the Oxford Street, Regent Street, Holborn, City and Westminster areas and the later attractions of South Kensington and Chelsea remained throughout the whole period. The growth of London to incorporate previously separate settlements added new areas of attraction. In particular, Islington, Nottinghill, the East End, St John's Wood and the area immediately to the north of Oxford street became areas of concentration from the late 1870s as London rapidly expanded.

The directory entries from the 1870s reveal the same street names appearing: High Street, Nottinghill; Upper Street, Islington; Deptford High Street; Queen's Terrace, St John's Wood. To the north of Oxford Street were Portman Square, Tottenham Court Road, Regent's Park Road, Edgware Road and Euston Road. These were local centres of trade and had their own local populations that could guarantee trade for the studio. The expansion of London had increased their population so that it could support a photographer. The area to the north of Oxford street represented the extension of the main London central area and could support a studio despite its greater distance from the prestigious central area.

The *Photographic News* (14 December 1888, p. 792) provided a summary of the situation: *"Regent Street still boasts its photographers, but their number is sadly reduced; Baker Street is but a ghost of its former self; while a writer in the Telegraph this week, describing the shops of North London, does not even mention the photographers of the Upper Street, Islington, and Euston Road. At one time, no one could walk down these two thoroughfares without being struck with the hosts of photographic studios...But like that of Regent Street and Baker Street, the glory of both Upper Street and Euston Road has departed, and the fortunes which were once made there are now amongst the traditions of photography"*.

THE LONDON PATTERN

The pattern observed lies with market forces. A simple correlation exercise clearly links population with the number of photographers through time, and herein lies the explanation of the observed pattern. Between 1851 and 1930 London's population increased from 2.36 million to 4.01 million with a peak of 4.54 million in 1901. This represents a major expansion in London which had to grow to accommodate this increase. An increase in area of London would provide an opportunity for a photographer to set up a studio in these new areas of population. The rise in population of a new area provided a market that could support a photographer and, as it grew still further, more photographers. Hence, a decline in the number of photographers in the West End is observed with an increase in the suburbs.

A further argument in support of this hypothesis is that once a certain concentration has been reached the level of photographers remains relatively constant - this is particularly so in the post-1919 period. A population threshold has to be reached before a photographer will set up a studio. Providing this threshold is maintained the number of photographers will remain constant in number (actual firms may come and go but the numbers remain constant). The West End has a lower threshold and can support far more studios than would be expected because of the large numbers that come to the area and are only temporary migrants or commuters. The area has a higher population and potential demand because of these temporary visitors than its actual population would suggest.

Such a situation may exist for London as a whole, with the whole city having a lower threshold level than other cities by virtue of a greater level of demand resulting from its temporary population.

This hypothesis also explains why certain postal districts will not have or have not had any photographers located within them. Either they do not have a sufficient population to reach the threshold needed for a photographer to set up a studio or the population may in absolute numbers reach the threshold but in terms of spending power and wealth may not be sufficient to support a studio. Some of the poorer areas of East London such as E14 (the Isle of Dogs) in 1959 did have a large population but its spending power was not sufficient to support a photographic studio. The problems of population and personal wealth have been discussed by Phillips and Walton.[14]

The location of photographic studios at the street scale supports these reasons. Demand related to population levels is important and appears to explain the location of studios at the street level.

LONDON AS AN INNOVATIVE CENTRE

There are a number of reasons why London should have been the innovative centre for photography. London, as the capital city of Britain, was the political, educational, social and economic centre of the country. Political figures could and did provide the encouragement and support an art such as photography would need to become accepted and established. Government influence was important with respect to the Patent Office and patronage.

Photography was a luxury and its success may be in part due to the early support it received from the Queen, Prince Albert and the Royal family during the 1840s. This, together with reports of such visits by royalty and notable figures of the age, undoubtedly attracted people to have their 'likeness' taken.

A demand was created that allowed more photographers to enter the market. Economic factors such as backing for a studio would be most likely found in London together with sufficient demand to make a venture worthwhile.

Other centres such as Liverpool, Manchester and Birmingham had some of these factors but not all and, as a result, they became secondary centres of dispersal and not the initial innovative centre. It is no coincidence that Beard became aware of the new daguerreotype patent. He was involved with the Patent Office with his own calico patents and was resident in London.

The first practitioners of the daguerreotype process already had a business in London. Hagerstrand's ideas on the communication of a new invention have, therefore, some relevance.[15] Miles Berry, through whom Daguerre patented his process was a London-based patent agent and Antoine Claudet, with a license direct from Daguerre, had founded a glass shop in London in 1834. Personal communication with Daguerre seems to have been important. Later, the dissemination of information about the new technique through newspapers and journals of the period such as *The Times*, and weekly magazines such as the *Art Journal, Saturday Review* and *Chamber's Edinburgh Journal* encouraged the spread of photography.

CONCLUSIONS

The trade directory is a useful tool, within certain limitations, to examine a particular industry. London is especially well-off in this respect with a long and comprehensive run of directories. The provinces are generally less well served. If they are used in conjunction with supplementary sources, for example, newspapers or photographic periodicals, a reasonably accurate picture of early photography can be built up.

London was the centre from where commercial photography spread to the rest of Britain. Scotland was free to practice daguerreotypy, England and Wales were not. One man, Richard Beard, controlled who was able to set up as a daguerreotype artist and where they did so through his purchase of Daguerre's patent. One exception to this was Antoine Claudet who had purchased a license directly from Daguerre in Paris. There were many itinerant photographers who illegally practised the daguerreotype process for a short time in a particular place before setting up in a new town with the intention of keeping one step ahead of Beard's patent protection efforts.

Beard, through his patent, limited commercial photography and vigorously defended his right to do so in the law courts. The introduction of Scott Archer's wet collodion process in 1851 and it's superiority over the daguerreotype in terms of sensitivity and operation immediately attracted operators. The expansion of photographic studios dates from this period.

London remained the dominant photographic city in Britain and many London studios set up branches in other towns and cities, for example, A. and G. Taylor.[16] Within London during the early period up to the 1870s the studios clustered along the main commercial and retail streets of the west end, the City and Westminster. With the expansion of the suburbs and expansion of the central area so the photographic studios moved out to where clusters of population existed. This study has proven a strong relationship of studio location to population after 1851.

London's dominant position in terms of numbers of studios and location at the political and social centre of the country has led to an over-emphasis of its position in modern photographic histories. The competence and portraiture skill of many London studios is without question but there were also many studios who produced work of a very dismal standard.

Many studios in other town and cities were of equal skill but they tend to be less well-known outside of their local area. The move amongst photographic historians towards more local histories of photographs should start to redress this balance.

THE FUTURE

This study is still very much on-going and a future editions will start to build on the expanded directory that follows. In particular company histories and those of individual photographers will be expanded. A companion volume looking at the period from 1908 is also a possibility. Information is still actively being collected and the author can be contacted at the address on the title page.

(left) William Gladstone photographed by T. R. Williams of 236 Regent street and published by Mason & Co. of 7 Amen Corner, Paternoster Row, London; (centre) a copy of a framed photograph, possibly an ambrotype, produced as a carte de visite; (right) an unidentfied man photographed by H. Turner of Bedford House, 245 Commercial Road E.

(left) Miss Whitelock photographed by Ayling of 493 Oxford Street; (centre) an unidentified child. The text on the carte back read 'Photographed by A. Fillan, Princess Gallery of Photography, 73 Oxford Street W. (Adjoining the Princess' Theatre) London'; (right) an unidentified lady seated at a typical studio prop by John & Charles Watkins of 34 Parliament Street, London S.W.

REFERENCES AND BIBLIOGRAPHY

TEXT REFERENCES

1. Pritchard, Michael (1986), *A Directory of London Photographers 1841- 1908*. ALLM Books, Bushey.

2. The Society of Genealogists is located at 14 Charterhouse Buildings, London. EC1M 7BA. Tel: 071-251 8799.

3. The Historical Group of the Royal Photographic Society can be contacted through the RPS at 46 Milsom Street, Bath. BA1 5DN. Membership of the Society is on payment of a subscription. The Group publishes a quarterly journal *The PhotoHistorian* and holds regualr meetings in London and occasional seminars around the country.

4. See, for example, Coe, Brian and Haworth-Booth, Mark (1983), *A Guide to Early Photographic Processes*. Victoria and Albert Museum, London; and Nadeau, L. (1990), *Encyclopedia of Printing, Photographic and Photomechanical Processes*, two volumes. Atelier, New Brunswick, Canada.

5. Lansdell, Avril (1985), *Fashion à la Carte: 1861-1900*. Shire Publications, Princes Risborough. A general book on dating photographs is Robert Pols (1992), *Dating Old Photographs*. Federation of Family History Societies, Birmingham.

6. Shaw, Gareth (1982). *British Directories as Sources in Historical Geography*. Historical geography research series No.8. April.

7. Goss, Charles W. F. (1932). *The London Directories 1677-1855*. Denis Archer, London.

8. Norton, J. E. (1950). *Guide to the National and Provincial Directories of England and Wales Published Before 1856*. Royal Historical Society, London.

9. Oliver, J. L. (1964). 'Directories and their use in Geographical Enquiry'. *Geography*, 49, p. 400-409.

10. Sources for photographic research are discussed in Pritchard, Michael, 'The Rise of British Photographic Manufacturing' in Pritchard, Michael (editor) *Technology and Art. The Birth and Early Years of Photography*.

11. Pritchard, Michael (1986), *Innovation Diffusion - A case study of photography*, Department of Geography, University of Hull, Hull.

12. Good histories of photography dealing with this early period include Gernsheim, Helmut & Alison (1955 and 1969). *The History of Photography*. Oxford University Press, London; Newhall, Beaumont (1983). *Latent Image - the discovery of photography*. Albuquerque; Eder, J M (1978), *The History of Photography*. Transl. Edward Epstein. Dover Publications Inc, New York; Gernsheim, Helmut (1956), *L. J. M. Daguerre. The History of the Diorama and the Daguerreotype*. London.

13. Heathcote, Bernard V. and Pauline F. (1979). 'Richard Beard: an ingenious and enterprising patentee'. *History of Photography*, 3, 4, p. 313-329.

14. Phillips, A. D. M. and Walton, J. R. (1975). 'The Distribution of Personal Wealth in English Towns in the mid-nineteenth Century'. *Transactions of the Institute of British Geographers*, 64, p. 35-48.

15. Hagerstrand, T. (1967). *Innovation Diffusion as a Spatial Process*. University of Chicago Press, Chicago.

16. Gill, A. T. (1985-1986). 'Andrew and George Taylor', *Royal Photographic Society Historical Group Quarterly*, No. 70 Autumn 1985, p. 6; No. 71 Winter, 1985, pp. 4-5; No. 73 Summer 1986, pp. 10-11; No. 75 Winter 1986, pp. 10-11.

GENERAL SOURCES

This bibliography notes some of the published material relating wholly or largely to London photographers and photographic companies. It also includes significant references which are of relevence, such as Audrey Linkman's guide to photograph formats. References about non-London aspects of London photographers'work, for example Stephanie Spencer's article on Francis Bedford, are also included where they list further relevant sources and references. The bibliography is not definitive but may prove a useful starting point for further research.

Adamson, K. I. P. (1988), 'More Early Studios. Part 1' in *Photographic Journal* 128, 1, January 1988, pp. 32-36 and 'More Early Studios. Part 2' in *Photographic Journal* 128, 7, July 1988, pp. 305-309.

Arnold (1977), *William Henry Fox Talbot*. Hutchinson Benham, London.

Bolas, Thomas (1895). *The Photographic Studio*. Marion and Company, London.

Castle, Peter (1973). *Collecting and Valuing Old Photographs*. The Garnstone Press Ltd, London.

James, H. A. (19—). *The Price Guide to Photographic Cards*. Bishopsgate Press, London.

Lee, David (1986), 'The Victorian Studio', two parts in *British Journal of Photography* 7 February 1986, pp. 152-165 and 14 February 1986, pp. 188-199.

Linkman, A. E. (1990), 'The Itinerant Photographer in Britain 1850-1880' in *History of Photography* 14, 1, January-March 1990, pp. 49-68

Linkman, Audrey (1991), *Nineteenth Century Card Formats in Britain*. Supplement No. 92. RPS Historical Group, Bath.

Linkman, Audrey (1993), *The Victorians. Photographic Portraits*. Tauris Parke Books, London.

Palmquist, Peter E. (1991), *Photographers: A Sourcebook for Historical Research*. Carl Mautz Publishing, Brownsville, CA. Includes an important world bibliography of directories of photographers by Richard Rudisill.

Prescott, Gertrude Mae (1985), *Fame and Photography: Portrait Publications in great Britain 1856-1900*, unpublished doctorate thesis. Faculty of the Graduate School of the University of Texas at Austin.

Pritchard, H. Baden (1883). *The Photographic Studios of Europe*. Piper and Carter, London.

Pritchard, H. Baden (1883) *About Photography and Photographers*. Piper and Carter, London.

Robinson, H. P. (1885). *The Studio: and what to do in it*. Piper and Carter, London.

Wall, John (1977), *Directory of British Photographic Collections*. Royal Photographic Society and William Heinemann, London.

Welford, Sam (1991). 'The Cost of Photography in the Period 1850-1897' in *The PhotoHistorian* No. 92 Spring 1991, pp. 15-17.

Witkin, Lee D. and London, Barbara (1979). *The Photograph Collectors Guide*. Secker and Warburg, London.

Wood, R. Derek (1979). 'Daguerreotype Shopping in London in February 1845'. *British Journal of Photography*, 9 November, p. 1094-1095.

Wood, R. Derek (1980). 'The Daguerreotype Patent, the British Government and the Royal Society'. *History of Photography*, 4, 1, p. 53-59.

LONDON STUDIOS

Bennett, Stuart (1977). 'Jabez Hogg Daguerreotype'. *History of Photography*, 1, 4, p. 318.

Blackmore, Anet (1989), 'Photographs by Henry Bedford-Lemere' in *History of Photography* 14, 4, October-December 1989, pp. 369-371.

Darrah, William C. (1981), *Cartes de Visite in Nineteenth Century Photography*. William C. Darrah, Gettysburg, PA.

Elwall, Robert (1984). "The foe to graphic art': the rise and fall of the Architectural Photographic Association'. *The Photographic Collector*, 5, 2, p. 142-164.

Fielding, A. G. (1987), 'Rejlander in Wolverhampton: His Sponsorship by William Parke' in *History of Photography* 11, 1, January-March 1987, pp. 15-22.

Gill, A. T. (1966). 'J. F. Goddard and the Daguerreotype process - part 1'. *Photographic Journal*, 106, 11, p. 370-376.

Gill, A. T. (1966). 'J. F. Goddard and the Daguerreotype process - part 2'. *Photographic Journal*, 106, 12, p. 389-395.

Gill, A. T. (1967). 'Antoine Francois Jean Claudet (1797- 1867)'. *Photographic Journal*, 107, 12, p. 405-409.

Gill, A. T. (1975). 'Richard Beard' (pamphlet). *Royal Photographic Society Historical Group Newsletter*, December, London.

Gill, A. T. (1977). 'Wolcott's Camera in England and the Bromine-iodine Process'. *History of Photography*, 1, 3, p. 215-220.

Gill, A. T. (1979). 'Further discoveries of Beard Daguerreotypes'. *History of Photography*, 3, 1, p. 94-98.

Gill, A. T. (1985-1986). 'Andrew and George Taylor', *Royal Photographic Society Historical Group Quarterly*, No. 70 Autumn 1985, p. 6; No. 71 Winter, 1985, pp. 4-5; No. 73 Summer 1986, pp. 10-11; No. 75 Winter 1986, pp. 10-11.

Haaften, Julia Van (1980). 'Francis Frith and Negretti and Zambra'. *History of Photography*, 4, 1, p. 35-37.

Hallett, Michael (1986), 'Major British Photographic Collections', three parts in *British Journal of Photography*, 1 August 1986, pp. 894-897, 8 August 1986, pp. 923- 925 and 15 August, pp. 950-951.

Haworth-Booth (1992), *Camille Silvy: River Scene*. Getty Museum, Malibu.

Heathcote, B. V. & P. F. (1988), 'The Feminine Influence: Aspects of the Role of Women in the Evolution of Photography in the British Isles' in *History of Photography*, 12, 3, July-September 1988, pp. 259-273.

Henisch, B. A. & H. K. (1980). 'A. J. Melluish and the Shah'. *History of Photography*, 4, 4, p. 309-311.

Hercock, R. J. and JoneS, G. A. (1979). Silver by the Ton. A History of Ilford Limited 1879-1979. McGraw-Hill, London.

Hooper, David and Linkman, Audrey (1986). 'Brown, Barnes & Bell' in *RPS Historical Group Quarterly* No. 74 Autumn 1986, pp. 10-11; and follow up letter from Adamson, K. I. P. in *RPS Historical Group Quarterly* No. 72 Spring 1986, p. 12.

Johnson, Christine (1985). 'George Shadbolt. Victorian Photographer of Hornsey' in *RPS Historical Group Quarterly* No. 71 Winter 1985, pp. 2-3; reprinted from *Bulletin of the Hornsey Historical Society* No. 25 (1984), pp. 25-27.

Jones, Edgar Yoxall (1973), *Father of Photography. O. G. Rejlander 1813- 1875*. David & Charles, Newton Abbot.

Lambert, Miles (1991), *Fashion Photographs 1860-1880*. Batsford and National Portrait Gallery, London.

Levitt, Sarah (1991), *Fashion Photographs 1880-1900*. Batsford and National Portrait Gallery, London.

Lloyd, Valerie *et.al.*, *The Camera and Dr Barnardo*, Dr Barnardo, 1975.

McCauley, Elizabeth Anne (1985), *A. A. E. Disdéri and the Carte de Visite Portrait*. Yale University Press, Newhaven, U.S.A.

Negretti, P. A. (1985). 'Henry Negretti - Gentleman and Photographic Pioneer'. *The Photographic Collector*, 5, 1, p. 96-105.

Odgers, Stephen L. (1978). 'A Labelled Wolcott Daguerreotype'. *History of Photography*, 2, 1, p. 19-21.

Osman, Colin (1991), 'Thomas Sims 1826-1910' in *The PhotoHistorian* No. 94 Autumn 1991, pp. 82-83.

Pritchard, Michael (1988), 'Commercial Photographers in Nineteenth Century Britain' in *History of Photography* 11, 3, July-September 1987, pp. 213-215 and follow-up correspondence from B. V. and P. F. Heathcote in *History of Photography* 12, 1, January-March 1988, p. 89.

Reynolds, Leonie and Gill, Arthur T. (1985). 'The Mayall Story'. *History of Photography*, 9, 2, p. 89-107.

Reynolds, Leonie and Gill, Arthur T. (1986). 'The Mayall Story: a postscript'. *History of*

Photography, 11, 1, January-March 1987, pp. 77- 80.

Sansom, Leslie (1965), 'One Hundred Years of Portraiture [Bassano's studio]' in *British Journal of Photography*, 14 May 1965, pp. 418-423.

Spencer, Stephanie (1987), 'Francis Bedford's Photographs of North Wales: Selection and Interpretation' in *History of Photography* 11, 3, July-September 1987, pp. 237-245.

Steel, Jonathan (1982), 'T. R. Williams: The first master of the Stereograph' in *The*

Photographic Collector 3, 1, Spring 1982, pp. 91-101.

Stirling, Alec (1990), 'Philip Henry Delamotte: artist and photographer' in *RSA Journal*, CXXVII (June 1990), p. 491-495.

Welford, Sam (1989), 'B. J. Edwards, Victorian Photographer, Inventor and Entrepreneur' in *History of Photography*, 13, 2, April-June 1989, pp. 157-163.

Welford, Sam and Lansdell, Howard (1992), 'A Biography of Alfred Harman Founder of the Britannia Works Co.' in *The PhotoHistorian* No. 98 Autumn 1992, pp. 61-64.

CARTES DE VISITE: A SELECTION - BACKS

A rare carte showing a photographer's advertisement (left) and recording an historic event (right). Timms's advertisement has been added to the omnibus by retouching.

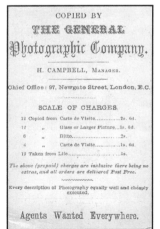 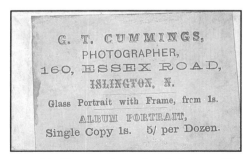

(left) The General Photographic Company's scale of charges. The front of the card is a copy from an earlier photograph; (above) a label applied by the photographer to a carte back. Cummings is not recorded at 160 Essex Road in the Post Office directories but appears from 1874 elsewhere in the vicinity.

LONDON PHOTOGRAPHERS 1841-1908

The names are listed and contracted using the conventions in the London Post Office directories of the period. This usually involves the removal of vowels, and then the remaining letters. Where space has permitted some words have been re-expanded to aid readers. The original alphabetical sequence of the Post Office directories has been retained.

A

Abbott, William
110 Richmond Road S.W.   1881

Absell, George
45 Newington Causeway S.E.   1864-65

Absell, James
83 Upper Street, Islington N.   1864-65

Adams and Cusden
20 Orchard Street W.   1882-83

Adams, Edward
142 Upper Street N.   1877-79

Adams, Miss Isabella, and Co.
151 Upper Street N.   1874-76

Adams, J.
20 Orchard Street W.   1884

Adams, John (senior)
19 Esmond Road E.   1866-68
75 Roman Road E.   1869-73

Addy, William
4 King's Road, Chelsea S.W.   1873-75

Aglio and Absolon
201 Piccadilly   1857

Akerman, James
51 Gray's Inn Road W.C.   1874-76

Aland and Co
5 New Oxford Street W.C.   1884

Aland, John
119 Camberwell Road S.E.   1890

Albert, E., and Co.
1 Park Side, Knightsbridge S.W.   1878-80

Albert Gate Photo Co.
45 St George's Place S.W.   1902

Alberto and Co.
41 New Oxford Street W.C.   1894-95

Album Portrait Co.
David Taylor, manager, 1864
George Robert Fitt, manager 1865-66
100 Regent Street W.   1864-67

Alder and Co.
9 Strand W.C.   1881-83

Aldis, Elijah
47 Baker Street, Portman Sq. W.   1864

Aldridge, George
408 Edgware Road W.   1876-80

Alexander, Chas.
5 Church St, Shoreditch   1857

Alfieri, Bernard
70 Mortimer Street W.   1899-00

Allan and Hudson
134 Kingsland High Street N.E.   1890-92

Allan, Robert L.
13 Murray St., Camden Town N.W.   1864-69

Allard, Frederick
55 Homerton Terr., Homerton N.E.   1907
116 Wick Road, Hackney N.E.   1908-

Allen, Dave
335 Albany Road, Camberwell S.E.   1892

Alliance Limited
115 Newgate Street E.C.   1904

Altman, Abraham
12 Richard Street, Commercial Rd. E. 1900-03

Amateur Association
16 Brook Street W.   1905

Angerers, Son, Fruwirth and Co.
146 Cheapside E.C.   1866-67
1 Palace Road, Upper Norwood S.   1866-67

Angle, Henry
6 Westland Place W.   1870
22 Bishop's Road W.   1871-76

Angle, Sidney Butler
40 Walworth Road S.E.   1904-08-
110 Southwark Park Road S.E.   1905-08-

Anglo-American Photo Co.
Richard P. Estabrooke, manager
153 Fleet Street E.C.   1880-84
272 Regent Street W.   1880-83

Anglo-Continental Co.
23 Brooke Street   1897

Anthony, Simon
344 Fulham Road S.W.   1878-80

Antill and Smith
83 Newington Causeway S.E.   1888

Antill, Herbert
83 Newington Causeway S.E.   1890-91

Antrobus, Miss Dora
26 New Cavendish Street W.   1906

Archard, Leonard
69 South Audley Street W.   1869-70

Archer, Argent A.
48 Lime Street E.C.   1888-91
7A Bath Place, Kensington Rd. W.   1892-94
195 Kensington High Street W.   1895
195A Kensington High Street W.   1896-07
140 Kensington High Street W.   1907-08-

Archer, Fredk S.
105 Great Russell Street   1855-57

Archibald, Walt, and Co.
538 Kingsland Road N.E.   1907

Architectural Photographic Association
Wm Lightly, Hon. secretary,
Henry Moody, curator
9 Conduit Street, New Bond St W.   1861-64

Armstead and Maltby
173 Upper Street N.   1865-66

Army and Navy Auxiliary Co-Operative
Supply Ltd.
Francis St, Victoria Street S.W.   1902-08-
Horwick Place, Victoria Street S.W.   1907-08-

Arndt, Wolfgang
10 Nugent Terr., St John's Wd. N.W.   1894-98

Art & Decorative Photographic
Co. Ltd, The
John James Harris, secretary
41 Threadneedle St E.C.   1866

Art Light Photo Co.
21 Piccadilly W.   1901

Art Photographic Association, The
James Michael Rourke, manager
51 Threadneedle Street E.C.   1886-89
52 Cheapside E.C.   1889

Art Room Co.
271 Kentish Town Road N.W.   1907

Arter, Thomas
146 Euston Road N.W.   1889

Artistic Photographic Co. Ltd
72 Oxford Street W.   1895-00
90 & 92 Oxford Street W.   1901-07
63 Baker Street W.   1908-

Artists Co-Operative Assoc., The
William Henry Silvester, manager
204 Regent Street W.   1880

Artlett, Richard
110 Westbourne Grove W.   1881-82

Ash, William *57 Clapham Road*
119 Newington Causeway S.E.   1881-87
Hampton Street, Walworth S.E.   1887-88

Ashby, George
84 King's Road, Chelsea S.W.   1861-64
36 Elizabeth Street, Pimlico S.W.   1867-76

Ashdown, Henry
1 Waverley Place, St Johns Wd. N.W. 1869-80
42 Harrington Road S.W.   1889
Queen's Gate Hill, Harringtn Rd. S.W.   1890

Ashdown, Henry
74 Baker Street W.   1882-84

Ashdown, Thomas Edward
205 City Road E.C.   1871-76

Atkins, George Jones
335 City Road E.C.   1874-78

Attwood and Co.
113 Pentonville Road N.   1881-83

Attwood, William
113 Pentonville Road N.   1871-80

Austen, George William
15 Highbury Place N.   1891-06

Austin, Rodney, and Co.
140A Jamaica Road S.E.   1900-01

Avery, Mrs Elizabeth
24 Ladbroke Grove Road W.   1880-81

Avery, Frederick George
237 East India Dock Road E.   1902-08
28 Jubilee Street E.   1904-05

Avery, George Frederick
40 Lillie Road, Fulham S.W.   1907

Avery, John
209 King's Road W.C.   1908-

Avery, John H., & Co
164 Strand W.C.   1900-01

157 Strand W.C.   1902-05
9 Parkhurst Road, Holloway N.   1906-08-

Avery, John James
106 Holland Park Avenue W.   1897-98
237 East India Dock Road E.   1899-01
28 Jubilee Street E.   1899-08
26 Junction Road N.   1902-08-

Avery, Thos Porter
8 Railway Pl, Ladbroke Gr. Rd. W   1868-69
3 Upp. Railway Tr, Ladbroke Gr. W.   1870-72
24 Ladbroke Grove Road W.   1873-79
26 Ladbroke Grove Road W.   1875-79

Avins, John
114 Tyers Street, Lambeth S.E.   1871-79

Ayling, Joseph
4 Crane Court, Fleet Street E.C.   1885

Ayling, Stephen
493 Oxford Street W.   1860-70
6 Augustus Square N.W.   1862-76
3 & 6 Augustus Square N.W.   1871-72

Ayres, Wm Mountford
10 Boundry Rd, Nottinghill W.   1895-96

Azulay, Henry
36A Queen St, Brompton Rd. S.W.   1872

Azully, Mrs Clara
184 Fleet Street E.C.   1883-84

B

Bagnelle and Small
22 Baker Street W.   1890

Bailey, Alfred Jas.
17 Hindon Street, Pimlico S.W.   1881-89
35A Hindon Street, Pimlico S.W.   1890-08-
Noted as being established in 1880.

Bailey, Charles
17 Hindon Street, Pimlico S.W.   1902

Bailey, Mrs Emily
4 Newland Terr., Kensington Rd. W.   1875-83

Bailey, Henry
4 Newland Terr., Kensington Rd. W.   1866-74

Bailey, Thomas
39 Spring Street, Paddington W.   1864

Bailey, William
36 Chandos St, Covent Gdn. W.C.   1889-90
4 High Street, Nottinghill W.   1890-93
37 Chandos St, Covent Gdn. W.C.   1891-92
225 Westminster Bridge Rd. S.E.   1894
85 Praed Street W.   1895-96

Baker and Dixon
152 Fleet Street E.C.   1906

Baker and Muggeridge
152 Fleet Street E.C.   1907

Baker, Frank Andrew
152 Fleet Street E.C.   1908

Baker, Gabriel Augustine
28 Jubilee Street E.   1872-98

Baker, Philip (junior)
263 Fulham Road S.W.   1866-84

Baker Street Photographic Co., The
20 Upper Baker Street N.W.   1881

Ball, James
17 Regent Street S.W.   1892-06
11 Wilton Road, Pimlico S.W.   1907-08-

Ballenger, James
17 Mabledon Place W.C.   1901

Banfield, Miss Violet
304 Regent Street W.   1903-05

Barat, George
110 Westbourne Gr., Bayswater W.   1871

Barber, William
32 St Martin's le Grand E.C.   1859-65

Barclay Brothers
47 Old Broad Street E.C.   1897-99
79 Mark Lane E.C.   1900-08-
3 Minories E.   1902-04

Barker and Pragnell
162 Sloane Street S.W.   1892-93

Barker, Arthur
56 Holloway Road N.   1884

Barker, Charles
49 Brecknock Road N.   1901

Barker, Miss Ethel
196 Brompton Road S.W.   1901
4 Onslow Pl., South Kensington S.W.   1902-03

Barker, Wm Jas
242 St Paul's Road, Islington N.   1898-01

Barlow, Jas
75 Cambridge Street, Pimlico S.W.   1867

Barnard, Mrs Hebe
140 Regent Street W.   1856
188 Regent Street W.   1857-60
131 Regent Street W.   1861-72

Barnard, Philip Augustus
140 Regent Street W.   1856
188 Regent Street W.   1857-60
131 Regent Street W.   1861-75

Barnes and Judge
4A New Bond Street W.   1857-58

Barnes, Forrester Seeley
39 King's Road. S.W.   1898-00

Barnes, James Alfred Sleeman
56 Poplar Road, Camberwell S.E.   1907-08-

Barnes, John
141 Caledonian Road N.   1908

Barnes, Robert F.
64A New Bond Street W.   1860-62

Barnes, Robert F., & Co.
64A New Bond Street W.   1859

Barnes, Thomas, & Co.
9 Cornhill E.C.   1878-79

Barnes, Thomas J.
3 Hope Place, Mile End Road E.   1859-62

Barnes, Thomas John, and Son
6 Bedford Place, Commercial Rd. E.   1865-66
422 Mile End Road E.   1866-88

Thomas Barnes was the first full-time photographer to work for Dr Barnardos, the homeless childrens charity. Originally in business on his own account he began working for Barnardo from about 1870 and he moved completely on to Barnardo's premises around 1874 when the charity set up its own photographic department. Barnes worked for Barnardos except on Thursdays and Saturdays when, presumably, he attended to his own business.

Barnardos changed photographer in 1883 to Roderick Johnstone *(q.v.)* who may have been Barnes's assistant.

Barnes, William Aug.
6 North Street, Westminster S.W.   1868

Barnett, Alexander
239 New Kent Road S.E.   1898-99

Barnett, Henry Walter
1 Park Side, Hyde Park Corner S.W.   1899-03
12 Knightsbridge S.W.   1904-08-
95 Gloucester Road S.W.   1905-06

Barnett, M.
3 Hayfield Place, Mile End Road E.   1862

Barnett, Morris
198 Whitechapel Road E.   1863-64

Barrable, John George
244 Regent Street W.   1860-74

Barratt, J.
222 Regent Street W.   1848

Barraud and Jerrard
96 Gloucester Road, Portman Sq. W.   1874-81

Barraud and Robertson
120 Fulham Road S.W.   1908-

Barraud, F., Mayall and Co. Limited
126 Piccadilly W.   1898

Barraud, Herbert Rose
96 Gloucester Pl, Portman Sq. W.   1883
263 Oxford Street W.   1883-91
73 Piccadilly W.   1893-96
126 Piccadilly W.   1897

The *Photographic News* (16 February 1883) paid a visit to Mr Herbert Barraud's studio in Oxford Street and compared it favourably to Van Bosch's Paris studio *"it is newly constructed, with taste and style, and indicates a spirited desire to make a step forwards beyond conventional limits"*. According to the journal the studio had been newly constructed and had been planned throughout. In order to maximise the light available for portraiture Barraud had, as one would expect, constructed a glass room at the top of his building *"so well that he looks down on everybody around him, his side-light coming in directly due north. The light, indeed, floods in from both sides and from the roof in such a manner that means have been employed for modifying it, similar to those we have seen in use in Southern Europe."* A gas engine had been installed to power a lift to take sitters to the studio.

Barraud enjoyed a high reputation. The *Photographic News* stated *"We have no need to tell that Mr Barraud does excellent work, for of that our readers are already aware"* and at modest prices. In 1883 Barraud was charging for a sitting, two proofs and six cartes-de-visite half a guinea or for twenty-four copies one guinea.

Barrauds Limited
263 Oxford Street W.   1892-04

Barratt & Stanley
145 Regent Street   1854-57

Barratt, J.
222 Regent Street   15 October 1846

Barrett, Mrs Eugene V.
6 Felix Pl, Liverpool Road N.   1862-69

Barrett, Michael
104 Grand Jnctn Terr., Edgware Rd.   1858

Barrett, Wm
6 Felix Pl, Liverpool Road. N.   1864-67

Barrington, Benedict and Co.
20 Upper Baker Street N.W.   1877

Barry, James
404 Strand W.C.   1864-65
352 Strand W.C.   1868-69

Bartier, William
134 East India Dock Road. E.   1874-08-

Barton, George
22 Harleyford Road S.E.   1908

Barton, Jas
8 Stephenson Terr., Caledonian Rd.   1858

Basebe, Athelstane
199 Brompton Road S.W.   1878-83

Bassano, Alexander
122 Regent Street W.   1862-76
72 Piccadilly W.   1870-81
25 Old Bond Street W.   1878-03
182 Oxford Street W.   1889
42 Pall Mall S.W.   1891-92
18 Alpha Road N.W.   1892-96

The *Photographic News* (27 February 1880) gave an glowing report of a visit to Alexander Bassano's Old Bond Street studio *"it is exactly the sort of studio we should all of us like to have"* and *"a model establishment of the West End"*. Bassano's Old Bond Street studio was reserved for photographs taken by appointment while the Piccadilly studio undertook impromptu work. He had a separate printing establishment at Kilburn where negatives were sent as soon as they had been retouched and approved.

The studio was originally founded in 1850 in Regent Street and moved to Piccadilly from 1859- 1863. The studio then moved to Pall Mall before removing to 25 Old Bond Street in 1877. The studio was the society photographer from the 1850s throughout its history. The *Lady's Pictorial* (5 February 1921) reported on the studio's move to 38 Dover Street W1: *"The removal has not been quite to easy and simple as an ordinary member of the public would imagine it to be, because stowed away in Bassano's cellars in Old Bond Street were about a million negatives, all neatly numbered and arranged in such a way that their keeper could put his hand at once on any negative required. Not all these negatives have been removed, because some are never likely to be wanted again. On the other hand, some of the negatives are priceless, for to these studios have come numbers of very famous people. Bassano's have had has, in fact, done its part in perpetuating for posterity the portraits of all the great makers of Victorian and present times"*.

The company became Bassano & Vandyck Studio in 1964, Bassano & Vandyck Studio (incorporating Elliott & Fry) from 1965-1976 and Industrial Photographic at 35 Moreton Street SW1 from 1977. See separate entry for Elliott and Fry. The Vandyck Studio origins are unclear.

H. Goulton May a Bassano operator left to set up as a photographer at 11 Hill Rise, Richmond S.W.

The National Portrait Gallery has a substantial collection (presently uncatalogued) of the Bassano studio's later work from 1893-1949

Bassano and Davis
122 Regent Street W.   1866

Bassano Limited
25 Old Bond Street W.   1906-08-

Bassano's Studios Ltd.
25 Old Bond Street W.   1904-05

Bastain, Wm. Robert
85 Chalk Farm Road N.W.   1897

Bastain, Wm. Robert, and Sons
85 Chalk Farm Road N.W.   1898-03

Bates, William
68 London Road, Southwark   1855-56
9 Royal Road, Walworth S.   1859-60
264 High Holborn W.C.   1861-77

Bath, Mrs Maria
86 Farringdon Street E.C.   1877-80

Bath, William
44 Farringdon Street E.C.   1861-65
86 Farringdon Street E.C.   1865-76

Batiste, Maurice
440 Old Kent Road S.E.   1886

Batiste, Maurice, & Son
369 Edgware Road W.   1887-95
516 Oxford Street W   1887-01
369 Edgware Road W.   1888-94

Battersby, Frederick
29 Kensington High Street W.   1908-

Baugh & Bensley
22 Ludgate Hill E.C.   1860-64

Baugh, Spencer
22 Ludgate Hill E.C.   1859-65
41 Ludgate Hill E.C.   1866

Baum, Franz
4 Brook St, Hanover Square W.   1885-86

12 Old Bond Street W.   1887-97

Baumgart, Oscar
12 Little Alie Street E.   1900-02
118 Commercial Road east E.   1903-08-

Baumgart, Otto
12 Little Alie Street N.   1899

Baxter & Andrews
48 Stepney High Street E.   1889-93

Bayfield, James Slee
63 Westbourne Grove W.   1874-75
10 High Street, Nottinghill W.   1876-86

Bayne, Herbert
11 Bow Lane E.C.   1895-96
12 Bow Lane E.C.   1897-00

Beach, Charles Edward
107 Fulham Road S.W.   1889-96

Beadel, Victor
142 Bridge Street, Mile End E.   1905-08-

Beararni, John
147 Oxford Street W.   1865-66

Beard, Alex, and Co.
20 Green Street, Leicester Square   1855

Beard & Sharp
28 Old Bond Street W.   1859

Beard, Richard
309 Regent Street   1842-49
85 King William Street, City   1843-54
34 Parliament Street   1843-56
17 Wharf Road, City Road   1843-44
18.5 Wharf Road, City Rd   1845-48
Millman Mews, New Millman Street   1849-53
Royal Polytechnic Inst., Regent St.   1852-54
31 King William Street, City   1855-57

Beard Richard (junior)
31 King William Street, City E.C.   1858-69

Beattie, Alfred
10 Chapel Street, Preston   1883

Beau, Adolphe

283 Regent Street W.   1864-78

An established theatre photographer Beau purchased Camille Silvy's (*q.v.*) studio aound July-August 1868. Beau also ran or owned the Westbourne Studio, Kensington Gardens Square W. and also advertised as "Manager-intéressé for E. Cox, Sons & Stafford. Bayswater & Brighton".

Becker, Lewis

83 Charlotte St, Fitzroy Square W.   1898
11A Berners Street W.   1899-00

Beckett, Robert, and Sons

6 The Grace, Hackney N.E.   1899-02

Beckett, Samuel Joshua

20 Baker Street W.   1901-08-

Bedford, Francis

326 Camden Road N.   1876-83

"The bright landscape pictures of Mr Francis Bedford and of his not less talented son, Mr William Bedford, require no commendation...in the same way as Mr England appears to enjoy a sort of monopoly in Continental pictures, so the Messrs Bedford stand pre-eminent in reproducing the soft landscapes and craggy headlands of our own country." (Photographic News, 23 April 1880). Bedford acquired fame when he accompanied Prince Albert, the Prince Consort, on a journey to the Holy Land. A series of 210 plates were secured of which 175 were selected for publication.

Bedford Lemere & Co

137 Regent Street   *c*.1865-70
4 Featherstone Buildings, W.C.   1868
78 Albert Street N.W.   1872
147 Strand W.C.   1872-08-

Bedford Lemere senior (1839-1910) established the company in the mid-1860s at 147 Strand where it remained until 1946. Henry [Harry] Bedford Lemere was born in 1865 and effectively took over the running of the firm during the 1880s by which time the architectural specialisation had already been established. The company remained the leading purveyor of domestic, commercial and industrial images until his death in 1944. The compay moved to 3 Park Labe, Croydon from 1947-1957 and South Park Hill Road, South Croydon from 1957. Most of the surviving 20,000 plus negatives and prints (as well as daybooks) are held by the Royal Commission on the Historical Monuments of England.

Beech & Shaw

149 Fleet Street E.C.   1890

Beechey, Clement

16 Cromwell Place S.W.   1905

Beethoven, Carl

118 New Bond Street W.C.   1888-89
20 Baker Street W.   1890-91

Beethoven, Morris

22C Ebury Street S.W.   1904

Beleno, Harry

40 Walworth Road S.E.   1872

Bell & Co.

78 New Cross Road S.E.   1887

Bell & Dixon

147 Strand W.C.   1872

Bell, Miss Annie

179 Regent Street W.   1906
92 Victoria Street S.W.   1907-08-

Bell, Edwin

47 Kentish Town Road N.W.   1875-76

Bell, John

295 Strand W.C.   1873

Bell, Sidney

334A Essex Road N.   1904-05

Bellgrove, Geo. W., & Co.

81 Fulham Palace Road W.   1905
135 Fulham Palace Road W.   1906

Belton & Reed

57 Oxford Street W.   1867-69

Belton, William
19 Octavius Street, Deptford S.E.   1895-05

Belton, William John
57 Oxford Street W.   1870
26 St Paul's Cres., Camden Sq. N.W. 1878-94

Bender, Joseph, & Co.
181 City Road E.C.   1908-

Benn & Cronin
149 Great Titchfield Street W.   1907-08-

Bennett, Henry Watson
3 Chandos St, Covent Garden W.C.   1889
10 & 11 Bedford St, Covent Garden   1890-91
Dacre House, Arundel Street W.C.   1892

Bennett, James
124 & 126 High Road, Kilburn N.W.   1899

Bennett, James, & Co.
124 & 126 High Road, Kilburn N.W. 1900-03

Bennett, William
27 Sloane Street S.W.   1866-67
30 Sloane Street S.W.   1868

Bennetts, William
92 Brompton Road. S.W.   1874-75

Benson, Joseph Richard Chas.
78 Chalk Farm Road N.W.   1873-80

Bequet, Frederick
5 Duke Street, Tooley Street S.E.   1856-59

Beresford, George Charles
20 Yoeman's Row, Brompton S.W.   1903-08-
The Hulton-Deutsch Collection have the Beresford archives of Society portraits and personalities from 1902-1931.

Bergamasco, Charles
3 King Street, Covent Garden W.C.   1875-79

Berners Portrait Co.
John Werge, manager
11A Berners Street, Oxford Street W. 1874-75

Bernhardt, Charles
10 Upper Street, Islington N.   1881

Bernieri, Caldesi & Co.
13 Pall Mall east S.W.   1869-70

Bernowski, Maurice
235 High Holborn W.C.   1888

Berry & Sharp
16 & 17 Poultry E.C.   1892

Berry, Alfred
37 Albion Grove, Barnsbury N.   1905-08-

Berry, George
88 Jamaica Level, Bermondsey S.E.   1877-79

Berry, George
445 Southwark Park Road S.E.   1880-86

Bertolacci, Misses C. M. & I.
25 Redcliffe Road S.W.   1884-90

Bertolle & Son
268 Caledonian Road N.   1903-04

Bertolle, James
268 Caledonian Road N.   1893-02

Bertolle, James, & Son
268 Caledonian Road N.   1905-08

Bertolle, James, & Son
8 Stephenson Terr., Caledonian Road 1859-60

Bertolle, James Lewis Wm.
226 Caledonian Road N.   1877-85
268 Caledonian Road N.   1886-91

Bertolle, Louis
331 Caledonian Road N.   1863-65

Bessent, Thomas
152 Goswell Road E.C.   1878

Best, John Bird
4 Nottinghill Terrace W.   1882-91

Bex Brothers
56 High St, Camden Town N.W.   1886

Biddle & Dowdall
49 King William Street E.C.   1899-01

Biddle, Chas. Geo., & Co.
49 King William Street E.C.   1902-08-

Bijou Photo Co.
William Crouch, manager
204 Regent Street W.   1884-86

Birchall, Thos
19 St Martin's le-Grand E.C.   1866-68
79 Cheapside E.C.   1870-72

Bird, Henry Wm., & Co.
16 & 17 Poultry E.C.   1878-85

Birnstingl, Louis, & Co.
230 Regent Street W.   1864

Bishop, J. & Co.
13 Lancashire Court, New Bond Street 1894
19 Princess Road, Regents Park N.W. 1894
113 Park Street, Camden Town N.W. 1895
87 Park Street, Camden Town N.W. 1896

Bishop, John
44 St George's Road, Regents Park 1893

Bishop, Robert
29 Kennington Park Road S.E.   1869-79

Blackburn, Wm.
High Street, Clapham S.   1858-59

Blake, Frank
132 Camberwell Road S.E.   1906-07

Blake, Leonard
4 Coburg Pl, Bayswater W.   1885-88

Blampey Brothers
106 Upper Street, N.   1898-00

Blanchard, Valentine
147 Strand W.C.   1859
1A Brecknock Pl., Camden Tn. N.W. 1865
12 Camden Cottages, Camden Town 1866-71
128 Camden Road N.W.   1866-68
9 Albany Courtyard, Piccadilly W. 1871-75
48 Piccadilly W.   1871-75
289 Regent Street W.   1876-84

'Mr. Blanchard has achieved a very extensive reputation. His large direct portraits - massive,

dignified, full of life - are, indeed, too well known to require any detailed description here, for every visitor to the Pall Mall Exhibitions during the past half-dozen years must have witnessed examples of his handiwork. Mr. Blanchard is, to some extent, a disciple of Adam-Salomon, the well-known sculptor and photographer of Paris.' (Photographic News 19 March 1880, p. 137.

This visit by the journal to Blanchard's Regent Street studio described the studio in glowing terms, particularly his methods for diffusing daylight and his own process of producing photographs on opal. At this time Blanchard was charging £2 2s per dozen cabinet cards and £1 1s for cartes.

Blanche, Mrs Mary
110 Southgate Road N.   1904-05

Blayney, Charles
35 Upper Street N.   1880

Blennerhassett, John Fredk.
62 Upper Street, Islington N.   1872
1A Vernon St, King's Cross Rd   1872-75

Blewett, William
299 Euston Road N.W.   1869-71

Bolak, George
10 Bolt Court, Fleet St E.C.   1906-08-

Bolas, S. B., & Co.
3 Creed Lane E.C.   1898
11 Ludgate Hill E.C.   1898
77 Oxford Street W.   1899-01
68 Oxford Street W.   1902-08

Bond, James Wm.
2 Gwynne's Pl., Hackney Road N.E. 1856-63
501 Hackney Road N.E.   1864-75

Bond Street Photographic Co., The
69 New Bond Street W.   1895-97

Bondonneau, Emile
213 Regent Street W.   1869-73

Boning & Small
22 Baker Street W.   1879-95
22 & 71 Baker Street W.   1891

Boning, Robert
16 Wellington Square, Chelsea S.W.   1863

Boning, Robert, & Co
112 Cheapside E.C.   1864
13 & 16 Wellington Square, Chelsea   1864
162 Regent Street W.   1868

Bonner & Covell
83 High Holborn   1857
86 Whitechapel Road E.   1858-60

Bonner, George
86 Farringdon Street E.C.   1856-64

Booker & Sullivan
67 & 69 Chancery Lane W.C.   1903-08-

Bool, Alfred
86 Warwick Street, Pimlico S.W.   1867-69

Bool, Alfred & John
14 Stockbridge Terrace S.W.   1870-78
86 Warwick Street, Pimlico S.W.   1870-78

Bool, George
110 Richmond Road S.E.   1877-80

Bool, John
86 Warwick Street, Pimlico S.W.   1886-08-

Bordone, Paris
235 High Holborn W.C.   1889-90

Boresoff, Lewis
66 Fieldgate Street, Whitechapel E.   1898-99

Bosley, William
26 Westbourne Grove W.   1873-77

Bossoli, Claude
92 Brompton Road S.W.   1868-69
138 Brompton Road S.W.   1870-71

Boucas, George
120 Mile End Road E.   1900-08-

Bouell, Charles Von
492 Oxford Street W.C.   1874

Bourdon, Miss Rosa A.
7 City Terrace, City Road   1854-56

Boursnell, Robert
15 Richmond Road, Shepherds Bush   1904-08-

Bower, Alfred
86 Whitechapel Road E.   1865-82
87 Whitechapel Road E.   1862-64

Bowerman, Charles
391 Hackney Road N.E.   1907-08-

Bowers, Edmund
154 Euston Road N.W.   1888-90

Bowers, John
175 Regent Street W.   1902

Bown, Henry (senior)   *298 Clapham Road SW*
14 Jamaica Road S.E.   1877-78
33 Jamaica Level S.E.   1884
33 Jamaica Road S.E.   1885-08-
Rockingham St, Newngtn Causeway   1888
43 New Kent Road S.E.   1889-08-
31 Spa Rd, Bermondsey S.E.   1889-90
63 Spa Rd, Bermondsey S.E.   1891-94
31 Jamaica Road S.E.   1895-08-

Bown, Henry (junior)
400 Evelyn Street, Deptford S.E.   1907-08-
116 Walworth Road, S.E.   1908-

Bown, H., Ltd.
31 & 33 Jamaica Road S.E.   1908
43 New Kent Road S.E.   1908

Box, Robert George
40 Charing Cross S.W.   1871-77
Box was a pupil of T. R. Williams of Regent Street.

Boxall, George
246 Old Kent Road S.E.   1905-08-

Brabazon, George
440 Old Kent Road S.E.   1890

Brabazon, George Henry
131 Fleet Street E.C.   1889-07
440 Old Kent Road S.E.   1891-03
246 Old Kent Road S.E.   1895-03

Braconyer, Edward Alfred
38 Clerkenwell Close E.C.   1905

Bradley, Daniel
40 Cannon Street Road E.   1865

Bradshaw & Godart
103 Newgate Street E.C.   1877-78
Successors to the London School of
Photography.

Bradshaw, Wm. Stephen
103 Newgate Street E.C.   1879-03

Braine, Robert
4 Conduit Street east W.   1863

Brandon, Jonathan
193 Piccadilly W.   1858

Branston, Charles
80 Cornhill E.C.   1858

Bray & Wakefield
84 Newgate Street E.C.   1880

Bremner & Rouch
162 Regent Street W.   1859

Brent, Fredk. Josiah
390 Southwark Park Road S.E.   1880
449 Southwark Park Road S.E.   1881-85

Brett, John
42 Ball's Pond Road N.   1868-72

Brewes, Samuel
9 Chiswell St, Finsbury E.C.   1855-59

Bridge, Fredk A.
30 Dalston Terrace, Dalston Lane E. 1871-75

Bridge, Fredk Albert
55 Dalston Lane N.E.   1899-08-

Briggs, Frank
15 High St, St. Johns Wood N.W.   1859-69

40 High St, St. Johns Wood N.W.   1870-72

Briggs, Frank, & Son
40 High St, St. Johns Wood N.W.   1873-01
10 Queen's Terrace, St Johns Wood   1902-03

Briggs, Netterville
20A Baker Street W.   1873-74
20 Baker Street W.   1875-89

Bright, G. M.
183 Strand   25 February 1847

Bright, James
183 Strand   2 December 1845

Brightman, Charles Ariel
13 St John Street, Westminster   1906

Brine, George Harrison
5 High Road, Kilburn N.W.   1906-07
398 Harrow Road W.   1909

British Art Co.
61 Essex Road N.   1904-07
61 & 63 Essex Road N.   1908

British Automatic Photograph Co. Ltd.
C. O'Neill Crowley, secretary
31 Lombard Street E.C.   1904
26-31 Eyre Street Hill E.C.   1904

British Biograph Co.
12 Charing Cross Road W.C.   1902

British Fine Arts Society Limited
S. Powell, secretary, 1895;
H. W. Anderson, secretary, 1896
7 Union Court, Old Bond St. E.C.   1895-96

British Industrial Photo Co.
32 Craven Street, Strand W.C.   1902

British Solar Printing Co.
66 Pentonville Road N.   1906

Brittleneck & Co.
4 & 5A Tottenham Court Road W.   1882

Brittlebank, Arthur
3A Tottenham Court Road W.   1876
2 Aldgate High Street E.   1877-81

4 Tottenham Court Road W. 1877-81
5A Tottenham Court Road W. 1878-81

Brock & Evitt
6 Queen's Road, Bayswater W. 1877-78

Brock, Herbert, & Co.
26 New Cross Road S.E. 1899-02
840A Old Kent Road S.E. 1903-05

Brock, Walter Bino
Miles Street, South Lambeth S.W. 1879-82
3 Miles Street, South Lambeth S.W. 1883-88
162 King's Road, Chelsea S.W. 1889
76 Wandsworth Road S.W. 1889-08-

Brockley, Charles
295 Edgware Road W. 1898-99

Brodie, Vere
22 Baker Street W. 1894

Brokenshir
256 Strand 18 August 1846

Brooker, George
44 Regent Street W. 1854

Brookes, Mrs Ann Hannah
387 Kingsland Road S.E. 1889

Brookes, Arthur
369 Kingsland Road E. 1878-83

Brookes, Arthur
12 Bath Place, New Road 1855-56
312 Oxford Street W. 1858
199 Oxford Street W. 1859-60

Brookes, Charles
438 Mile End Road E. 1893

Brookes, Edward Arthur
10 Downham Road N. 1891-92

Brookes, Frederick
197 Borough High Street S.E. 1887-91
79 Oxford Street W. 1893-96
401 Strand W.C. 1897

Brookes, Frederick
351 Oxford Street W. 1856-61

Brooks, Albert
129 Westminster Bridge Road S.E. 1897-03

Brooks, Mrs Hannah
261 Goswell Road E.C. 1890-99

Brooks, J.
3 Lower Nottinghill Terrace W. 1859

Brooks, Vincent, Day and Son
Gate Street, Lincoln Inn Fields W.C. 1869-77
68 & 10 Gate Street W.C. 1878-98
48 Parker Street W.C. 1898-03

Brothers, Mrs Annie
22A Mortimer Street W. 1872-73

Brown & Bennett
27 Sloane Street S.W. 1865

Brown, Barnes & Bell
220 & 222 Regent Street W. 1880-85
62 Cheapside E.C. 1881-89
12 Baker Street, Portman Square W. 1886-01

With their head office in Liverpool Brown, Barnes and Bell established a network of ranches around the country. The London branches were responsible for their own photo-finishing while the northern branches all returned their negatives to Liverpool. The *Photographic News* 17 September 1880, pp. 447-448 surveyed the Liverpool operation and company's philosophy. The company's objective was the cater for the mass market, producing good quality work at a moderate cost.

The same journal (22 February 1884, p. 127) reported that a proposal had beem made to transfer the business of the firm to a joint stock company, having a capital of £130,000 and that it was intended to issue shares to the value of £30,000. The reason for this was to raise capital to develop the photo-filigrane process and the manufacture of phototype blocks (Luxotype).

Brown, Frederick
10A Blenheim Place N.W. 1890
83 Newington Causeway S.E. 1894
30 Newington Green Road N. 1904-05

Brown, James
132 Camberwell Road S.E.   1886-87
327 Vauxhall Bridge Road S.W.   1887
148 Camberwell Road S.E.   1888-89

Brown, Joseph
13 Sloane Street, Chelsea S.W.   1866-69
32 Sloane Street, Chelsea S.W.   1870-72

Brown, Thos J.
11A Tottenham Court Road W.   1856

Brown, William
41 Kennington Oval S.E.   1873

Brown, William
16 Kennington Oval S.   1865-66

Brown, Wm. Arthur
148 Camberwell Road S.E.   1890-99
102 London Wall E.C.   1890-92

Brown, Wm. Arthur & Son
148 Camberwell Road S.E.   1900-08-
146 Camberwell Road S.E.   1903-08-

Browne, Miss Frances
135 Regent Street W.   1893-96

Brunelliere, Hy. Antoine
125 Regent Street W.   1865

Bryant & Co.
66 Old Kent Road S.E.   1908

Buck, Sidney
4 Newton Terr., Westbourne Gro W.   1863-64

Bulbeck, John, & Co.
167 Strand W.C.   1898-01
158 Strand W.C.   1902-08-

Bull, George
110 Richmond Road S.E.   1876

Bull, John & Alfred
14 Stockbridge Terr., Pimlico S.W.   1869

Bullingham, Henry
25 Harrington Road S.W.   1891-98
21 Harrington Road S.W.   1899-08-

Bullock, James
56 High Street, Camden Town. N.W.   1869

Bunnett, Wm. Henry
145 Hammersmith Road W.   1904-08

Burford, Frank Wm.
109 Great Russell Street W.C.   1905-08-

Burge, Geo Henry
154 Newington Butts S.E.   1869-71

Burghall, Geo. J.
1 Belmont Row, Vauxhall S.   1866

Burke, Edward
316 High Holborn   1853
47 Ludgate Hill E.C.   1854-58
211 Upper St, Islington N.   1859

Burlington Photographic Rooms
William M'Dougall, proprietor
174 Regent Street W.   1856-57

Burnett, Poole
11A Berners Street W.   1897

Burow, Ralph, & Co.
304 Regent Street W.   1898

Burrows & Colton
22 Baker Street W.   1877

Burrows, Mrs Eliza
12 Somerset Place, Commercial Road 1856-60

Burrows, Fredk. Thomas
22 Baker Street W.   1878

Burstein, William
422 Mile End Road E.   1905

Burton, Edward
47 Church Street, Minories E.   1864

Burton, James
410 Euston Road N.W.   1867

Burton, James Davies
194 Oxford Street W.   1864

Burvill, Wood
45 Brompton Road S.W.   1870-71

Butcher, Isaac
101 East India Dock Road E.   1880-89
142 East India Dock Road E.   1885-94

Butcher, Wm. Fredk
100 High Street, Nottinghill W.   1865

Butler & Dyer
26 Walnut Tree Walk S.   1864-73

Byzanotype Portrait Co.
61 Knightsbridge S.W.   1906-08

C

Caeser, Thomas
61 Upton Road, Kingsland N.   1907-08-

Caldesi & Co.
13 Pall Mall east S.W.   1871-75

Caldesi, Blanford & Co.
13 Pall Mall east S.W.   1861-62
6 Victoria Grove, Kensington Gate   1861-62

Caldesi, Leonida & Co.
13 Pall Mall east S.W.   1860-68
6 Victoria Grove, Kensington Gate   1863-66

Caldesi & Montecchi
13 Pall Mall east S.W.   1858-59
38 Porchester Terr., Bayswater W.   1859

The studio was acquired by Camille Silvy around August 1859 (see Haworth-Booth (1992), p. 72).

Calvert & Timms
87 Farringdon Street   1856-57

Calvert, Richard Isaac
87 Farringdon Street E.C.   1858-65

Cameo Miniature Co.
18 & 19 Newcomen Street, Borough   1908-

Cameron & Smith
20 & 70 Mortimer Street W.   1891-94

Cameron, Henry Herschel Hay
70 Mortimer Street W.   1886-90

20 & 70 Mortimer Street W.   1895-97
31 George St, Hanover Square W.   1898-01
20 Mortimer Street W.   1898-99

Cameron Studio Ltd.
195 & 196 Brompton Road S.W.   1902

Campbell & Grey
17 Cheapside E.C.   1903-04

Campbell-Gray & Edwards-Duncan Ltd.
17 Cheapside E.C.   1905

Campbell-Gray Ltd.
17 Cheapside E.C.   1906-08-

Campbell, John
14 High Holborn W.C.   1863

Campbell, Luke
M'Lean's Building, New Street Sq.   1856

Campbell, William
85 Hyde Road, Hoxton N.   1876

Campbell, William Sidney
2 Creed Lane E.C.   1903-08-

Campbell, William Sidney & Alfred Joseph
2 Creed Lane E.C.   1897-02

Candland, James
34 Cheyne Walk, Chelsea S.W. 1873

Caney, William Laws
151 Upper Street N. 1878

Cannon, Miss Miranda
18 King William Street 1854
In business from 1853-1854 she occupied Antoine Claudet's former studio.

Cannon, Thomas
190A Broadhurst Gardens, Hampstead 1904

Carder, Henry
5 College Street, Chelsea S.W. 1871-73
3 Terrace, Earls Court, W. Brompton 1875
189 Earl's Court Road S.W. 1880
268 King's Road, Chelsea S.W. 1881-82
368 King's Road, Chelsea S.W. 1883-90
317 King's Road, Chelsea S.W. 1892

Carder, Robert
189 Earl's Court Road S.W. 1879

Carder, William
189 Earl's Court Road S.W. 1877

Carlin & Woods
71 Upper Street N. 1907

Carlin, Leon
171 Upper Street N. 1908

Carlton & Co.
240 Edgware Road W. 1907

Carpenter, Harry
120 Mile End Road E. 1885

Carpenter, Harry, & Co
120 Mile End Road E. 1886-93

Carpenter, Henry, & Co.
153 Deptford High Street E.C. 1889-91

Carr, Miss Elizabeth
16 Edgware Road W. 1901-02

Carter, Mrs Charlotte
37 Norton Folgate N.E. 1894-95

Carter, Christopher
51 Tottenham Court Road W. 1886

Carter, Frank
132 Camberwell Road S.E. 1897-05

Carter, George
44 Lillie Road, Fulham S.W. 1905-06

Carter, John Edward
20 Lower Philimore Place W. 1876

Carter, Thomas
107 Euston Road N.W. 1890

Carter, Major William
167 Old Kent Road S.E. 1907-08-

Cartwright, Richard
349 Kingsland Road E. 1874-87
333 Kennington Road S.E. 1878-79
10 Upper Street N. 1881-82
34 Upper Street N. 1883-87
184 Fleet Street E.C. 1887

Casbon, Charles & Co.
94 Waterloo Road S.E. 1894

Casket, Portrait Co. Ltd.
Thos. Edward Golding, secretary, 1864;
Henry Swan, manager, 1866-68
40 Charing Cross Road S.W. 1864-68

Cason, James
33 Carmen Street, Poplar E. 1906

Cassels, Miss Amy
67 & 68 New Bond Street W. 1906-08-

Castle, Alfred
282A New Cross Road S.E. 1904-08-

Castle, Chas (junior)
41 Castle Street, Holborn E.C. 1865

Caswall-Smith, John
309 Oxford Street W. 1904-08-

Catlin, Mrs Mary
4 Albion Street, Rotherhithe S.E. 1862
Lower Road, Rotherhithe S.E. 1863-65
7 Albert Place, Union Rd, Rth S.E. 1866

38 Union Road, Rotherhithe E. 1867-77

Cave, Joseph
376 Oxford Street W. 1872
146 Euston Road N.W. 1875-78

Cave, Joseph Hy.
17 Portman Place, Edgware Rd. W. 1856-58

Celleriers Syndiate Ltd.
57 Pall Mall S.W. 1887-89
16 & 17 Poultry E.C. 1888

Central Art Gallery
49 Southampton Row W.C. 1908

Ceramic Stained Glass & Vitrified Photograph Co.
Alfred Rands, manager
19 Finsbury Circus E.C. 1885

The *Photographic News* (14 November 1884) visited the company's main office at Finsbury Circus and the works at Chingford. The company largely worked from the negatives of customers with the greater number of pictures being applied to glass, including opal glass) or on to articles of crockery. At the time Mr Rands, the manager, said *"vitrified pictures are coming much into use for placing on graves and mounting on tombstones, an application of them which has been common on the Continent for some years."*

The works, located in cottages were largely staffed by young ladies engaged in retouching, painting and colouring ceralic pictures. The works were looked after by Mr. H. N. White who explained the process to the *PN* and also undertook the furnace work.

Chamberlaine, John
66 Marylebone Road N.W. 1870-73

Chamberlaine, John Wm.
41 Euston Road N.W. 1877-79

Chamberlaine, William
84 King's Row, Chelsea S.W. 1871

Chancery Photo Co.
10 Chicester Rents W.C. 1907-08

Chandler, Alfred
8 Richmond Street, Walworth S.E. 1875-79

Chandler Brothers
5 Mitre Court E.C. 1891-97
175 Fleet Street E.C. 1898

Chandler Brothers & Williams
175 Fleet Street E.C. 1899-00

Chanoch, Max
76 Finsbury Pavement E.C. 1892

Chappius, Paul Emile
69 Fleet Street E.C. 1860-68

Chappius, Paul Emile, & Co.
69 Fleet Street E.C. 1869-72

Charles, Madame Lallie
The Nook, 1 Titchfield Road, N.W. 1902-07
Known as Lallie Garet-Charles in 1897 when she had work published she died in 1897.

Charles, William
21 Piccadilly W. 1902

Cheetham, George Robert
77 Roman Road E. 1886

Cherry & Fleming
204 Pentonville Road N. 1861-73

Chesherton, William
13A Hereford Place, Commercial Rd. 1872-74

Chesterton, William
159 St. Georges Street E. 1859

Chevalier, Bertram
22 Bishop's Road, Paddington W. 1892

Chic Photo Co.
422 Strand W.C. 1904

Churchill, James
304 Regent Street W. 1902

City Central Photographic Studio
James Leath, proprietor
6 Dean's Court, Doctors' Commons 1864

City Of London Fine Art Assoc., The
Argent A. Archer, manager
48 Lime Street E.C.	1888-90
7A Bath Place, Kensington Road W.	1892-94
195 Kensington High Street W.	1895-96
193A Kensington High Street W.	1897
195A Kensington High Street W.	1898-00

City Of London Institute of
Photography
John Griffiths, manager
41 Ludgate Hill E.C.	1865
30 New Bridge Street E.C.	1866

City of London Photographic Co.
98 Cheapside E.C.	1876-79

City of London Photographic
Copying Co.
Wm. Anderson, manager, 1865-70
Wm. Henderson, manager, 1871
18 Queen Street, Cheapside E.C.	1865-67
2 Queen Street, Cheapside E.C.	1868-71

City Photographic Co.
Andrew Windsor, manager
52 King William Street E.C.	1872

City Studio
George Richard Mainwaring
63 St Paul's Churchyard E.C.	1865

Claflin, Corliss
150 Strand W.C.	1900-02

Clark & Mann
6 York Buildings, Adelphi W.C.	1908-

Clark, George
135 Tottenham Court Road W.	1859-61

Clark, James
129 New North Road N.	1881-84

Clark, John
113 Fleet Street	1857

Clarke Brothers
307 Essex Road N.	1891

Clarke, Archer
5 Woburn Bldngs, Euston Sq. W.C.	1874-75

Clarke, Charles Donald
12 Cartusian Street E.C.	1883

Clarke, Miss F. E.
5 Woburn Bldngs, Euston Sq. W.C.	1876-77

Clarke, Grayson
9 Claro Terrace, Richmond Road S.W.	1895

Clarke, John
89 Strand W.C.	1854
140 Strand W.C.	1858

Clarke, John Joseph
54 Chancery Lane W.C.	1863-65

Clarke, William
29 Kennington Park Road S.	1868

Clarkington & Co.
246 & 248 Regent Street W.	1863-70

According to a *carte* back the company removed to 118 New Bond Street W. In addition to a general studio they specialised in Parliamentary portraits and published a series of portraits of the British legislature.

Clarkington, Charles
183 Strand W.C.	1853-56
4 Lyon's Inn	1855
69 Regent Street W.	1856-58
246 & 248 Regent Street W.	1859-62

Class, Jacob
55 Greenfield Street, Whitechapel E.	1905-08-

Claudet & Jerrard
107 Regent Street W.	1883

Claudet, Antoine F. J.
18 King William Street, Strand	1848-51
107 Regent Street W.	1852-68

Claudet, Henri
107 Regent Street W.	1869-84

Clempson & Hutchinson
Chancery Lane W.C.	1906

10 Chichester Road   1906

Clerke & Co.
15 Islington High St N.   1890-94
429 New Cross Road S.E.   1891-92
4 Tottenham Court Road W.   1892-94

Clerke, Miss M. Shadwell
117 Ebury Street S.W.   1907-08-

Clifford, Charles E.
30 Piccadilly W.   1857-59

Clowes & Edwards
238 East Street, Walworth Road S. 1868-70

Clowes, Edward Stephen
238 East Street, Walworth Road S.E. 1871-73
224 Walworth Road S.E.   1873-81

Club Photo Co.
98 Cheapside E.C.   1900

Coates, Lois & Co.
16 Tottenham Court Road W.   1905-08

Cocke & Lewis
44 Regent Street W.   1848

Cocke, A. J.
44 Regent Street W.   30 March 1847-1850

Cocke, A. J. & A. L.
44 Regent Street W.   1849

Cocke, Archibald Lewis, and Co.
179 Regent Street   1855

Cockrum, Wm. Porter
63 Charing Cross S.W.   1864

Cohen, Martin
4 Bickley Row, Rotherhithe S.E. 1863-87

Cohn, George
42 Cannon Street Road E.   1864

Colas, Louis Ferdinand
105 Cheapside E.C.   1856-60

Cole, Charles
15 Church Row, Limehouse E.   1874

Cole, Frederick
150 Brompton Road S.W.   1866-67
124 Brompton Road S.W.   1869-70
380 Euston Road N.W.   1871-82
378 Euston Road N.W.   1883-08-

Cole, Richard
17 Waterloo Place, Shepherds Bush   1861

Cole, Wm. Harold Hastings
83 Cheyne Walk S.W.   1886-89
10 Church Street, Chelsea S.W. 1889-04

Coleman, James
10 Brunswick Place, City Road N.   1868

Coleman, Thomas
4 Craven Buildings, City Road. E.C. 1861-67
19 Brunswick Place, City Road. N. 1869-90

Colinette, Charles
1 College Crescent, Hampstead N.W.   1907

Collen, Henry
29 Somerset Street, Duke Street   1841-45
Collen was the first professional Calotypist and his agreement with William Henry Fox Talbot, the inventor and patentee, to operate the process began in August 1841. He was also the first licensee. Collen was an established miniaturist and member of the Royal Academy, and had been drawing master to the Princess Victoria. Collen's business relationship with Talbot lasted until at least 1844 (see Arnold (1977), pp. 138-140). Between 16 August 1841 and 24 June 1842 Collen took 209 portraits and for Collen's total business over the three years to August 1844 Arnold estimates that only 650 portrait sessions took place.

Colliere & Purdue
435 Fulham Road S.W.   1889

Colliere, Charles, & Co.
70 Lillie Road S.W.   1899-02
40 Lillie Road S.W.   1903

Colliere, Gwyn
148 Sloane Street S.W.   1861-67
97 Fulham Road S.W.   1863-64

223 Fulham Road S.W. 1865-77
83 Gracechurch Street S.W. 1868
162 King's Rd, Chelsea S.W. 1869-70
138 Brompton Road S.W. 1873
45 St Georges Place, Knightsbridge 1876-81
14 Stockbridge Terrace, Pimlico S.W. 1880-84
327 Vauxhall Bridge Road S.W. 1885

Colliere, William
299 Euston Road N.W. 1892

Collier, John Thomas
56 Paddington Street W. 1866-72
12 Columbia Market, Hackney Rd. E. 1871

Collings, Arthur Esme, Limited
69 New Bond Street W. 1891-93
175 New Bond Street W. 1895-05
52 & 175 New Bond Street W. 1903
171 New Bond Street W. 1906

Collings, J. W. & A. E.
69 New Bond Street W. 1889

Collings, Keturah
16 North Audley Street W. 1905-08-

Collings, Whyte, Limited
69 New Bond Street W. 1890
404 Oxford Street W. 1890
53 Kensington High Street W. 1891

Collins, Fredk James
238 Upper Street N. 1904-08-

Collins, George
130 Culford Road N. 1875-81

Collins, Tom John
56 Cochrane Street N.W. 1878-83

Collins, William
6 Colvill Terrace, Kings Rd, Chelsea 1858

Collis, George
77 Cornhill E.C. 1875
80 Cornhill E.C. 1880-82

Collis, George Lestock
1 Sun Ct, Cornhill E.C. 1859-79

Colloff, Robert John
51 Hind Street, Poplar E. 1905-08

Colman, Arthur
38 Brecknock Road N. 1873

Colnaghi, Bernard
62 Piccadilly 1853-55

Colnaghi, Martin Hy., and Co.
62 Piccadilly 1856-57

Colnaghi, Oswald
62 Piccadilly 1852

Color-Photo Co.
Birkbeck Bank Chambers, Sthmptn 1901-02

Colour Photographic Co.
Major Hughes Hallett, manager
1 Park Side, Knightsbridge S.W. 1881

Colson, Charles Fage
11 Gould Square E.C. 1857-62

Combs, John Nelson
39 King's Road, Chelsea S.W. 1891

Comer, Elles
2 Langley Place, Commercial Rd. E. 1866-68

Commercial Photographic Co.
40 Fetter Lane E.C. 1907

Compton, Mrs Norah
69 Marlborough Road, Old Kent Rd. 1898-05

Compton, Robert
59 Catlin Street, Rotherhithe Rd. S.E. 1900-08-

Compton, Robert
19 Barkworth Rd., Bermondsey S.E. 1886-87

Compton, William Chas.
69 Marlborough Road, Old Kent Rd. 1897
440 Old Kent Road S.E. 1905-08-

Coney, John Fredk.
92 Farringdon Street E.C. 1858

Connaught Studios
A. H. Tee, secretary
7 Edgware Road W. 1908-

Connell, Frederick
69 Abbey Road N.W. — 1892-93
3 Blenheim Pl., St. Johns Wd. N.W. — 1894-01
50 Grove End Road. N.W. — 1902

Connell, Miss Lena
50 Grove End Road. N.W. — 1903-08-

Conner, John, & Co.
228 Westminster Bridge Road S. — 1868-69

Constant, Michael
125 Newgate Street — 1853

Cook, Edwin
319 Fulham Road S.W. — 1908-

Cook, Arthur D.
22 Newman Street, Oxford Street W. — 1869-70

Cooke, Duncan
22 Newman Street, Oxford Street W. — 1872

Cooke, William
307 North End Road W. — 1908-

Cooke, William
15 Warwick Street, Pimlico S.W. — 1908-

Cooper & Humphreys
71 Newman Street W. — 1907-08-

Cooper, Bernard J., Ltd.
133 Finchley Road N.W. — 1903-04
74 Baker Street W — 1906
31 York Place W. — 1907-08

Cooper, Charles John
31 Spa Road S.E. — 1885-88

Cooper, Frederick
304 & 312 Euston Road N.W. — 1867-68
304 Euston Road N.W. — 1869-91

Cooper, Mathew Felton
41 King William Street E.C. — 1869-76

Co-Operative Photographic Society
Edward Sands, manager
3 Postern Row E.C. — 1871-74

Coote, Edward
33 Ovington Square W. — 1885

Coppin, Henry
16 & 17 Poultry E.C. — 1890-91

Cordova, Ernest
17 Regent Street W. — 1888

Cork, Charles Sawyer
154 Euston Road N.W. — 1876-81

Cork, George William
58 Fleet Street E.C. — 1894-97
153 Fleet Street E.C. — 1899-08-

Cornhill Photographic Co.
60A Cornhill E.C. — 1880

Corri & Lancaster
83 Fleet Street E.C. — 1865

Cosway, Paul
25 Harrington Road S.W. — 1900-01

Cosway, Richard B.
171 New Bond Street W. — 1907-08

Cottee, Fk. Cuthbert
19 Willims Terr., Blue Anchor Road — 1863-71
Blue Anchor Road S.E. — 1872-75
147 Blue Anchor Road S.E. — 1876-79
147 Southwark Park Road. S.E. — 1880-85

Cotton & Wall
90 Cannon Street, west E.C. — 1857-61

Cotton, John A., & Co.
119 Westbourne Grove W. — 1865
90 Cannon Street, west E.C. — 1866
76 Cannon Street, west E.C. — 1867

Cotton, John A. Edwd., & Co.
90 Cannon Street, west E.C. — 1865

Cotton, John Anderson, & Co.
35 Westbourne Grove W. — 1864

Cotton, John Anderson
Cannon Street, west — 1855-56
90 Cannon Street, west E.C. — 1862-64

Cotton, Miss Violet
16B Fulham Road S.W. 1904-07
16 Fulham Road S.W. 1908-

Cottrell, William
145 Fleet Street 1854

Covell & Thompson
137 Edgware Road W. 1857-59
297 Oxford Street W. 1858-59

Covell, John William
113 Whitechapel Road E. 1867

Covell, William
81 High St, Whitechapel E. 1856-58
83 High Holborn 1856
4 New St, Covent Garden 1856-57
86 Whitechapel Road E. 1861-62
47 & 113 Whitechapel Road E. 1863-65
113 Whitechapel Road E. 1866

Cowderpy, Thomas
7 Everett Street, Brunswick Sq. E.C. 1861

Cowper & Baker
127 Queen's Road, Bayswater W. 1878-80

Cowper, James
81 Lupus Street, Pimlico S.W. 1881

Cowper, Thomas Wm.
43 Markham Street, Chelsea S.W. 1873-81

Cox & Frier
313 City Road E.C. 1885

Cox & Palmer
20 Upper Street, Baker Street, W. 1884

Cox, Henry
11 Alfred Place, York Road N. 1869
34 Brecknock Rd, Camden New Tn. 1870
118 New Bond Street W. 1871-72

Cox, James Mitchell
55 Baker Street, Portman Sq. W. 1863

Crabb, Henry
142 Grundy Street, Poplar E. 1878

Craig, George
14 High Holborn W.C. 1861-69

Craig, William Erwin
62 Cheapside E.C. 1894-95

Craig, Charles
26 Westbourne Grove W. 1879

Crane, Henry
287 Walworth Road S.E. 1880-91

Crayon Art Co., The
49B Brecknock Road N. 1902-03
25 Evershott Street N.W. 1904-08-

Crayon Ltd.
49 Brecknock Road N. 1900
49B Brecknock Road N. 1901

Creed, George & Mrs Sophia
135 Regent Street W. 1878-82

Crellin, Philip (junior)
162 Regent Street W. 1866-67
87 Regent Street W. 1868-71

Crews, William
2 Camden Rd., Camden Town N.W. 1864

Crisp, Charles
131 Shirland Road, Paddington W. 1889

Croachley, Thomas Geoffrey
293 King's Road S.W. 1891-95

Croal, John T.
40 & 42 Harrington Road S.W. 1888

Crook, Henry
122 Newington Butts S.E. 1871-89
6 Westminster Bridge Road S.E. 1882
7 Lower Sloane Street S.W. 1885

Cross, Charles Jospeh
114 Campbell Road E. 1891-08-

Croucher, John Honor, & Co.
22 Ludgate Hill 7 April 1847-49

Crowhurst, James
96 Prince Of Wales Road N.W. 1900-02

Crown Art Society Ltd.
15B James Street, Haymarket   1906

Croydon, James
94 Cornwall Road W.   1891-94

Croydon, James, & Sons
398 Harrow Road W.   1895-98

Croydon, Walter
94 Cornwall Road W.   1878-90

Cubbitt, Charles
626 Old Kent Road S.E.   1897

Cubitt, —
Edgware Road   21 August 1846

Cumby, William Adolphus
82 Bayham St., Camden Town N.W.   1870-71

Cummings, George Thos.
60 Pentonville Road N.   1874-80
181 Kentish Town Road N.W.   1884

Cundall & Co.
168 New Bond Street W.   1872

Cundall & Downes
168 New Bond Street W.   1860-62
10 Bedford Place, Kensington W.   1861-62

Cundall & Fleming
168 New Bond Street W.   1868-71

Cundall & Howlett
168 New Bond Street W.   1856-57

Cundall, Downes & Co.
10 Bedford Place, Kensington W.   1863-64
168 New Bond Street W.   1863-65
19 Bedford Gardens, Kensington W.   1865

Cundall, Howlett & Downes
168 New Bond Street W.   1858-59

Cundell, Joseph, & Co.
19 Bedford Gardens, Kensington W.   1866-67
168 New Bond Street W.   1866-67

Curd, John James
5 Coburg Place, Bayswater W.   1860

Curling, Geo. John
169 Fleet Street E.C.   1890-06
17 Furnival Street E.C.   1897
16 to 20 Farringdon Avenue E.C.   1907-08-

Curran, James Corls
2 Provindence Place, Limehouse E.   1868-74
678 Commercial Road east E.   1875-77

Curran, Mrs Jane
678 Commercial Road east E.   1878-00

Currie, John Barton
16 Edgware Road W.   1881-94

Curtis, Mrs Annie
111 Grove Road, Bow E.   1895-96

Curtis, John Henry
30 Albany Road S.E.   1886-91
111 Grove Road E.   1889-04

Curtis, John Henry & Co.
111 Grove Road E.   1905-08

Curzon, Eustace, & Co.
119 Pall Mall S.W.   1896

Curzon, Robey & Co. Ltd.
7 Newman Street W.   1898-02
4 Newman Yard W.   1898-02

Cyrus & Cuffell
209 King's Cross Road W.C.   1906

Cyrus, John
209 King's Cross Road W.C.   1907

D

Dadd, John
Lower Road, Rotherhithe S.E.   1872

Dade, Frederick
2 Grove Place, Holloway Road. N.   1872

Dale, Augustus
74 St Johns Road, Hoxton N.   1863-65

Dalziel, John		**Daverson, Henry**	
369 Strand W.C.	1864	127 Great Portland Street W.	1883-84
Daniels & Blaber		**Davidson, Reginald**	
38 Tachbrook Street S.W.	1896-99	214 Seven Sisters Road N.	1902
Daniels, Arthur Joseph		**Davidson, S.**	
38 Tachbrook Street S.W.	1900-08-	2 Claremont Terrace, New Road	1855
D'Anter & Thomas		**Davis & Crompton**	
147 Seven Sisters Road. N.	1899-03	19 Barkworth Road, Rotherhthe S.E.	1884-85
D'Arcis & Whyman		**Davis & Stedman**	
162 Sloane Street S.W.	1894	180 Tottenham Court Road W.	1906
D'Arcis, Frederick		**Davis, Miss Annie, & Co.**	
121 Pall Mall S.W.	1895-97	267 Fulham Road S.W.	1866-67
D'Arcis, Frederick, & Co. Ltd.		**Davis, Arthur D. & Ernest J.**	
3 Waterloo Place S.W.	1898-01	267 High Holborn W.C.	1900

Darke & Rodmill
15 Camden Road N.W.   1866-67

Davis, Arthur

Darke, Thomas
15 Camden Road N.W.   1868-69

Post Offce, Tube Bdgs, Newgate St	1902-05
15 Newgate Street E.C.	1903-04
180 Tottenham Court Road W.	1905
85 Newgate Street E.C.	1906
134 Cheapside E.C.	1906-08
97A Regent Street W.	1907
95A Regent Street W.	1908-

Darlington & Miller
454 Kingsland Road N.E.   1902

Darlington, Miss Gertrude Mary
454 Kingsland Road N.E.   1901

Davis, David
470 Mile End Road E.   1904-06

Darnell & Morgan
216 Kennington Road S.E.   1880

Davis, Henry
24 Cornhill E.C.   1862-69

Darnell, William

756 Old Kent Road. S.E.	1874-76
216 Kennington Road S.E.	1881-83

Davis, Hyman
35 Bruton Street, Berkeley Square W.   1863-76

Davis, Thos
35 Bruton Street, Berkeley Square W.   1862

Darnell, William, & Co
106A Ladbroke Grove Road. W.   1887

Davis, Wm.

3 Bentinck Place, Portland Town	1856-57
10 Great Titchfield Street W.	1866

Dashwood, Christian
1A York Place, Kensington Road   1857

Daubray, Henry

70 Regent Street W.	1864-68
90 Westbourne Grove W.	1869-82

Davis, William, & Son

3 Bentinck Place, Portland Tn. N.W.	1858-59
10 Great Titchfield Street W.	1860-65

Davey, William
106 Upper Street, Islington N.   1901-08-

Davison, Edward James
310 High Road Kilburn N.W.   1899-00

Davison, Misses Jane & Margaret
309 Regent Street W.   1875-76

Dawson, Alfred & Charles
3 Ludgate Circus Buildings E.C.   1889-91
23 Farringdon Street E.C.   1884-85
St Dunstans Court, Fleet Street E.C.   1884-85

Dawson, Alfred & William
23 Farringdon Street E.C.   1886-88
St Dunstans Court, Fleet Street E.C.   1886
160 Fleet Street E.C.   1887
3 Ludgate Circus Buildings E.C.   1890

Dawson & Edis
91 Sloane Street S.W.   1859

Dawson, James
312 Kingsland Road N.E.   1908

Day & Son Ltd.
43 Piccadilly W.   1867-68

Day, Hamilton, Smith & Co.
14 Piccadilly W.   1862-64

Day, Hamilton, Smith & Son
14 Piccadilly W.   1856-61

Day, Albert
43 Kenton Road, S. Hackney N.E.   1899-01
165 Well Street, S. Hackney N.E.   1902-08

Day, Arthur
14 Piccadilly W.   1865-66

Day, Charles Wm.
82 New Bond Street W.   1858-59

Day, Henry Valentine
Trafalgar Bdgs., Northumberland Av.   1900-01

Day, John B.
3 Savoy Street, Strand W.C.   1869-72

Day, John B., & Son
3 Savoy Street, Strand W.C.   1873-78

Day, Joseph
209 Shoreditch High Street N.E.   1860

Death, Hy
5 Addington Place,Cmberwell Rd. S   1857-64
119 Camberwell Road S   1865-88

Debenham & Gabell
158 Regent Street W.   1884-90

Debenham, Arthur
158 Regent Street W.   1891-92

Debenham, Wm. Elliott
158 Regent Street W.   1863-83
4 Powis Place, Haverstock Hill N.W.   1865-76
188 Regent Street W.   1871-72
46 Haverstock Hill N.W.   1877-04

Decours & Co.
16 & 17 Poultry E.C.   1886-87

Decours & Hovey
125 Hammersmith Road. W.   1899-03

Deighton & Dunthorne
320 High Holborn W.C.   1879

De La Motte, Philip Henry; also
Delamotte, Philip Henry
168 New Bond Street   1855
King's College, Strand W.C.   1856-58
38 Chipstone Place, Bayswater W.   1856-61

Delamotte, Freeman
15 Beaufort Buildings W.C.   1857-59

Delmen Art Studios Co. Ltd.
470 & 472 Holloway Road N.   1894-01

De Mauny, Louis
16 Fitzroy Terrace, New Road   1857
374 Euston Road N.W.   1858-66
4 Orange Row, Kennington Road S.   1864-65
333 Euston Road N.W.   1867-77
313 Euston Road N.W.   1876-78
326 Euston Road N.W.   1878-08-

Demezy & Co.
179 Regent Street W.   1870-78

Demezy & Hemery
179 Regent Street W.   1868-69

De Mouxy, John Marie
125 Regent Street W.   1864-65

De Mouxy, Joseph
19 Strand W.C.   1857-62

Dench, Edward
326 Oxford Street W.   1862
Mornington Pl., Hampstead Rd. N.W.   1863
245 Hampstead Road N.W.   1864

Deneulain & Blake
147 Strand W.C.   1877-84

Deneulain, Albert
147 Strand W.C.   1876
147 Strand W.C.   1885-94
22 Baker Street W.   1895-01

Denison, Edwin Henry
9 Charing Cross S.W.   1854-62

Denman, John Flaxman & Son
61 Bancroft Rd., Mile End Rd. N.E.   1865
238 Mile End Road. E.   1866-68

Dennis, William
6 Queen's Road, Bayswater W.   1883

Dennis, William, & Co.
26 Westbourne Grove W.   1884-85

Dickins & Glasse
27 Sloane Street S.W.   1891-92

Dickins, Frank
27 Sloane Street S.W.   1893-97

Dickinson Brothers
114 New Bond Street W.   1855-58
174 Regent Street W.   1855

Griffith, an operator working for Dickinson Brothers, left to set up his own studio in Margate.

Dickinson Brothers & Foster
114 New Bond Street W.   1876-77

Dickinson, George
161 Clarendon Road, Nottinghill   1880

Dietrichson & Co.
63 Westbourne Grove W.   1873

Dighton, Joshua
81 Lupus Street, Pimlico S.W.   1870

Dimberline, Richard
325 Old Ford Road, Bow E.   1882-93
75 Roman Road, Bow E.   1894-08-

Disdéri, A., & Co.
70, 71 & 72 Brook St, Hanover Sq.   1868
Hereford Lodge, Old Brompton S.W.   1868
4 Brook St, Hanover Square W.   1870-94

McCauley in her book on Disdéri (see bibliography) details his career in Paris and the opening of his London studios. From March 1865 Disdéri began converting a house on Brook Street which opened as his first London studio. A M. Léon was appinted to run it and the studio probably began serving customers from October 1865. An equestrian portrait branch was opened at Hereford Lodge, Old Brompton Road in early 1868.

Disderi, Adolphe
70, 71 & 72 Brook St, Hanover Square   1867
Hereford Lodge, Old Brompton S.W.   1867-69
4 Brook St, Hanover Square W.   1869

Diviani & Monte
Railway Place, Holloway Road N.   1867

Diviani, Gandenizio
Railway Pl, Holloway Rd. N.   1864-70
278 Holloway Road N.   1871
276 Holloway Road N.   1872-74

Dixon, Frederick
183 Regent Street   1856

Dixon, Henry
11 Sussex Terrace, Bayswater W.   1860-62
56 Albany Street N.W.   1864-65
112 Albany Street N.W.   1866-86

Dixon, Henry, & Son
112 Albany Street N.W.   1887-08-

Dixon, Montague, & Co.
15 Newgate Street E.C.   1907-08-

Dixon, Percy Goodchild
147 Strand W.C.   1873-75

Dixon, Richard H.
Temple Cmbrs, Falcon Ct, Fleet St.   1888-92
Falcon Court, 32 Fleet St. E.C.   1893-95

Dobbie, John
191 Fleet Street E.C.   1893

Dobie, Richard
13 Lower Sloane Street S.W.   1887

Dobbie, Richard Lizars
191 Fleet Street E.C.   1888-92

Dodge, Walter Parker
26 Stamford Road N.   1871

Dolamore & Bullock
30 Regent Street S.W.   1855-69

Dolamore, William
30 Regent Street W.   1870-73

Done & Ball
62 Cheapside E.C.   1890-93
12 Baker Street W.   1890-91

Done, John, & Co.
44 Baker Street, Portman Square W.   1877-79

Doran, Thomas
169 Essex Road N.   1888

Dore, James
78 Chalk Farm Road N.W.   1882-84
189 Earl's Court Road S.W.   1882

Dorman, George
90A Southgate Road N.   1902

Dorrett & Martin
60 Strand W.C.   1901-08

Dorrett was a partner of the well-known photographer, Paul Martin. He was born on 19 June 1870 and was apprenticed to a leading South Coast photographer. The *Photogram* (1899, p. 319) regarded him as one of the best technical photographers and lantern slide makers in London. He is listed at a studio in Clapham Junction outside of the main scope of this directory (see Appendix 1).

On 1 April 1899 Dorrett and Martin entered into a partnership taking over the premises of Fred Kingsbury at 16 Belle Vue Road, Upper Tooting and, for a short period, at 60 Strand W.

The partnership was dissolved on 31 December 1926. The *British Journal of Photography* (4 March 1927) reported that Dorrett was continuing alone at 382 Streatham High Road although this was subsequently denied in the issue dated 17 March 1929. Dorrett opened a studio in the Manor House, 341 London Road, Mitcham.

Douglas, Alfred
164 Sloane Street S.W.   1902-04

Dover Street Studios
38 Dover Street W.   1906

Dover Street Studios & Adart Ltd.
38 Dover Street W.   1907-08-

Downey, William & Daniel
61 Ebury Street, Pimlico S.W.   1872-08-
51 Ebury Street S.W.   1879
57 Ebury Street S.W.   1880-90

W. and D. Downey although known for their photography of Royalty and celebrities were, as the *Photographic News* (30 April 1880, pp. 206-207) was quick to point out happy to photograph anyone happy to tender one guinea. This gave the subject one position and a dozen cartes. The company occupied two modest houses in Ebury Street. Number 61 had two studios and number 57 which had only recently been completed had a glass house for photography. Downey's printing was largely done in Newcastle where all their pictures for publication were mounted and finished. One accessory employed by the firm (*PN* 16 September 1881, p. 439) was a trapeze, which was mainly used for posing ladies.

Daniel Downey died in July 1881.

The Hulton-Deutsch Collection have holdings of Downey's court and social work from c.1860-1920s.

Draycott Galleries
263 Oxford Street W.   1905-06

Dredge, George
449 Southwark Park Road S.E.   1891-92

Drewett, Edgar
4 Brunswick Place, Blackheath S.E.   1865-76

Driver, Albert Edward
291 New Cross Road S.E.   1904-08-

Droege & Wirth
201 Piccadilly   1854

Droege, Frederick
201 Piccadilly   1855

Dubisson, Walter
51 Oxford Street W.   1881
108 Oxford Street W.   1882-91

Dubourg & Veluti
143 Strand   1857

Dubourg, William
143 Strand W.C.   1858-60

Dudley, Philip
2 Knightsbridge Green S.W.   1902

Dudsman, James
1 Surrey Pl, Camberwell New Rd. S.   1856-60

Duffus, William
263 Oxford Street W.   1907

Dumain & Orchard, Misses
6 Bedford Place, Commercial Rd. E.   1867-69

Duncan, Charles William Walley
71 Newman Street W.   1906

Dundas, Miss Eleanor
10 Auriol Road, W. Kensington W.   1908-

Dunmore, Edward
280 Camden Road N.   1871
32 Great Coram Street W.C.   1872

Dunn, Clinton, & Co.
19 Grafton Square, Fitzroy Sq. W.   1882-83

Dunning, Henry
4 Bridge Street, Lambeth S.   1864
274 Westminster Bridge Road S.E.   1865-94

Durand, Francois
14 Blackfriars Road S   1856-62

Duros, Leon
408 Edgware Road W.   1902

Dutton, Miss Jane
3 Burton Hill Terrace S.   1857-60

Duval, Alexander
1 Hanway Street W.   1857-58
244 Regent Street W.   1858

Dyball, Robert H.
3 Lower Nottinghill Terrace W.   1860-83

Dyer Photographic Portrait Co.
A. Wood, manager;
E. G. Wood, proprietor
74 Cheapside E.C.   1868-74

Dyer, William
26 Walnut Tree Walk, Lambeth S.E.   1874
15 Canterbury Place, Lambeth S.E.   1876
53 Lambeth Road S.E.   1877-81
278 Kennington Road S.E.   1881-88

E

Eades, Richard E., & Co.
84 Newgate Street E.C.   1881

Eason, Arthur & Co.
9 Cornhill E.C.   1880

Eason, John
11 & 14 Lwthr. Arcade, Strand   1859-60

Eastham, John
122 Regent Street W.   1861

Edelstein, Willy
100 Westbourne Grove W.   1892-93

Edgar, James & Co.
121 Cheapside E.C.   1881-82

Edis, Charles
299 Euston Road N.W.   1872

Edis, Walter
91 Sloane Street S.W.   1860-65

Edisonograph Co., The
100 St Martin's Lane W.C.   1901-03
31 Maiden Lane W.C.   1904

Edmonds, Miss Catherine
118 Westbourne Grove W.   1900-03

Edmonds, Miss Cathrn.
31 York Place, Portman Square W.   1904-05

Edwards & Bult
20 Baker Street W.   1869

Edwards & Co.
12 Grove Road, Bow E.C.   1902-08-

Edwards, Ernest
20 Baker Street W.   1864-68

Edwards Fras. Wm.
341 Albany Road, Camberwell S.E.   1879-81

Edwards, John
1 Park Side, Knightsbridge S.W.   1882-98
For many years principal photographer for W.
& D. Downey.

Edwards, Lewis
21 Duke St, Manchester Square W.   1903

Edwards, William Henry
433 Strand W.C.   1867

Egerton, Jeremiah
443 Strand   1854-56
1 Temple Street, Whitefriars   1854-55

Ehn, Henry
58 Cheapside   1855-57

**Electric Light Enlarged Photo-
graphic Co. Ltd.**
40 King Street, Cheapside E.C.   1881-82

Electric Portrait Co.
149 Fleet Street E.C.   1897

Elite Portrait Co.
267 High Holborn W.C.   1901-08-
95 High Road, Kilburn N.W.   1905-08-

Elliott, James
9 Albany Court Yard   1856-61
48 Piccadilly   1856-61

Elliott & Fry
55 Baker Street, Portman Square W.   1865-86
55 & 56 Baker St, Portman Sq. W.   1887-08-
Park Rd, Barnet (works)   1886-88
7 Gloucester Terrace, Onslow Gdns.   1887-93

The Elliott & Fry partnership was founded in
1863 and the compay remained in Baker Street
at various numbers until 1963 when it was
incorporated into Bassano & Vandyck *(q.v.)*.

 The studio had a high reputation and was
visited by the *Photographic News* (30 January
1880) which was guided by the firm's
co-founder Clarence E. Fry. The premises in
Baker Street had three studios of various sizes
and charged one guinea for a dozen a a-half
cartes. The premises had four negative rooms
with the negatives being stored loose and open
in grooves. The firms printing was undertaken
at works in Barnet which carried out silver and
carbon work. The firm was also extensive
publishers of its photographs and this aspect of
the business was under the care of a Mr. Martin.

Elliott, Rollo
123B Pentonville Road N.   1869-78

Elliott, Rollo, and Co.
123B Pentonville Road N.   1879-82

Ellis & Burvill
45 Brompton Road S.W.   1872-83

Ellis, Alfred, & Walery
51 Baker Street W.   1900-08-

Ellis, Alfred
20 Upper Baker Street N.W.   1885-99

Ellis, Charles
9 Elgin Crescent W.   1908-

Ellsmoor, Miss Margaret
122 Regent Street W.   1903

Ellsmoor & Driver
122 Regent Street W.   1904

Elmes, Madame Eliza, & Co.
39 King's Rd, Chelsea S.W.   1890

Elmes, Sidney Walter
39 King's Rd, Chelsea S.W.   1881-89

Elwell, Francis Richard
44 Regent Street W.   1875-81
137 Regent Street W.   1882
122 Regent Street W.   1883-93

Elwell started his photographic career in Weston-Super-Mare and was linked through his wife's family to the Scottish photographer John Moffat.

Emberson, George, & Sons
6 Wilton Rd, Pimlico S.W.   1886-08-
83 Gracechurch Street E.C.   1894-97
62 Cheapside E.C.   1896-08-
12 Oxford Street W.   1905
129 Regent Street W.   1905
57 St Pauls Churchyard E.C.   1890-08-
358 Strand W.C.   1905
11 Wilton Road, Pimlico S.W.   1898-05

Emberson, George (junior)
9 Cornhill E.C.   1888-04
295 Edgware Road W.   1900-01
98 Cheapside E.C.   1905

Emberson, John
352 Strand W.C.   1893-00
60 Strand W.C.   1898-00
358 Strand W.C.   1901-08-
98 Cheapside E.   1901

Emberson, Thomas
83 Gracechurch Street E.C.   1898-04
179 Regent Street W.   1899-03
12 Oxford Street W.   1903-08-
129 Regent Street W.   1904-08-

Emery, Wilfred
24 South St, Manchester Square W.   1891-96
3 Soho Street, Soho Square W.   1897

Endacott, Alex
9 Claro Terrace, Richmond Rd. S.W.   1884-85

Endacott & Florkofski
9 Claro Terrace, Richmond Rd. S.W.   1886

Ennel, N.
7 Wellington St, London Bridge S.E.   1860-61

Ernst, Hermann
1 Waverley Pl, St Johns Wood N.W.   1891-03
14 Finchley Road N.W.   1904-08-

Esau, John
52 Mount Street, Lambeth S.   1864
127 Westminster Bridge Road S.   1865-69

Esme & Co.
405 Holloway Road N.   1889-91

Esme Collings Ltd.
5 Golding Square W.   1903

Essen & Pessarra
96 Aldersgate Street E.C.   1903

Estabrooke, Richard Parker
158 Fleet Street E.C.   1877
153 Fleet Street E.C.   1879-90

Estabrooke, Thomas Sherman
30 Regent Street S.W.   1874-76

Evans & Co.
36 Elizabeth St, Eaton Square S.W.   1884

Evans, M. E. & Co.
36 Elizabeth Street, S.W.   1878-80

Evans, Charles
2 Aldgate High Street E.   1882

Evans, Edmund William
24 Church Street, Kensington W.   1903

Evans, Frederick Wm.
4 Surrey Place, Old Kent Road S.E.   1860-63
246 Old Kent Road S.E.   1864-93

Evans, George Edward
27 Chancery Lane W.C. 1895-96

Eve, Mrs Sh.
4 Silver St, High Street, Nottinghill 1867

Eve, Charles
3 Kingsland Green 1857

Everett, Sydney T.
157 Morning Lane, Hackney N.E. 1905

Everitt, Henry
3 Cheapside E.C. 1867-74

Eyre, Arthur Stanlope
62 Piccadilly W. 1867-68

Eyre, John
105 Park St, Camden Town. N.W. 1906-07

F

Faithfull, Albert Edmund
2 Lower Nottinghill Terrace W. 1894

Fall, Thos.
9 Baker Street, Portman Square W. 1875-08-
10 Baker Street, Portman Square W. 1879-08-
10 High Street, Nottinghill W. 1887-90
6 Fitzjohn's Prom, Finchley Road 1890-93
474 Oxford Street W. 1890
233 Finchley Road N.W. 1892-95
42 High St, Nottinghill W. 1896-01
8 Grand Parade, Finchley Rd. N.W. 1897-98
180 Finchley Road N.W. 1899-08-

A reorganisation and extension of Fall's studio was undertaken in the Autumn of 1880 (*Photographic News* 29 October 1880, p. 528).

Faller, Frederick
118 Whitechapel High Street E. 1862-63

Fantini, Pasquale
435 Fulham Road S.W. 1886-87

Farmer, Hy.
11 Heresford Place, Commercial Rd. 1864-67

Farr, Henry
214 Grove Road E. 1886
216 Grove Road E. 1887-89

Fastowsky, Will
118 Cannon Street Road E. 1906

Faulkner, Charles
262 Seven Sisters Road N. 1899-08-

Faulkner, Robert
46 Kensington Gardens Square. W. 1864-77

Advertised on a carte (negative number 21323a) that on and after January 1st 1877 he would be lacated

Faulkner, Robert, & Co.
21 Baker Street, Portman Square. W. 1878-08-

Faulkner had a very high reputation amongst his contemporaries for the quality and success of his child studies. A number of his child studies were published as transparencies and as 'red chalk' carbon prints some of which, the *Photographic News* (22 October 1880, pp. 506-507) reported had sold over 10,000 copies.

Faust, Alfred
422 Mile End Road E. 1904

Fawn, William Henry
3 Black Prince Row, Walworth Road 1860-65
31 Walworth Road S 1867-70
Uxbridge Road, Bayswater W. 1872
Bayswater Road W. 1873-75
13 Evelyn Street, Deptford S.E. 1887-02
400 Evelyn Street, Deptford S.E. 1903-06

Feaks & Hiscott
84 Newgate Street E.C. 1882-83

Fearn, David, & Co.
50 High Road, Kilburn N.W. 1902-08-

Fehrenbach & Bernieri
45 St George's Place S.W. 1896

Fehrenbach, Edwin
111 Strand W.C. 1883-88

Fehrenbach, Emilian
111 Strand W.C.   1854-73

Emilian Fehrenbach died on 17 August 1867 and his trading name was carried by his wife Isabel for the next thirteen years. She was according to the Heathcotes "a reputable photographer, for when the premises were eventually acquired by Edwin Squire he continued to trade under the Fehrenbach name".

Fehrenbach, German
56 Chalk Farm Road N.W.   1868-70
64A New Bond Street W.   1871
45 St. George's Place S.W.   1897-00

Fehrenbach, Madame Isabel
111 Strand W.C.   1874-82

Field, Dudley
35 Buckingham Palace Road. S.W.   1883-86
69 New Bond Street W.   1889

Fielding, Henry Edward
235 Ball's Pond Road N.   1902

Fielding, Mrs Isabella
108 Hammersmith Road N.   1902

Fielding, Hy. Edward, & Co.
158 Stamford Street S.E.   1895

Fielding, Mrs Hy. Edward
158 Stamford Street S.E.   1896-00

Fillan, Andrew
73 Oxford Street W.   1864-67

Finch, Thomas
57 East Street, Walworth S.E.   1906

Fink, Philip
57 Oxford Street W.   1860-66

Finlayson, Jacob
62 Piccadilly W.   1858-72

Fish, William
73 Cross Street, Islington N.   1877

Fisher, Mrs Emma
108 Westborne Grove W.   1874-76

Fisher, John
90 Golborne Road W.   1894-08-

Fisher, Regnld Stanley
56 Seven Sisters Road N.   1904-06

Fisher, Robert
376 Oxford Street W.   1873
108 Westbourne Grove W.   1873-77

Fisher, Robert
31 Westbourne Grove W.   1859-61
40 Westbourne Grove W.   1862-63
28 Westbourne Grove W.   1864
90 Westbourne Grove W.   1865

Fisher, Thompson
174 Edgware Road W.   1896-00
54 Mare Street, Hackney S.E.   1899-06-

Fisher, Tom George
174 Edgware Road W.   1901-07

Flather, Henry
91 Regent Street W.   1866-68
109 Regent Street W.   1869-73

A *carte* advertised the fact Flather was "late Francis 91 (late 53) Regent St. W".

Flett, Henry
119 Cheapside E.C.   1898-07
103 Newgate Street E.C.   1904-08-

Flower, George
256 Westminster Bridge Road S   1866-72
258 Westminster Bridge Road S   1873-76

Folk, Emil
79 Minories E.   1862
3 Postern Row, Tower Hill E.C.   1862-63

Folker, John Herbert
12 Tottenham Court Road W.   1905-08-

Fontauella, Victor
12 Rathbone Place W.   1908-

Forester, Robert
100 Regent Street W.   1858-59

Fortman, Henry
98 Cheapside E.C.   1902

Fossick, Samuel
49 King William Street, City   1854-59

Foster, Gustav
228 Westminster Bridge Road S.E.   1872-73

Foster, Thomas
149 Ball's Pond Road N.   1866-70

Foster, W. H.
4 Upton Grove, De Beauvoir Tn. N.   1867-70

Foulsham & Banfield Ltd.
95 Wigmore Street W.   1906-07
2 Little Bruton Street W. (works)   1908-
49 Old Bond Street W.   1908-

Fowler, Thomas
18 Palmerston Road, Kilburn N.W.   1899-08

Fox & Hill
5 New Oxford Street W.C.   1893-95

Fox, Charles James
30 Finchley Rd, St Johns Wood N.W. 1872-74
34 Finchley Rd, St Johns Wood N.W.   1875

Fox, Thomas
233 High Holborn W.C.   1891-92

Foxlee, Miss Annie E.
124 High Road, Kilburn N.W.   1905-06

Foxlee, Edward William
98 Cheapside E.C.   1866-72

Fradelle & Leach
230 Regent Street W.   1870-72

Fradelle & Marshall
230 Regent Street W.   1873-77
246 Regent Street W.   1876-77

Fradelle & Young
17 Regent Street S.W.   1887
246 Regent Street S.W.   1887-97
283 Regent Street S.W.   1898-08-

Fradelle, Albert Eugene
19 Langham Place W.   1865-69
230 Regent Street W.   1878
246 Regent Street W.   1878-86
62 Cheapside E.C.   1880

A. E. Fradelle died in October 1884. He was the son and grandson of well-known artists. (*Photographic News* 31 October 1884, p. 704).

Francis & Co.
29 Ludgate Hill E.C.   1889-02
2 Creed Lane E.C.   1892-93

Francis, Henry
101 Great Russell St., Bloomsbury   1857

Francis, Leonard
243 Kentish Town Road N.W.   1905-08-

Frankel, Albert
39 Spring Street, Paddington W.   1867

Fraser, Mrs Flora & Jennings, Miss Agnes
9 Regent Street S.W.   1899-00
10 Charles Street, St James' S.W.   1901-02

Fraser, Mrs Flora
9 Regent Street S.W.   1898

Freedberg, Dan
20 Crellin St, Cannon Street Road E.   1906-08-

Freeman & Ayton
176 St John Street Road E.C.   1874

Freeman & Co.
176 St John Street Road E.C.   1875

Freeman, Frederick
6 Queen's Road, Bayswater W.   1879

Freeman, James
118 Praed Street W.   1881-82

Freeman, Richard Stanley
162 High Street, Nottinghill W.   1872-76
4 Nottinghill Terrace W.   1877-81

Freeman, William
15 Wells Street, Albany Road S.E.   1881-91

5 Neate Street, Camberwell S.E.   1892-96

French & Co.
82 King's Rd., Camden Town N.W.   1901-03

Frewing, Edward
16 Islington High Street N.   1872-76
189 Earls Court Road S.E.   1887

Frewing, Edward, & Co.
26 Westbourne Grove W.   1888

Frewing, Edwin, & Co.
17 Warwick Court W.C.   1891

Friedl, George
311 Kentish Town Rd. N.W.   1908

Frier & Parris
35 Ball's Pond Road N.   1890-92

Frier, Robert
35 Ball's Pond Road N.   1886-88

Frost, William
49 Brecknock Road N.   1891

Frost, William Row
16 & 17 Poultry E.C.   1873-77

Fruwirth, Daniel
146 Cheapside E.C.   1868

Fry, Alfred
105 Euston Road N.W.   1908

Fry, C. E. & Son
7 Gloucester Terrace, Onslow Gdns.   1894-08-

Fry, George & Co.
12 Lwr Seymour St, Portman Square   1874-77

Fry, Samuel & Co.
83 Gracechurch Street E.C.   1863-65

Fry, Robert
102 High Holborn   1863

Fry, Robert
19 Pleasant Row, Pentonville   1857

Fry, Samuel Herbert
5 Highbury Grove N.   1907

G

Gabell, Horace Victor, & Co.
22C Ebury Street S.W.   1891-97
13 Eccleston Street S.W.   1898-08-

Gabrielli, Enrico
9 Claro Terrace, Richmond St S.W.   1888-89
4 Vanston Place, Fulham S.W.   1903-05

Gabrielli, Rodalfo
132 Camberwell Road S.E.   1894

Gainsborough Studio
John Caswell-Smith, proprietor
309 Oxford Street W   1907-08-

Galea, Daniel
211 Clapham Road S.W.   1906-08
122 Regent Street W.   1906-08-

Gallo, Henry
6 Edgware Road, west W.   1866-67

Gally, John
6 Church Lane, Kensington W.   1860-64
6 Church Street, Kensington W.   1865-67
6 Wiple Street, Church St., Kens. W.   1868-73
48 Church Street, Kensington W.   1874-80

Gandy, Charles Alfred
5 Bishopsgate Street, without E.C.   1869-90
47 Old Broad Street E.C.   1892-93

Garford, Robert
4 Radnor Street, Chelsea S.W.   1907

Garner, William Myles
276 Holloway Road N.   1882-83
41 London Road S.E.   1885
250 Westminster Bridge Road S.E.   1885-86
298 Holloway Road N.   1887-89
40 London Road S.E.   1886-08
151 Upper Street N.   1890-91

Garrett, James
140 Deptford Lower Road S.E.   1884-86

Garrett, James, & Son
140 Deptford Lower Road S.E.   1887-95

Garstain, Miss Alice & Antrobus
Miss Dora
26 New Cavendish Street W.   1904-05

Gass, Frederick & Co.
112 Cheapside E.C.   1865
16 Wellington Square, Chelsea   1865

Gates, Henry, & Co.
229 Seven Sisters Road N.   1899-05

Gaubert, Edward
151 Fulham Road S.W.   1866-70
61 Cheapside E.C.   1872-76

Gaudin, Charles
384 Kennington Road S.E.   1874-75

Gay, David
74 Cheapside E.C.   1862-67
57 Cheapside E.C.   1868-69
39 Spring Street, Paddington W.   1870-73

Gearing & Sons
52 Regent Street W.   1898-08-
130 Ladbroke Grove W.   1908-
118 New Bond Street W.   1908-

Gearing, Charles
267 Fulham Road S.W.   1890-91

Gearing, Charles J., & Co.
52 Regent Street W.   1888-91
433 Strand W.C.   1888-91
343 Edgware Road W.   1889-91
343 Kentish Town Road N.W.   1890-92

Gear, Chidley & Co.
101 Great Portland Street W.   1900-07
8 Nottinghill Terr., Marylebone Road   1908-

Gearing, Mrs Emma Francis, & Sons
52 Regent Street W.   1892

Gearing, Mrs Emma Francis, & Co.
52 Regent Street W.   1893-97

General Photographic Co.
Hugh Campbell, manager
97 Newgate Street E.C.   1867-70

Genlain, Adolphus Frnes
119 Westbourne Grove W.   1867-68

Gent, Henry Johnson
448 Edgware Road W.   1870-72

Geobelhoff, William
307 Essex Road N.   1890

George, H.
Imperial Mansions, Oxford Street   1890

Gerlach, T.
10 Oxford Terrace, Kings Rd. S.W.   1862

German, James
230 Roman Road E.   1874

Gibbons, James Harper
3 Kensington High Street W.   1867-71
6 Kensington High Street W.   1872-72

Gibbs & Co.
454 Kingsland Road N.E.   1903-06

Gibbs & Muller
434 Kingsland Road N.E.   1907

Gibbs, Henry Richard
454 Kingsland Road N.E.   1892-00

Gibbs, John
24 Freeschool Street S.E.   1859-66
23 Freeschool Street S.E.   1867-70

Gibbs, Robert Henry
330 Mile End Road E.   1880-84

Gibson, Alfred Hy., & Co.
4 Crane Court, Fleet Street E.C.   1882

Gigney, Miss E.
8 Queens Buildings, Brompton S.W. 1859-62

Gilchrist, Napoleon Arthur
208 East India Dock Road E.   1908-

Gill, Charles
267 Fulham Road S.W.   1888-89

Gill, Edward Cope
38 Brecknock Road N.   1890

Gill, Fredk James
49 King William Street E.C.   1896-98

Gill, Geo. Reynolds
42 Islip St, Kentish Town Road N.W.   1866-67
381 Kentish Town Road N.W.   1868-78

Gill, John B.
37 Connaught Terrace, Edgware Rd.   1860
62 New Bond Street W.   1861-64

Gillard, William
263 Regent Street W.   1864-66

Gillard, William M.
106 Great Russell Street W.C.   1906

Gilling, Francis
158 Strand W.C.   1876-81

Gilson, Hy. Turner
80 Pitfield Street, Hoxton N.   1865-68

Gissing, John G.
4 Surrey Place, Newington Butts   1858-59

Gladwell, Harry Wm.
5 Ludgate Street E.C.   1859

Globe Enlarging Co.
27 Worship Street E.C.   1908

Glover, Bower & Miles
145 Regent Street W.   1858

Glover, Edward
51 Connaught Terr., Edgware Rd. W.   1859-68
83 Edgware Road W.   1869-71

Glynn Edward & Co.
117 Cheapside E.C.   1857-61

Gobbi, Bernardo
232 Euston Road N.W.   1875-77
221 Westminster Bridge Road S.E.   1879-85

Godart & Co.
154 Fleet Street E.C.   1899
30 Maiden Lane W.C.   1900-08-

Godart & Hay
39-41 Imperial Bdgs, New Bridge St.   1889-91

Godart Brothers
47 Imperial Bdgs, New Brdge St E.C. 1884-88

Godart, Thomas
39 & 40 Imperial Bdgs, New Brg St.   1892
149 Fleet Street E.C.   1893-94
58 Fleet Street E.C.   1895-97

Godart, Thomas & Co.
40 & 46 Ludgate Hill E.C.   1880
45 Imperial Buildings, New Brdge St. 1881-83

Godbold, Douglas
74 Baker Street W.   1904

Godbold, Henry James, & Son
74 Baker Street W.   1903

Goddard, Bernando
221 Westminster Bridge Road S.E.   1878

Godfrey, Frank
248 Caledonian Road N.   1894

Godon, Louis Nelson
293 King's Road, Chelsea S.W.   1896

Goebelhoff, Wilhelm
82 Pentonville Road N.   1896-01
34 & 82 Pentonville Road N.   1902-04
34 Pentonville Road N.   1905-08-

Goldbloom, Daniel
129 Westminster Bridge Road S.E.   1904-05

Goldesmann, Nachson
17 Hindon Street, Pimlico S.W.   1880

Good, William Thomas
7 Carlton Terrace, Harrow Road W.   1890-04
48 High Street, Nottinghill Gate W.   1904-06
25 Great Western Road W.   1906

Goodfellow, William
122 Regent Street W.   1878
179 Regent Street W.   1879-98

Goodman, Claudius E.
118 New Bond Street W.   1857-60
11 Lancaster Road, Nottinghill   1859

Goodwin, Edward Thomas Frederick
102 London Wall E.C.   1873-88
75 St Paul's Churchyard E.C.   1884-91

Goodwin, John
29 Jubilee Street, Commrcial Rd. E.   1878-85
43 Jubilee Street E.   1887-88

Gordon, Alex
24 Cannon Street west, City   1857

Gorsuch, John William
48 Junction Road N.   1899-01

Gosby, Tom
199 Brompton Road S.W.   1890

Gostick, Jesse
62 Upper Street, Islington N.   1863
832 Old Kent Road S.E.   1864

Gottheil, Elias
17A Jubilee St, Commercial Road   1859-62
23 Assembly Row, Mile End Road E.   1863-64
120 Mile End Road E.   1865-84

Gould, George
190 Shoreditch High Street E.   1905

Goulder, Chas
55 Douglas Street, Deptford S.E.   1867
341 New Cross Road S.E.   1868
24 Evelyn Street, Deptford S.E.   1872

Gover, Edward Thomas
28 Camomile Street E.C.   1876

Grabman, Joseph
22 Commercial Street E.   1903

Graham, G. C. & Co.
5 High Road, Kilburn N.W.   1904

Grant, Herbert, & Bros.
91 St Paul's Road N.   1865-66

Grant, James
35 Bridgport Place, Hoxton N.   1871-73

Grant, James Duncan
83 Newington Causeway S.E.   1902-08-

Grant, William
228 Westminster Bridge Road S.E.   1874

Gray & Davies
92 Queen's Road W.   1892-95

Gray & Jones
25 Old Cavendish Street W.   1867

Gray, Henry
Old Cavendish Street W.   1868

Gray, John Charles
512 Harrow Road W.   1900-08-
124 High Road, Kilburn N.W.   1904

Gray, John William
51 Popham Road, Islington N.   1906-07

Gray, Miss Lizzie
73 & 75 Bishops Road, Bayswater   1897-98

Gray, Misses Lizzie & Kate
100 Westbourne Grove W.   1895

Gray, William Edward
92 Queen's Road, Bayswater W.   1896-08-

Great Western Photo Art Co.
22 Bishop's Road W.   1882-88

Greatheed, William
174 Euston Road N.W.   1888

Greatrex, George William
224 Regent Street W.   1858

Greatrex, John Henry
196 Piccadilly W.   1856-58
79 Regent Street   1856
70 Regent Street W.   1857-60
162 Regent Street W.   1861

Green & Gilchrist
208 East India Dock Road E.   1907

Green, Robert Percy
294 Upper Street N.   1907

Greene, Friese, & Collings
69 New Bond Street W.   1888
92 Piccadilly W.   1888

100 Westbourne Grove W. 1888

Greene, Friese
69 New Bond Street W. 1886-87
92 Piccadilly W. 1887-92
100 Westbourne Grove W. 1889-91
110 Westbourne Grove W. 1889-90
20 Brook Street W. 1890-91
182 Oxford Street W. 1891
162 Sloane Street W. 1891
135 Regent Street W. 1892

Greene, Mrs Helena
39 King's Road, Chelsea S.W. 1893-97

Greener, James Henry
1 Belmont Row, Vauxhall S. 1859-65

Gregory, William, & Co.
51 Strand W.C. 1894-02

Gregory, William, & Co. Ltd.
51 Strand W.C. 1903

Griffiths, Alfred
204 King's Road S.W. 1877

Griffiths, Arthur
98 Amagh Road, Bow E. 1895-04

Griffiths, Arthur, & Son
98 Amagh Road, Bow E. 1905-08-
2 Gibralter Walk, Bethnal Green E. 1905-07

Griffiths, George
45 Cheapside E.C. 1865

Griffiths, John
32 St Martin's le Grand E.C. 1866-68
24 Cornhill E.C. 1870-78

Griffiths, John
89 Grove Road E. 1885-91

Griggs, Charles & W.
Elm Hse., Elm Grove, Peckham S.E. 1873-78

Griggs, William
Elm Hse., Hanover St, Peckham S.E. 1881-82
The Photo-chromo-lithographic establishment suffered a serious fire in June 1883

(*Photographic News* 15 June 1883). It was re-opened, after reorganisation early in 1884.

Grimston, Edward
79 Regent Street W. 1870-72

Grimwood, W.
10 Slades Place, High St., Deptford 1864-65

Grisdale & Fillan
73 Oxford Street W 1863

Gross, Geo.
3 Primrose Street, Bishopsgate 1856-57

Grossman, Alex James
197 Westbourne Grove W. 1902
22A Pembridge Villas, Bayswater 1903

Grove, W. H., & Boulton
174 Brompton Road S.W. 1906-08-

Grove, William Henry
174 Brompton Road S.W. 1889-05

Grunebaum, Joseph
6 Edgware Road W. 1865-68
16 Edgware Road W. 1869

Gubbins, William G.
22 Myddleton Square E.C. 1865-66
103 St Johns Wood Terrace N.W. 1865-66

Guggenheim, Jules M.
12 Pall Mall east S.W. 1858

Gumprecht, Louis
12 Cannon Street Road E. 1865-66
11 Cannon Street Road E. 1867-87

Gungler, Albert
116 Deptford High Street S.E. 1883

Gunn & Stuart
162 Sloane Street S.W. 1895-05

Gush & Co.
194 Regent Street W. 1872

Gush & Ferguson
179 Regent Street W. 1861-65
83 Gracechurch Street E.C. 1866-67

194 Regent Street W.   1866-71

Gush, Frederick
179 Regent Street W.   1860

H

Hadley, William Holke
5 Bridge Street, Lambeth   1854

Haes & Vandyk
19 Westbourne Grove W.   1875-81

Haes, Frank
41 St George's Place S.W.   1867-73
19 Westbourne Grove W.   1882-86

Haigh & Hemery
213 Regent Street W.   1878

Haigh, Edward
213 Regent Street W.   1875-77

Hailey, Clarence
51 Ordnance Road N.W.   1891-04

Haines, Frederick
61 Regent's Park Road N.W.   1888

Haines, Frederick, & Co.
61 Regent's Park Road N.W.   1889-90

Haines, Reginald
4 Southampton Row W.C.   1904-08-

Hains, David
28 Upper Phillimore Place, Kens. W.   1867-87
Originally from Lock and Whitfield's studio.

Halftones Ltd.
17 Fleet Street E.C.   1908-

Halksworth, Miss Jane
58 Fleet Street E.C.   1857-60

Hall & Co.
65 Haymarket S.W.   1904

Hall & Nightingale
20 Upper Baker Street N.W.   1880

Hall, Arthur
383 Wandsworth Road S.E.   1908

Hall, John
12 Red Lion Square, Holborn   1856-57
291 High Holborn W.C.   1864-65

Hall, Jospeh
159 Walworth Road S.E.   1889-93

Hall, Mrs L.
36 Russell Street, Covent Gdn. W.C.   1867

Halle, Samuel Baruch
133 Regent Street W.   1871
Originally worked at Mayer Brothers.

Halpen, Charles
22 Newman Street W.   1873-74

Hambley, William
116 Euston Road N.W.   1893

Hamerton, George
8 Burne Street, Edgware Rd. N.W.   1903-08

Hamilton, Miss
Frith Street, Soho   29 May 1848
The Heathcotes in their work on women in photography describe Miss Hamilton's activities. Originally a professional dancing teacher in the 1840s she became interested in photography and by the spring of 1848 was also offering lessons in photography.
    In July 1851 she announced that she had a photographic gallery at 147 Strand and remained in business for about two and one-half years.

Hamilton, Charles
22 Ludgate Street E.C.   1863-65
4 Ludgate Hill E.C.   1866-67

Hamilton, George
70 Regent Street W.   1863
39 Spring Street, Paddington W.   1865-66

Hamilton, James
248 Shoreditch High Street N.E.   1862

Hamilton, Miss Matilda
147 Strand W.C.   1852-54

Hamilton, T.
105A Bishopsgate St., without E.C.   1866-67

Hamly, William
116 Euston Road N.W.   1891-92

Hammond, Miss Mary
18 Yoemans Rw., Brompton Rd. S.W.   1901

Hammond, Miss May
122 Regent Street W.   1902

Hana, George Henry
443 Strand W.C.   1895-98

Hana Studios Ltd.
22 Bedford Street, Strand W.C.   1899-08-

Hancock & Williams
24 New Cross Road S.E.   1886-91

Hancock, Edward
24 New Cross Road S.E.   1892-93

Harding & Lawson
23 Liverpool Street E.C.   1897

Hardy, James D.
15 Victoria Terr., Hampstead N.W.   1864

Harford, Frank
6 Mildmay Road N.   1899-08-

Hargreaves, Mendelssohn
155 City Road E.C.   1894-98

Harman, Robert
11 Pleasant Row, Deptford High St.   1865-66
112 Deptford High Street S.E.   1867-72
116 Deptford High Street S.E.   1873-82

Harrington & Co.
36 Elizabeth Street, Pimlico S.W.   1882

Harrington, Frank, & Co.
31 Wilton Road S.W.   1884-98

Harris, Daniel
8 Newington Causeway S.E.   1859-65
31 Newington Causeway S.E.   1866-68

Harris, Gathorne
187 Roman Road E.   1887-89

Harris, Henry
74 Baker Street W.   1886

Harris, Percy
134 Kingsland High Street E.   1888-89

Harris, Tudor, & Son
40 Lillie Road S.W.   1904-06

Harrison, Cecil
29 Kennington Park Road S.E.   1880-83

Harrison, Henry
119 Roman Road, Bow E.   1905-08-

Harrison, John Ashworth
93 Rockingham St, Nwngtn Cswy.   1874-00

Harrison, Mrs My
191 Westminster Bridge Road S   1868-69

Harrison, Thomas James
307 Essex Road N.   1888-89

Harrison, Walter Geo.
Jamaica Level, Rotherhithe S.E.   1874-76

Harrison, Walter Hy.
4 Onslow Place, S. Kensington S.W.   1904-08-

Harrods Stores Ltd.
87 to 105 Brompton Road S.W.   1897-00

Hart, John
179 City Road E.C.   1886-98
181 City Road E.C.   1889-05

Harwood, George
153 Shoreditch High Street N.E.   1860-68

Hassan, Golam
20 Lower Phillimore Place W.   1865-66
13 Silver Street, High St. Nottinghill   1867-70

Hasset, John Fredk Blenner
62 Upper Street, Islington N.   1864-71
1A Vernon Street, Kings Cross W.C.   1865-71

Hatherill, John
8 Wynford Terrace, Lower Road S.E.   1862-68

Jamaica Level, Blue Anchor Rd. S.E. 1869-76
58 Jamaica Lvl., Blue Anchor Rd. S.E.1877-79
475 Southwark Park Road S.E.   1880-08-

Hatt, Robert
235 Balls Pond Road N.   1892-00

Havell, Edmund
31 Edgware Road W.   1868

Haves & Whiting
154 Euston Road N.W.   1891

Haviland Heath, John
7A Elm Tree Road N.W.   1900-01
15B James Street, Haymarket S.W.   1903

Hawes, Arthur
8 Grand Parade, Finchley Road N.W. 1894-96

Hawhes, William Thomas
16 Stamford Road N.   1907

Hawkins, Abdiel
65 Hatton Garden E.C.   1875

Hawkins, Henry
273 Portobello Road W.   1876-78
60 Evelyn Street, Deptford S.E.   1884-02
300 Evelyn Street, Deptford S.E.   1903-08-

Hay, George Heron
191 Regent Street W.   1865-70

Hayes, Charles
343 Edgware Road W.   1888

Hayler, Walter
36 Chandos St, Covent Garden W.C.   1879-83
40 Charing Cross S.W.   1885

Hayles, William Henry
20 Baker Street W.   1892-00

Hayward, Alfred Thomas
41 King William Street E.C.   1877-84

Heath & Beau
283 Regent Street W.   1862-63

Heath, Edgar
154 Great College Street N.W.   1878

Heath, Henry Charles
Chester Cottage, 7 Regents Park Rd.   1858
39 Great Marlborough Street   1858-61
11 Devonshire Terrace, Kensington   1860-62
153 Regent Street W.   1864-71

Heath, Vernon
43 Piccadilly W.   1863-76

Heath, Vernon, & Co.
43 Piccadilly W.   1877-85
37 Piccadilly W.   1887-88

Hebert, Frederick
89 Fulham Road S.W.   1869

Hedderly, James
2 Duke Street, Chelsea S.W.   1869-72
James Hedderly (*c*.1815-1885) was active as a
photographer in Chelsea from the mid-1860s to
the 1870s. He particularly photographed the
Chelsea Embankment and river frontage. A
small collection of his work is held by at the
Chelsea Reference Library, Old Town Hall,
Kings Road, London SW3 5EZ. A report
appeared in *The Local Historian* 18 (1988), 3,
pp. 142-144.

Hedges, Robert Thomas
985 High Street, Camden Town N.W.   1870
215 High Street, Camden Town N.W.   1871
279 High Street, Camden Town N.W.   1872-83

Heilbrom & Allerton
8 Coburn Road, Bow Road E.   1872

Hellery, James Spencer
48 Priscilla Road, Bow Road E.   1894
18 Bishops Rd, Cambrdge Rd. N.E.   1902-08-
                                13 Silver Street •

Hellis, Robert, & Sons
309 Euston Road N.W.   1890-08- •
211 Regent Street W.   1890-91 ~
213 Regent Street W.   1890-06 —
1 Deptford Bridge S.E.   1891-99 — •
63 St Pauls Churchyard E.C.   1891-05 —•
26 Westbourne Grove W.   1891-02 —
160 High St., Camden Town N.W.   1892-08- —
107 Fulham Road S.W.   1897-07 —
30 Clapham Road
6 The Pavement, Clapham Common ~
211 Queen's Road, Peckham •
688 Fulham Road
71 Green Lanes, Stoke Newington

232 Mare Street, Hackney N.E. — 1899-08-
49 Deptford Bridge S.E. — 1900-08-
24 Westbourne Grove W. — 1903-06 ,

Hellis, Mrs Gertrude
13 Silver Street, Kensington W. — 1897-99

Hellis, R.
13 Silver St, High Street, Nottinghill — 1871-96 ,

Hellstern, Arthur
436 New Cross Road S.E. — 1904-06

Helsdon Bros
146 Euston Road N.W. — 1902-03

Hemery, Thomas George
204 Regent Street — 1856
213 Regent Street W. — 1879-80

Hemming, Alfred
190 Great Dover Street S.E. — 1880

Henderson, Alexander L.
49 King William Street E.C. — 1863-88
3 Amersham Road, New Cross S.E. — 1876-88

The *Photographic News* described Henderson's methods of making photo-enamels at his King William Street premises in its issue of 16 March 1883.

Henderson, Andrew
184 Fleet Street E.C. — 1854-59

140 Strand W.C. — 1857

Henderson, James
204 Regent Street W. — 1854-55

Henderson, Joseph
61 Regents Park Road N.W. — 1877
40 Charing Cross S.W. — 1878-80

Henderson, Thomas
25 Islington Terrace N. — 1864-66

Henderson, William Boyd
110 Westbourne Grove W. — 1900-05
108 Westbourne Grove W. — 1906-08-

Henderson, William
2 Queen Street, Cheapside E.C. — 1872-73
15 Queen Street, Cheapside E.C. — 1874-76

Henneman, Nicholas, & Co.
22 Regent Street — 1852-54
122 Regent Street W. — 1855-58

Henri & Co.
314 Holloway Road N. — 1890

Hentschel, August
168 Fleet Street E.C. — 1878

Hepworth & Co. (cinematographers)
17 Cecil Court, Charing Cross Road — 1903-04

Hepworth Manufacturing Co. Ltd. (cinematographers)
17 Cecil Court, Charing Cross Road — 1905-07
15 & 17 Cecil St., Charing Cross Road — 1908-

Herbert, Frank
240 Oxford Street W. — 1868-69

Herbert, George
Old Ford Road E. — 1871-72

Hering, Frank
137 Regent Street W. — 1857-74

Heritage, Thomas
3 Addington Road, Bow E. — 1864-66

Herman, Raivid
77 Turner St, Commercial Road E. — 1903-07

83 Gracechurch Street E.C.	1905-07

Herve, Charles Stanley

213 Oxford Street W.	1855-56
256 Oxford Street W.	1858-60

Hewett, Edward

4 Rutland Terrace, Abbey Road N.W.	1869-71

Hewett, Edward

134 Edgware Road W.	1877-79

Heymann, Madame Marie

322 Upper Street N.	1894

Hicks, John Arthur

291 New Cross Road S.E.	1890-03

Higdon, Thomas

83 Fleet Street E.C.	1856-59

Higginson, Thomas Walter

520 Kingsland Road N.E.	1908-

Hilder, Charles John

77 Sheriff Road, Kilburn N.W.	1901-08-

Hildesheimer, Albert

2 & 4 New Zealand Avenue E.C.	1896
2 New Zealand Avenue E.C.	1897-98

Hill & Scott

139 & 141 Brompton Road S.W.	1887-89

Hill, Frank

39 Kings Road, Chelsea S.W.	1905-08-

Hillman, Walter, & Co.

112 Pentonville Road N.	1901

Hills & Saunders Ltd.

48 Porchester Terrace, Bayswater W.	1869
36 Porchester Terrace, Bayswater W.	1870-87
47 Sloane Street W.	1894-96

"Messrs. Hills and Saunders have always taken a high rank in London...They may be found 'at home' at other places besides Bayswater, at Eton, Aldershot, Sandhurst, Oxford, and Cambridge; but the studio in Porchester Terrace is, we believe, the headquarters."

(Photographic News 7 May 1880, p. 218). The studio was run by a Mr. Cowan. and last yea

Hilton, John Deane

115 Strand W.C.	1881-85
443 Strand W.C.	1886-88

Hinton, Chas

29 Great College St, Camden Town	1855-57
34 Gt. College St, Camden Tn. N.W.	1858-60
72 Gt. College St, Camden Tn. N.W.	1861
73 Gt. College St, Camden Tn. N.W.	1862-64
154 Great College Street N.W.	1869-72

Hinton, Wm. Ernest, & Co.

54 Mare Street, Hackney N.E.	1907-08-

Hiron, Russell

17 Hindon Street S.W.	1897-01

Histed & Co.

42 Baker Street W.	1901-08-

Histed, Ernest Walter

42 Baker Street W.	1900

Hitchcock, George

205 Walworth Road S.E.	1894-95

Hoather, William Henry

104 Leighton Road N.W.	1897-03

Hobbs & Barratt

16A Bouverie St, Fleet Street E.C.	1905

Hobbs, James

198 Shoreditch High Street N.E.	1867-71
135 Tottenham Court Road W.	1873-74

Hobbs, William

81 High Street, Whitechapel E.	1861-86

Hobcraft, Edward

419 Oxford Street W.	1855

Hobcraft, William

419 Oxford Street W.	1856-72

Hobkirk, Robert

156 Kentish Town Road N.W.	1907

Hoeck, Hermann
147 Seven Sisters Road N.   1905

Hogg, Robert
55 Fleet Street   1856

Hoffman, Otto
7A Mornington St, Regents Pk. N.W. 1876-77

Holbrook, Albert Hy.
14 Danvers Street, Chelsea S.W.   1876-78
17 Church Street S.W.   1879-80

Holland, Walter
11 Poultry E.C.   1907

Holloway, Chas. Wykeham
107 Clarendon Road W.   1878-79

Hollyer, Frederick
8 Bartholomew Villas, Kentish Tn.   1869
9 Pembroke Square W.   1873-08-

Holman, William
26 Pentonville Road N.   1900-03

Holmes, James
2 Prospect Terrace, Holloway Rd. N. 1882-83

Holt, George
116 Euston Road N.W.   1888-89
236 Westminster Bridge Road S.E.   1890-91

Holt, George Frederick, & Son
48 New Kent Road S.E.   1885

Holyoake, Walter Rowland
45 Westbourne Grove W.   1871

Home & Co.
162 Kings Road, Chelsea S.W.   1887-88

Homes, Henry
75 Blackfriars Road S.E.   1880-92

Hood, John
36 King William Street, City E.C.   1865

Hoole, Henry Fredk. & Co.
40 Queens Road, west S.W.   1897-99

Hooper, Turner & Co.
3 Cheapside E.C.   1877-80

The company was formerly Geo. Hooper of Winwood House, 68 Canonbury Park south N.

Hooper, George
13 Silver Street, Kensington W.   1900-08
422 Mile End Road E.   1903

Hooper, George
246 & 248 Regent Street W.   1867
68 Canonbury Park, south N.   1869-76
3 Cheapside E.C.   1877-80

Hope, Morton
512 Harrow Road W.   1898-99

Horne & Thornthwaite
213 Regent Street W.   1864

Horse Shoe Photographic Co.
Henry Bedford Lemere, manager
4 & 5A Tottenham Court Road W.   1883-84

Hoskins, Edward
448 New Cross Road S.   1884-86

Houghton, Thomas Rd.
2 Montpeliar Street, Walworth S.E.   1880-81

Hoult, Charles
18 Bishops Road, Cambridge Rd. E.   1901

Howard & Saunders
7 Garnault Place, Clerkenwell E.C.   1873

Howell, Thomas
299 Euston Road N.W.   1881-89

Hubbard, John
1 Oxford Street W.   1861-81
4 Oxford Street W.   1882-85
Hubbard died in November 1884. He had *"for many years maintained a well- deserved repute for his negative and retouching varnishes"*.

Hubere, Hubert
12 Baker Street W.   1892

Hubert, Joseph
304 Regent Street N.   1899-00

Hudson, Fredk. Augustus
177 Holloway Road N.   1871-74

2 Kensington Park Road W. 1875-77

Hudson, William
97 Hackney Road E. 1872

Hughes, Alfred
433 Strand W.C. 1892-08-

Hughes, Cornelius Jabez
433 Strand W.C. 1856-61

Hughes was born in 1819 and trained as a daguerreotypist with J. E. Mayall at his Lowther Arcade, Strand, studio. After working as a photographer for himself in Glasgow he returned to London in 1855 and set up in business on the Strand, moving to Oxford Street in 1859. He purchased the business of the Isle of Wight photographer W. G. Lacy in 1862 and practised photography from 6 Royal Victoria Arcade, Union Street, Ryde. Queen Victoria was a regular patron. Hughes was an important early figure in photography as a contributor to journal and was active within the Photographic Society. He died on 11 August 1884.

Hughes, Edward James
147 Strand W.C. 1861

Hughes, Edward S.
433 Strand W.C. 1862

Hughes, John Cartwright
14 Edith Villas, W. Kensington W. 1905
95 Gloucester Road S.W. 1908-

Hull, Henry Edmonds
135 Holland Park Avenue N.W. 1899
136 Holland Park Avenue N.W. 1900-08-

Hum & Bishop
90 Newgate Street E.C. 1877-80

Hum & Roberts
90 Newgate Street E.C. 1876

Hum, David, & Co.
90 Newgate Street E.C. 1881-89
52 Cheapside E.C. 1892

Humfrey, Harold
418 Strand W.C. 1905-06

Humphreys, Henry
46 Guildford Pl, Lwr Kennington Ln. 1867
143 Lower Kennington Lane S. 1868

Hunt, Alfred W., & Co.
99 Trafalgar Rd, Old Kent Rd. S.E. 1900-06

Hunt, Charles
30 Piccadilly W. 1866-70

Hunt, Henry Doddridge
349 Harrow Road W. 1895
389 Harrow Road W. 1896

Hunt, Henry William
59 & 60 Cornhill E.C. 1884
10 London Road S.E. 1894-04

Hunt, James Ernest
100 Clarendon Road W. 1889-93
141 Clarendon Road W. 1894-08-
127 Ladbroke Grove W. 1906-08-

Huntly, John Lysnar
238 Upper Street N. 1896-03
470 & 472 Holloway Road N. 1904-08-

Hutchings & Orchard
756 Old Kent Road S.E. 1877-83

Hutchings, Thomas
756 Old Kent Road S.E. 1884-85

Hutchinson & Svendsen
115 & 116 Strand W.C. 1906-07

Hutchinson, Hugh
10 Upper Street N. 1883-85

Hutchinson, William
313 City Road E.C. 1887

Huxley, Henry
Old Ford Road, Bow E. 1873-77
548 Old Ford Road, Bow E. 1878-85

Hyatt, Hallett
95 Gloucester Road S.W. 1907
111 Oxford Street W. 1907-08-

Hyatt, James H. L.
47 Great Russell Street W.C.   1894-97
70 Mortimer Street W.   1902-06

Hyde, James
103 Holborn Hill E.C.   1864-67

I

Imperial French Photographic Co.
Charles Orsich & Co, proprietor
131 Fleet Street E.C.   1868-70
4 Haymarket S.W.   1868-70
352 Strand W.C.   1870-77
151 Fulham Road S.W.   1873
52 King William Street, City E.C.   1875-76

Imperial Photographic Co.
A. M. West, manager, 1880-82
R. W. Thomas, manager, 1883
J. D. O. Connor, manager, 1884
44 Baker Street W.   1880-84

Ingle, Walter
29 Bessborough Place, Pimlico S.W.   1891-08-

Inglis, Byng
293 Kings Road, Chelsea S.W.   1897-08-

Inow, Jacob
30 Lambeth Road S.E.   1905

Institute Of Photography
Herbert Watkins, proprietor
179 Regent Street   1856-57

International Photo-Sculpture
Co. Ltd, The
Joseph E . Allen, secretary
66 Marylebone Road N.W.   1866
61A York Terrace, Regents Park N.W.   1866

Ireland, Jospeh
94 Bridge Road, Lambeth S.   1864
250 Westminster Bridge Road S.   1865-70

Iris, Henry
34 Upper Street, Islington N.   1871-72
10 Upper Street, Islington N.   1872-80

---

170 Holloway Road N.   1884-87

Ivimey & Ward
154 Newington Butts S.   1866-68

Izard, Edwin
141 High Holborn W.C.   1856-59

J

Jacks, J., & Co.
22 Glasshouse Street W.   1902-08-

Jackson, Charles
34 Cheyne Walk, Chelsea S.W.   1874-76

Jackson, Thomas C.
172 Kings Road, Chelsea S.W.   1865-69

Jacolette, Martin
42 Harrington Road S.W.   1891-08-
38 & 40 Harrington Road S.W.   1902-08-

James, Alfred
1 Buckingham Palace Road S.W.   1888-97
87 Buckingham Palace Road S.W.   1892-93

James, Arthur
1 Buckingham Palace Road S.W.   1901-02

James, Charles
32 Edgware Road W.C.   1857-58

James, D. Brook, & Co.
76 Cannon Street E.C.   1868-80

James, Frederick
226 Oxford Street W.   1870

James, George
130 Euston Road N.W.   1875-83

James, Joseph Rd.
11 Mount Row, Liverpool Road N.   1859-63

James, Mrs Hannah
130 Euston Road N.W.   1873-74

James, Oliver, & Co. Ltd.
154, 155, 156 & 157 Fleet St. E.C.   1902-03
154 Fleet Street E.C.   1904

Jaques, William Henry
20 East Street, City Road. N. 1906
279 High Street, Camden Town N.W. 1908

Jarchy, Arnold
42 Union Road, Rotherhithe S.E. 1894
45 Union Road, Rotherhithe S.E. 1895-08
Tower Bridge Approach S.E. 1899-02
Tower Bridge Road S.E. 1903-07

Jedwabnitsky, Stanislas
143 Brompton Road S.W. 1888

Jee, Thomas
Deptford Bridge S.E. 1865-90
440 New Cross Road S.E. 1891

Jefferys, William
28 Church Street, Lisson Grove N.W. 1871-80

Jeffrey, William
114 Great Russell Street W.C. 1863-77

Jenkins, Wilfred Lawrence
116 Cromwell Road S.W. 1901-08-

Jenner, Misses Phoebe & Oliva
411 Mare Street, Hackney N.E. 1904

Jennings, Miss Agnes
10 Charles Street, St. James' W. 1903-08-

Jennings, George
38 Brecknock Road N. 1893

Jerrard, George
107 Regent Street W. 1885-99
105 Regent Street W. 1900-02
78 Sutherland Avenue W. 1903-08-

Job, James
37 High Street, Bow S 1865-66

Johnson, Alfred
57 Broadway, London Fields N.E. 1908

Johnson, Frederick
133 Portobello Road W. 1875-78
108 Westbourne Grove W. 1880

Johnson, Robert
292 Kings Road, Chelsea S.W. 1900-08-

Johnson, Roderick
367 Mile End Road E. 1888-96

Johnstone began working for Dr Barnardo from c.1883 taking over from Thomas Barnes *(q.v.)*. He started his own commercial studio in 1887 but gave it up in 1896 when he worked full-time for the charity. He remained with Barnardo until 1906.

Johnson, William
467 New Cross Road S.E. 1881-82

Johnston & Hoffmann
31 Devonshire St, Portland Place W. 1903-07

Jonas, Alexander
87 Kingsland High Street N.E. 1906-08-

Jones & Co.
176 Upper Street N. 1905

Jones, Alfred Percy
Barnsbury Street, Islington N. 1899-01

Jones, Miss Alice Lawton
176 Upper Street N. 1906-08-

Jones, Charles
235 High Holborn W.C. 1882-84

Jones, Charles Joseph
75 Essex Road N. 1893-04

Jones, Frederic
146 Oxford Street W. 1862-68

Jones, John
37 Lambeth Road S.E. 1888-93

Jones, Mrs Agnes
53 Burdett Road, Mile End E. 1876-77

Jones, Thomas
498 Oxford Street 1850
537 Oxford Street 1854-56

Jones, William Bonner
Westbourne Grove W. 1871-72

Joselyn, Alfred
49 Brecknock Road N. 1902

Joseph, —
62 Piccadilly   25 April 1846

Joyce, Helen, & Son
307 High Holborn   1856

Joyce-Barrett, Frank & Marie
22 Bishop's Road W.   1893-94
41 Torriano Ave, Camden Tn. N.W.   1895

Jules, Albert
121 Edgware Road W.   1899-04

Juliane, Louis
8 Regent Street W.   1858-64
133 Regent Street W.   1865-68

K

Katz, David
24 New Road, Whitechapel E.   1903

Katzman, Jacob
87 Leman Street E.   1891-94

Kay, Arthur
88 Edgware Road W.   1893-94

Kaye, Vernon
4 Onslow Place, S. Kensington S.W.   1889-00

Keen, Charles Job
64 High Street, Nottinghill W.   1902

Keen, Thomas
64 High Street, Nottinghill Gate W.   1903-08-

Keens, John
151 Culford Road N.   1871-72

Kemp, John Rd.
24 John Street, Commercial Road E.   1859
25 Jubilee Street, Mile End Road E.   1860-63

Kennett Bros.
119 Westbourne Grove, Bayswater W.   1866

**Kensington Photographic Co., The
Wren & Co, proprietor**
24 Ladbroke Grove Road W.   1883

Kent, William
147 Oxford Street W.   1857-64
52 St Georges Place S.W.   1868-69

Kilburn, W. E.
Not given   9 February 1847

Kilburn, William E.
234 Regent Street   1852-55
222 Regent Street W.   1856-64

Killick, John Henry
399 Holloway Road N.   1889-08-

King, Arthur
6 Norland Terrace, Nottinghill W.   1875-82
7 Norland Terrace, Nottinghill W.   1883-95
136 Holland Park Avenue W.   1896-98

King, Edward
80 Cornhill E.C.   1859

King, Horatio-Nelson
188 Regent Street W.   1873-74

King, Thomas
109 Cheapside E.C.   1879-80

Kingsbury & Notcutt
45 St Georges Place S.W.   1886-90

Kingsbury, Edward R.
45 St Georges Place, Knightsbridge   1871-75

Kingsbury, Frederick
45 St Georges Place S.W.   1891-95
120 Fulham Road S.W.   1898-99

Kinninmont & Taylor
19 Regent Street S.W.   1905

Kinninmont, Kenneth
19 Regent Street S.W.   1906

Kirby, John
346 New Cross Road S.E.   1889-90

Kirby, Theophilius
346 New Cross Road S.E.   1891

Kirkby, Samuel
164 New Kent Road S.E.   1886-93

Kirkwood, James
99 Regent Street W.   1903

Kitchener & Salmon
30 New Bond Street W.   1901

Klic, Karel
9 Barnsbury Park N.   1888

Klose, Detlef
186 New Kent Road S.E.   1893-95

Knapp, Miss Henrietta
48 Church Street, Kensington W.   1890-91

Knibb, Charles
56 Holloway Road N.   1876-83

Knight, Richard
31 Edgware Road W.   1867

Knowles, Francis James
343 Edgware Road W.   1886
80 Kennington Road S.E.   1886-87

Koenig & Lloyd
17 Hindon Street, Pimlico S.W.   1891-93

Koenig, Lloyd & Hiron
17 Hindon Street, Pimlico S.W.   1894

Koenig, Charles
131 Church Street, Paddington   1878
373 Edgware Road W.   1879-08
375 Edgware Road W.   1886-04

Koenig, Charles, (senior)
205 Edgware Road W.   1868

Koenig, Gasper
199 Oxford Street W.   1866-67

Koenig, Gasper, & Son
226 Oxford Street W.   1855-64

Koenig, Siegmund
26 Westbourne Grove W.   1890

Kohn, Miss Rose
184 Kings Road, Chelsea S.W.   1908-

Kotch, Francis
48 Junction Road N.   1902-08-

75 Essex Road N.   1908-

Kotch, Frederick
75 Essex Road N.   1905-07

Kresovsky, Woolf
87 Leman Street E.   1895-02

Krever, Mark
2 Newington Green N.   1908-

Krumer, Max & Joseph
422 Mile End Road E.   1907

L

Lacey & Son
140 Jamaica Road S.E.   1894

Lacey, William
20 Blackfriars Road S.E.   1888-93

Lacy, John, & Co
20 Blackfriars Road S.E.   1882-87

Lafayette, James
179 New Bond Street W.   1897-98

Lafayette Limited
179 New Bond Street W.   1899-08-
178 New Bond Street W.   1908-
The National Portrait Gallery and the Victoria
and Albert Museum have important holdings of
this studio's work.

Laib, Paul
8 Haverstock Hill N.W.   1898
50 Clareville Grove S.W.   1899-00
3 Thistle Grove Lane S.W.   1901-08-

Laidlaw, Andrew Elliot
435 Fulham Road S.W.   1888

Lake, Thomas
161 Kingsland Road N.E.   1869-74

Lale, John Henry, & Co.
129 New North Road, Hoxton N.   1871-72

Lambert & Okey
56 High Street, Camden Town N.W.   1888-90

Lambert, Edward James
56 High Street, Camden Town N.W.   1891-08-

Lamercier, Louis
131 Fleet Street E.C.   1870-75

Lamont & Ross
56 Huntley Street W.C.   1898

Lamotte, Claude
148 Sloane Street, Chelsea S.W.   1859

Lancaster, Edward
22A Endell Street W.C.   1887-89
5 New Oxford Street W.C.   1890-91
233 High Holborn W.C.   1893
235 High Holborn W.C.   1894

Lancaster, Richard Stuart
120 Mile End Road E.   1894-97

Landor, Edmund
61 Knightsbridge S.W.   1905

Lane, John
54 Hatfield Street, Blackfriars Road   1855
143 Blackfriars Road S.   1856-68

Langfiar Limited
23A Old Bond Street W.   1899-08-

Langfiar, Adolph
154 Holland Park Avenue W.   1906-07
95 Wigmore Street W.   1908

Langfiar, Pearl
24 Westbourne Grove W.   1907-08

Langford, George
17 Hindon Street, Pimlico S.W.   1890
1 Caroline Street, Pimlico S.W.   1896-08-

Langton, Arthur James
35 Buckingham Palace Road S.W.   1887-08-

Langton, James Arthur
307 & 309 Euston Road N.W.   1884-88
369 Euston Road W.   1885-86
309 Euston Road N.W.   1887-89

Lansdell, George
10 Stonefield Street, Islington N.   1893-04

Laporte & Stanley
172 Kings Road S.W.   1862-64

La Porte & Thompson
1 Buckingham Palace Road S.W.   1882

La Porte, Charles
204 Kings Road, Chelsea S.W.   1866-76

La Porte, John
84 Kings Road, Chelsea   1867
Wandsworth Road S.W.   1869-70
1 Buckingham Palace Road S.W.   1872-83

La Porte, John, & Co.
1 Buckingham Palace Road S.W.   1884-85

Lapparini, Attilio
42 Tottenham Court Road W.   1903-08-

Larmuth, T. H.
5 Carpenter Buildings, London W.   1854

Laroche, Martin
65 Oxford Street W.   1852-62

Laroche, Silvester
65 Oxford Street   23 August 1848
W. H. Silvester-Laroche practised the daguerreotype from 1845 was assisted Scott Archer in his work in developing the collodion process. In 1854 was resisted Talbot's patent claim over the new collodion process and was sucessful in defending the Talbot's claim for infringement of the patent - spending over £2000 in the process. This action was instrumental in opening up photography for professional practise free of any restriction. He died in Birmingham on 10 November 1886 at the age of 77 years. A relative, W. S. Laroche, practised as a photographer in Llandudno.

Laroche, Thomas
191 Newington Butts S.E.   1887-88
199 East India Dock Road E.   1889-00

Larritt, John James
12 Hannibal Road, Stepney Green E.   1864-74

Lascelles, Henry
34 Howland Street W.   1864-67

Lattimer, John Freeman Latham
307 Essex Road N.   1873-81

Laurens, Glanville
189 Earls Court Road S.W.   1894-99

Lavis, George & Mrs Rebecca
135 Regent Street W.   1864-77
See Creed, George.

Lawrence, George Henry
40 Walworth Road S.E.   1899-02

Lawrence, John
411 Mare Street, Hackney N.E.   1905

Leakey, Alfred Henry
99 Harrow Road W.   1904-08-

Lean, Charles
170 Holloway Road N.   1898-00

Le Beau
Hackney Road   12 February 1846

Le Beau & Rust
11 Westbourne Grove W.   1863-64
26 Westbourne Grove W.   1865

Lee, George
204 Kings Road, Chelsea S.W.   1879-81
182 Kings Road, Chelsea S.W.   1882-87

Lee, James
47 Whitechapel Road E.   1858-61

Lee, James Hy.
2 Prospect Terrace, Holloway Rd. N. 1884-85
553 Holloway Road N.   1886-02
72 Seven Sisters Road N.   1905-07

Lee, John Hy.
147 High Street, Shoreditch N.E.   1868

Lee, William John
72 Seven Sisters Road   1908-

Leech, George Walter
252 Cambridge Road E.   1880

Leigh, Harry
159 Stamford Street E.   1896

Leigh, Herbert, & Co.
6 Dean Street, Soho W.   1908-

Lemaire, Henry
3 Blackfriars Road S.   1856-59

Leman, Edward
2 Camden Rd, Camden Town N.W.   1863

Leman, Herbert Thomas
135 Oxford Street W.   1903-06
304 Regent Street W.   1907-08-

Lemere, Bedford
78 Albert Street, Regents Park N.W. 1867-72
4 Featherstone Buildings W.C.   1868
147 Strand W.C.   1869-72

Lemere, Bedford, & Co.
147 Strand W.C.   1873-08-

Le Mesurier & Marshall, Misses
Red Brick House, Campden Hill Rd.   1897-04
9 Kensington High Street W.   1905-08-

Lenthall, Henry
222 Regent Street W.   1862-78

Leo, Victor
83 Newington Causeway S.E.   1889

Leon, Miss Marie
30 Regent Street S.W.   1901-08-

Leon, Victor
140A Jamaica Road S.E.   1899

Leonard, William Miles
246 High Holborn W.C.   1857-60

Le Roi, Claude, & Co.
16 & 17 Poultry E.C.   1872

Leroux, Pierre
133 Queens Road, Bayswater W.   1907

Levinne, William
148 Holborn Bars E.C.   1859-61

Lewis, Fredk. Wm., & Co.
93 Whitechapel High Street E.   1901-07

Lewis, James
30 Stephenson Terrace, Caled. Rd. N.   1858

Lewis, Thomas James
21 Great Marylebone Street W.   1896-97

Leyland, Miss Edith
120 Fulham Road S.W.   1901-07

Leyland, Edward
120 Fulham Road S.W.   1900

Lile, John Hy., & Co.
129 New North Road, Hoxton N.   1873-78

Lindell, Mrs E.
10 Queens Terr., St Johns Wd. N.W.   1866-67

Lindsey, Crawford
124 Old Kent Road S.E.   1871-72

Lindsey, Frederick
16 Coventry Street, Haymarket W.   1859
8 Queens Buildings, Brompton S.W.   1863
45 Brompton Road S.W.   1864-68
84 Kings Road, Chelsea S.W.   1865-66
219 Fulham Road. S.W.   1866-68

Linforth, Miss Florence
61 Prince of Wales Road. N.W.   1900-08

Lintott, Madame Anna
118 New Bond Street W.   1902

Lintott, Arthur
118 New Bond Street W.   1903-06

Liverpool & London Photographic Co.
Edward Leman, manager
98 Cheapside E.C.   1875

Lloyd, Edward
6 Kensington High Street W.   1878-79

Lloyd, William
17 Hindon Street, Pimlico S.W.   1895-96

Lock & Whitfield
178 Regent Street W.   1857-95
24 Edwardes Square, Kensington   1866-69

Mr. G. S. Crawford Barnes acted as chief operator to Lock and Whitfield until his death in January 1883. He had been one of the pioneers of commercial photography practising the daguerreotype. *Photographic News* 26 January 1883, p. 63).

Lock, Samuel Robert
100 Regent Street   1855
178 Regent Street   1856

Lock was born in London in 1822 and was educated at Kings's College. After travelling and working in Tasmania and the Pacific he returned to England where he found employed with Nicholas Henneman (*q.v.*). He stayed with Henneman for some time where "society hailed with delight the softening influence of the brush which Mr. Lock had brough tto bear with an excellent eye for colour". He left to open a studio of miniature painting opposite Claudet's studio in the Quadrant where he quickly gained a reputation for converting Talbotypes into beautiful miniatures. Having no studio he painted the sitter's own photographs or accompanied them to a photographer to be taken.

He met George C. Whitfield who had just built a studio in Regent Street and a formal partnership was commenced on 1 September 1856 at 178 Regent Street. A studio was later opened at King's Road, Brighton. Lock was a favoured miniature painter to the Queen and Prince and Princess of Wales. He was also a partner in the Woodbury Company.

Lock died on 9 May 1881. (*Photographic News* 20 May 1881, p. 230).

Locke, Henry
209 High Street, Shoreditch N.E.   1861
206 High Street, Shoreditch N.E.   1862-64
248 High Street, Shoreditch N.E.   1863-69

Locke, William
215 Regent Street W.   1875-78

135 Regent Street W.	1883-84

Lombardi & Co.
13 Pall Mall east S.W.	1893-95

Lombardi, Caldesi, & Co.
13 Pall Mall east S.W.	1896-98
27 Sloane Street S.W.	1900-01

Lombardi, Eugenio, & Co
27 Sloane Street S.W.	1899

Lombardi, Weston, & Son
27 Sloane Street S.W.	1902-05

Lomnitz, Miss E.
26 Victoria Street S.W.	1897-08-

London & County Photographic Copying Co.
Fredk S. D. Phillips, manager
17 Warwick Court, High Holbrn W.C.	1867

London & County Portrait & Co.
Albert Baker, managing director
Fredk S. D. Phillips, manager
63 St Pauls Churchyard E.C.	1877-88
75 St Pauls Churchyard E.C.	1880
52 Cheapside E.C.	1881-82
304 Regent Street W.	1885
1B Norfolk Terr., Westbourne Gr.	1885

London Electrotype Agency Ltd.
31 St Bride Street E.C.	1902-07
10 St Brides Ave, Fleet Street E.C.	1908-

London Institute of Photography, The
Grant & Johnson, managers;
Joseph Johnson, 1866
10 & 11 Upper Street, Islington N.	1865-66

London & Paris Photographic Co., The
90 Newgate Street E.C.	1865-66

London Photographic Copying Co.
Lawrence Phillips, manager
Fredk S. D. Phillips, manager, 1870-
302 Regent Street W.	1865-66
304 Regent Street W.	1867-72
1 Norfolk Terr., Westbourne Grove	1872

London Photographic Co. Ltd.
Fredk Wm. Vidler, manager
304 Regent Street W.	1873-84
1 Norfolk Terr., Westbourne Gr. W.	1873-75
1B Norfolk Terr., Westbourne Grove	1876-84
224 Regent Street W.	1897-01
12 Baker Street W.	1902-08-

London Photogravure Syndicate Ltd.
5 Victoria Grove, Chelsea S.W.	1893-02
164 Regent Street W.	1895
5 Netherton Grove, Chelsea S.W.	1903-08-

London Portrait Co.
Fredk. Thos. Newcombe, manager;
Francis Gilling, manager, 1867;
W. E. Parker, manager, 1886
68 Cheapside E.C.	1864-76
7 Carlton Terrace, Harrow Road W.	1886
88, 89 & 90 Chancery Lane W.C.	1903

A *carte* from the 68 Cheapside address advertised the fact that "The Manager of this Company was formerly with the Stereoscopic Company but has now no connection with the same".

London & Provincial Photograph Co.
235 Balls Pond Road N.	1901

London & Provincial Photographic Co.
Jas. Russell Williams, manager, 1864-66;
Jas. Jones, manager;
Maurice Welfare, manager, 1868
443 Strand W.C.	1864-68

London & Provincial Photographing Co.
Fredk Lindsey, proprietor
443 Strand W.C.	1873-75

London School Of Photography
Saml Prout Newcombe & Co, props.
78 Newgate Street E.C.	1858-60
174 Regent Street W.	1858-76
142 Upper Street, Islington N.	1858-76
103 Newgate Street E.C.	1861-91
23 Poultry E.C.	1861-66
52 Cheapside E.C.	1862-86
Pantheon, Oxford St W.	1865-67

Soho Bazaar, Oxford St W.   1868-74

See also Bradshaw and Godert.

London Stereoscopic Co.
54 Cheapside E.C.   1860-62
313 Oxford Street W.   1860-61

London Stereoscopic & Photographic
Co. & C. de V. Institute
G. S. Nottage, managing partner
54 Cheapside   1863·
110 Regent Street W.   1863·

London Stereoscopic & Photo-
graphic Co. Ltd.
G. S. Nottage, managing partner
54 & 53 Cheapside E.C.   1864-66
110 Regent Street W.   1864·
108 & 110 Regent Street W.   1865-89
54 Cheapside E.C.   1867-08
108, 110 & 106 Regent St W.   1876-90
2 Bow Churchyard E.C.   1886-95
106 & 108 Regent Street W.   1891-08-

The London Stereoscopic Company, together
with its slight changes of name was a substantial
company almost from its inception in 1854. In
addition to its photographic studio it was also a
significant retailer of photographic equipment -
many purchased from the maker and re-badged
with the LSC logo. The company was founded
by George S. Nottage who became an Alderman
of the City of London and was described the the
Photographic News (13 February 1880) as one
of the most commercially successful
photographic companies. The company's studio
was not substantially different to many others
but the business success in all branches of
photography - from retail to publishing to studio
work was unsurpassed. The company stored
their negatives at Kingsland where their printing
establishment was also located.

The Hulton-Deutsch Collection have the
bulk of the London Stereoscopic Company
archives of from 1854-1914. Included in the
LSC collection is William England's
topographical work of the 1850s and 1860s and
William Grundy's 'English Views' (of the Uk
and Ireland) from the late 1850s.

Long, Arthur Spencer
19 St Leonards Terrace, Chelsea   1901-04
3B Stewarts Grove, Chelsea S.W.   1905
169A Fulham Road S.W.   1908-

Long, Charles Edmund
60 Bow Road E.   1896-05

Long, James Frederick
15 Finsbury Place E.C.   1858
3 James Place, Hoxton N.   1857-59
26 City Terrace, City Road   1859

Long, R. W. R.
15 Percy St, Tottenham Court Road 1867

Lonsdale & Nafzger
55 Carr Street, Limehouse Fields E.   1902
51 Carr Street, Limehouse Fields E.1903-08-

Lonsdale, John Smith
100 Fleet Street E.C.   1864-65
54 Chancery Lane W.C.   1866-67

Lord, Frederick
34 Aldgate Street E.   1880
6 Westminster Bridge Road S.E.   1885

Lord, Frederick, & Sons
314 Walworth Road S.E.   1894

Lorne, Alfred, & Co.
454 Kingsland Road E.   1885-91

Lovell, Alexander
84 Kings Road, Chelsea S.W.   1872

Low, Edmund
31 King William Street E.C.   1870-7

Lowe, Lawrence
10 Queens Terr., St Johns Wd. N.W.   1868-94
8 Abbey Gardens N.W.   1898-08-

Lowrie, James Frederick
83 Fleet Street E.C.   1878-85
184 Fleet Street E.C.   1880-81

Lucas & Box
40 Charing Cross S.W.   1869-70

Lucas & Groom
37 Wigmore Street W.   1866-67

Lucas & Ohrly
5 Coburg Place, Bayswater W.   1879
4 Coburg Place, Bayswater W.   1880

Lucas & Tuck
7 Haymarket S.W.   1870-72

Lucas, Arthur
37 Wigmore Street W.   1868-69
49 Wigmore Street W.   1870-71
31 New Bond Street W.   1883-84

Lucas, Arthur
127 Queens Road, Bayswater W.   1882-84

Luckin, Thomas
9 Holborn Bars E.C.   1861

Lund, Percy, & Co.
21 Imperial Buildings E.C.   1891-92
Memorial Hill Buildings, Frrngdn St.   1893

Lupson, Augustus
34 Upper Street N.   1888-93
9 Camden Street, Islington Green N.   1894

Luton, Percy William
34 New Cross Road S.E.   1908-

Lynde, Fredk. Raymond
408 Edgware Road W.   1881-92
244 Regent Street W.   1890-91

M

McAllum, John
47 Old Broad Street E.C.   1894-95

Macalpine, Charles
4 Silver Street, High St, Nottinghill   1862-66

Macandrew, James Grant
44 Regent Street W.   1868-74
31 Osnaburgh Street N.W.   1869-77
11 Osnaburgh Street N.W.   1878-82

McArdle, Peter
151 Upper Street, Islington N.   1879-85

McArdle, Mrs Peter
151 Upper Street, Islington N.   1886-87

McCave, Joseph
19 Bayswater Terrace, Bayswater Rd.   1867

McCaul, Miss Helen
34 Victoria Street S.W.   1899-08-

McCree, William
196 Piccadilly W.   1860

Macdonald, Henry
9 Claro Terrace, Richmond Rd. S.W.   1893-94

Mace, Thomas
256 Oxford Street W.   1868-71

McKenzie, Alex
36 Chandos St, Covent Garden W.C.   1886-88

McKenzie, Alex
10 Alice Street, Bermondsey S.E.   1886

Mackenzie, Alexander
79 Oxford Street W.   1890-92

Mackey, George
97 Hackney Road E.   1870-71

Mackintosh, John Alex
13 Chalk Farm Road. N.W.   1868-72
2 Prospect Terrace, Holloway Rd. N. 1873-81

McMillan, Daniel
132 Fleet Street   1854

McMullen & Staker
78 New Cross Road S.E.   1885-86

McMullen, John
492 Old Kent Road S.E.   1880

Macnaghten, Miss Ellen
83A Gloucester Road S.W.   1905-08-

McNamara, John
101 Shoreditch High Street E.   1884

McRae, Duncan Forbes
109 Cheapside E.C.   1892-99

Macy, William
440 Edgware Road N.W.   1876-83

Mahy, Hippolite
73 Newgate Street   1857

Mainwaring, George R.
63 St Pauls Churchyard E.C.   1865-67

Major, John
50 Bemerton Street, Caledonian Road 1865-74

Malby, Walter
155 City Road E.C.   1868-72

Malkin, Albert
2 Skinner Place, Holloway Road. N.   1861-62
2 Francis Place, Holloway Road. N.   1863-64
168 Holloway Road N.   1865-67

Mallia & Galea
211 Clapham Road S.W.   1905
122 Regent Street W.   1905

Mallia, John
285 Oxford Street W.   1906-08-

Maltby, William
Barnsbury Hall, Barnsbury Street N. 1869-71

Maltby, William Flower
176 Upper Street N.   1877-82

Maltby, Glasse & Co.
176 Upper Street N.   1883

Maltby, Wm. F., & Co.
Barnsbury Hall, Barnsbury Street N. 1872-76

Manchee, Peter
14 Arbour Terr., Commercial Road   1866-67

Manders, Arthur
Barnsbury Hall, Barnsbury Street   1887-88

Manders, Ernest Walter
213 Regent Street W.   1907-08-

Manders, Frederic
3 Sarah Place, Old Street Road E.C. 1860-65

Mansell, Edward, & Co.
151 Upper Street N.   1877

Mansion House Photographic Co.
16 Poultry E.C.   1894-00

Mapel, Fed, & Co.
135A High Road Kilburn N.W.   1908

Margand, Alfred
115 Seven Sisters Road N.   1904-07

Margetts, Joseph William
12 Prospect Place, Kingsland Road   1865-66
404 Kingsland Road N.E.   1867-69

Maries & Nield
397A Kingsland Road N.E.   1907

Marioni, Giovanni D.
24 Edgware Road W.   1865-66

Marks, George
75 St Pauls Churchyard E.C.   1870-79

Marshall, Hy.
18 Bishops Road, Cambridge Rd. E.   1885-00

Marshall, William Shury
34 Parliament Street S.W.   1878-80
40 Charing Cross S.W.   1881

Martel, Madame Anne C.		**Mathews & Simpson**		
1 Berkeley Villas, Lghbrgh Park S.	1858-60	79 Rotherfield Street N.		1874-75

Martel, Madame Anne C.
1 Berkeley Villas, Lghbrgh Park S. 1858-60

Martin & Sallnow
416 Strand W.C. 1885-08-

Martin, Mrs Emma
12 Grove Road, Bow E. 1900

Martin, Isaac
152 Cannon Street Road E. 1882-88
231 Commercial Road east E. 1882-84

Martin, Israel
245 Commercial Road east E. 1887-92

Martin, John
261 Commercial Road east E. 1893
245 Commercial Road east E. 1894-08-

Martin, Joseph
186 Commercial Road east E. 1879-80
11 Cannon Street Road E. 1888-94
37 Norton Folgate N.E. 1893
14 West India Dock Road E. 1895-06
62 West India Dock Road E. 1907-08-

Martin, Miss Rita
74 Baker Street W. 1907-08-

Martyn, Frank
242 St Pauls Road, Islington N. 1890-97
Trafalgar Bldgs, Northumberland Av. 1894

Martyr & Morgan
143 Queens Road, Bayswater W. 1866-70

Mason, R. & F.
8 High Street, Nottinghill W. 1902-03

Mason, Robert H., & Co.
28 Old Bond Street W. 1865-74

Massey, Edward Easterby
14 High Holborn 1855-57
114 High Holborn 1860-61

Massey, Mrs Jane Emma
14 High Holborn W.C. 1862

Masters, William
3 Douglas Street, Deptford S.E. 1866

Mathews & Simpson
79 Rotherfield Street N. 1874-75

Mathiew, James
30 Oxford Street W. 1868

Mathieu, Francis
90 Newgate Street E.C. 1865
30 Oxford Street W. 1867-69

Mathews, Charles Fredk.
51 Tottenham Court Road W. 1887-95

Mathhyssen, Miss Gherrada
109 Regent Street W. 1875

Mattype Co.
30 New Bond Street W. 1908-

Maud, Madame Stephanie
16 Brook Street W. 1906-

Maull & Co.
62 Cheapside E.C. 1873-78
187A Piccadilly W. 1873-78

Maull & Fox
62 Cheapside E.C. 1879
187A Piccadilly W. 1879-08-

Maull & Polybank
55 Gracechurch Street E.C. 1856-65
187A Piccadilly W. 1858-65
Tavistock House, Fulham Road S.W. 1865

Maull, Henry, & Co.
62 Cheapside E.C. 1866-72
187A Piccadilly W. 1866-72
Tavistock House, Fulham Rd. S.W. 1866
252 Fulham Road S.W. 1867-70

Mavetti, Henry
Westbourne Hall, Westbourne Gr. 1870

Mavis, Louis Charles
440 Old Kent Road S.E. 1880-85

Mavor & Meredith
12 Furnival Street E.C. 1893-95

May, George William
188 Regent Street W. 1864

May, Henry & Philip
83 Newington Causeway S.E.   1896

May, John
382 Euston Road N.W.   1867
38 Euston Road N.W.   1868-69

May, Robert C.
5 Sloane Terrace, Sloane St. S.W.   1858-69

May, Samuel F.
5 Bishopsgate Street, without E.C.   1866-68

Mayall, John & Edwin, & Collins, Thomas Henry
224 Regent Street W.   1869-75

Mayall & Co.
H. R. Barraud, manager, 1894-97
F. Barraud, manager, 1898-
164 New Bond Street W.   1887-92
73 Piccadilly W.   1893-96
126 Piccadilly W.   1897-08-

Mayall, John
224 Regent Street W.   1876-94

Mayall, John & Edwin
224 & 226 Regent Street   1868

Mayall, John E.
164 New Bond Street W.   1881-83

Mayall, J. E.
Also known as **Professor Highschool**
433 West Strand   18 May 1847

Mayall, John Edwin
224 Regent Street W.   1853-89
433 Strand   1853-55
224 & 226 Regent Street W.   1857-67
15 Argyll Place W.   1859-67

Mayall, John Jabez E.
164 New Bond Street W.   1881-86
Mayall's studio was amongst the first four 'electric studios' in in London - including Negretti and Zambra's at Crystal Palace. The *Photographic News* made a visit in it's issue of 12 May 1882. According to the journal the studio had spared neither expense nor trouble in it's installation and decoration. The Bond Street studio took over the whole building which had formerly been occupied by Ross and Co. the opticians. From this period all portraits were taken by electricity - with an exposure of three or four seconds. An announcement in the same journal on 6 October 1882 reported that Mayall's studio was using the Swan electric lamps run by a ten-horse engine.

Mayer Brothers
133 Regent Street W.   1855-69
See Halle, S. B.

Mayhew, Julius
6 Old Bond Street W.   1857-61

Mayland, William
236 Regent Street W.   1881-82
Mayland was reported as leaving London for a new studio in Deal, Kent, in May 1882 (*P.N.* 26 May 1882, p. 303). His collection of negatives was taken over by Samuel
    Walker of Regent Street.

Maynall, Joe Parkin
548 Oxford Street W.   1883-89

Mayman, Alfred
170 Fleet Street E.C.   1877-89

Meadows, James
141 Holloway Road N.   1886

Meadows, James Francis
129 New North Road N.   1879-80
34 Guildford Road, Poplar E.   1891

Meagher, P. & Co.
1A Coppice Row, Clerkenwell E.C.   1859

Medlen, James
Barnsbury Hall, Islington N.   1867-68

Meeks & Hughes
433 Strand W.C.   1870-72

Meeks, Ferdinand James, & Co.
433 Strand W.C.   1873

Meisenbach Works (Carl Hentschel Ltd.)

182, 183 & 184 Fleet Street E.C.	1907-08
West Norwood S.E.	1907-08

Meisenbach Co. Ltd.

31 Farringdon Street E.C.	1888
57 & 59 Ludgate Hill E.C.	1889-91
West Norwood S.E.	1889-06
108 Fleet Street E.C.	1892
Wolfington Road West Norwood	1892-93
188 Fleet Street E.C.	1893-01
173 Fleet Street E.C.	1902
173-175 Fleet St E.C.	1903-06

The Meisenbach Company Ltd. removed their City office to 188 Fleet Street in August 1891.

Melanographic Portrait Co.
Christian Krumbein, manager

283 Regent Street W.	1879

Melhuish & Gale Ltd.

68 Pall Mall S.W.	1895
58 Pall Mall S.W.	1896

Melhuish, Arthur James

9 Holborn Bars E.C.	1860
12 York Place, Portman Square W.	1864-86
12 Old Bond Street W.	1888-89
58 Pall Mall S.W.	1891-94

Mendelssohn, Hayman Selig

27 Cathcart Road, South Kens. S.W.	1883-88
14 Pembridge Crescent, Bayswater	1886-08-

Mendelssohn had been practising as a photographer in Newcastle before opening his South Kensington studio in June 1882 (*P.N.* 30 June 1882). Of Polish extraction he took part in a Polish uprising before fleeing to London via Hamburg. On arrival he worked for the Downey studio before setting up on his own account (P.N. 13 March 1891, p. 198).

Mendelssohn, Hayman Selig & Herman E.

14 Pembridge Crescent W.	1887

Mendelssohn, Herman E.

14 Pembridge Crescent W.	1886-88

Menrant, Rosney & Durand

69 Regent Street W.	1854

Menzies, William

213 Upper Street, Islington N.	1866

Merchants Portrait Co.

106 & 271 Kentish Town Road. N.W.	1908-

Merick, Moses

Bayswater Road W.	1876

Merralls, Joseph

309 Regent Street W.	1858-59

Merrett Brothers

140 Jamaica Road S.E.	1885

Metropolitan Photo Co.

22 Chapel Street, Edgware Rd. N.W.	1905

Meurant, Joseph

6 Cumberland Place, Newington Butts	1855-60

Meves Brothers

10 New Street, Covent Garden W.C.	1858

Meves, Louis Charles

70 Albany Street, Regents Park N.W.	1867-76
440 Old Kent Road S.E.	1877-79

Meyerstein, Emil

280 High Holborn W.C.	1884-85
Tichborne Court W.C.	1884-85

Michaelis, Mathias

186 Commercial Road. east E.	1887-93

Middleton, Albert George

312 Kingsland Road. E.	1888-06

Middleton, Richard

143 Brompton Road S.W.	1887

Mildmay, Paulet St. John

67 Elizabeth Street S.W.	1894

Miles, Arthur

369 Strand W.C.	1857-59

Millard & Co.

6 Queens Road, Bayswater W.	1876

Miller & Vesey
36 Baker Street, Portman Square W. 1865-66

Miller, Joseph
45 High Street, Camden Town. N.W. 1882-93
38 Brecknock Road N. 1894-95

Mills, George Wm., & Son
170 Holloway Road N. 1894-97

Mills, Thomas Robert
65 Upper Street, Islington N. 1865-67
30 Cross Street, Islington N. 1868-69

Milton, Frederick
45 St Georges Place S.W. 1882-83

Milton George
258 Westminster Bridge Road S.E. 1880

Mitchell & Debanham
68 London Road, Southwark 1857

Mitchell, Thomas
51 Green Street, Stepney E. 1865

M'Lean & Haes
26 Haymarket S.W. 1864
7 Haymarket S.W. 1865-66
Frank Haes *(q.v.)* MD was well-known for his
animal studies. Examples of his work are held
at the Zoological Society of London.

M'Lean, Melluish & Co.
26 Haymarket S.W. 1862

M'Lean, Melluish, Napper & Co.
26 Haymarket S.W. 1861

M'Lean, Melluish & Haes
26 Haymarket S.W. 1863

M'Lean, Thomas, & Co.
7 Haymarket S.W. 1867-69

Moeser, Charles
152 Cannon Street Road E. 1879-81

Mohr, John M.
Regina House, Upper Holloway N. 1865

Moira & Haigh
1 Lo Seymour St, Portman Square W. 1864-68
12 Lowr Seymour St, Portman Sq. W. 1869-70

Moloney & Taylor
3 Victoria Terrace, Lower Road S.E. 1874

Moloney, James
140 Jamaica Road S.E. 1878

Monck, Basil
100 Westbourne Grove W. 1897-98
435 Fulham Road S.W. 1899

Monger, Arthur Peter
67 & 69 Chancery Lane W.C. 1897-98
8 Breams Buildings E.C. 1899-08-

Montague, John
2 Postern Row, Tower Hill E.C. 1862

Monte & Russell
56 High Street, Camden Town N.W. 1875

Monte, James
56 High Street, Camden Town N.W. 1870-85
78 Chalk Farm Road 1871-72
335 City Road E.C. 1873
221 Westminster Bridge Road S.E. 1875-77
313 City Road E.C. 1880-90
38 Whitechapel Road E. 1882-89

Montes, James
4 Greenland Pl, Camden Town N.W. 1869

Monteney, Jacob
5 Sidney Place, Commercial Road E. 1862-63

Montgomery, Henry
311 Oxford Street W. 1864

Moody, William
111 Grove Road E. 1892

Moore, Alfred
283 Regent Street W. 1858-61

Moore, Henry
9 St Ann's Place, Limehouse E. 1868-73

Moore, Samuel
222 Bethnal Green Road N.E. 1863-68

Moore, Sidney James
Barnsbury Hall, Barnsbury Street   1889

Moorecroft, William
8 Eastwd Terrace, Hornsey Road N.   1869-70

Mora, Walter Henry
3 Lower Nottinghill Terrace W.   1891

Morgan, Percy George
147 Kennington Road S.E.   1869-77
17 New Street, Kennington S.E.   1878

Morgan, William
77 Holborn Hill E.C.   1858

Morganti, Alfred
176 Tottenham Court Road W.   1855-59

Morganti, Miss R.
176 Tottenham Court Road W.   1860

Morpeth, John
432 Strand   1856

Morrall & Jones
245 Poplar High Street E.   1881

Morrall, Amos
245 Poplar High Street E.   1882

Morris, Edward
45 Cheapside E.C.   1866

Morris, George
19 Tachbrook Street S.W.   1866-69

Moryson, Thomas Arthur
47 Old Broad Street E.C.   1902-05

Moss, Harry
17 Green St, Leicester Square W.C.   1906

Moul, Frederick
6 Queens Road, Bayswater W.   1875

Mouque & Colas
105 Cheapside   10 May 1849-55

Muckell, Samuel
146 Euston Road N.W.   1879-88

Muggeridge, Claud
152 Fleet Street E.C.   1908-

Muir, George Thomas
6 High Street, Kensington W.   1883-85

Muir, Richard
25 Hanway Street, Oxford Street W.   1873-83

Muller, Louis Edward
454 Kingsland Road N.E.   1908-

Mullins, Henry
230 Regent Street W.

N

Nancy, J. J.
5 & 6 Benyon Cts, Hertford Road N.   1861-62

Nansen & Co.
78 Camberwell Road S.E.   1899-03

Nastrowsky & Co.
204 Regent Street W.   1882

Nastrowsky, Baron
88 Cheapside E.C.   1876
76 Rotherfield Street N.   1876

Nastrowsky, Wm. Charles
9 New Bond Street E.C.   1877-80
27 New Bond Street E.C.   1881-82

National Photographic Co.
Wm. Anderson, manager
33 Bucklersbury E.C.   1866

National Photographic Co. Ltd.
J. W. Bryan, secretary;
H. W. Anderson, secretary, 1896
7 Union Court, Old Broad Street E.C. 1895-98

Naudin, Adolph
124 Brompton Road S.W.   1865-67

Naudin & Co.
13 The Terrace, Kensington Rd. W.   1884-94
169 Kensington High Street W.   1895-08-

Nayer, Philip
106 Kensington Park Road N.W.   1869-70

Nayler, Robert
178 Great Portland Street W.   1861

Neale, Wm. Browne
369 Strand   1854-55

Neaves, Louis C.
70 Albany Street, Regents Park N.W.   1866

Negretti & Zambra
59 Cornhill E.C.   1860-72
1 Hatton Garden E.C.   1860-69
107 Holborn Hill E.C.   1860-61
122 Regent Street W.   1862-76
153 Fleet Street E.C.   1865-73
Holborn Circus, Holborn Vdct. E.C.   1870-76
Charterhouse Street E.C.   1870-76
45 Cornhill E.C.   1873-76
Crystal Palace, Sydenham   1883-99

Negretti and Zambra secured the rights to photography at Crystal Palace from its opening and were still exercising them in December 1881.

Nelson, Horatio
37 Westbourne Grove W.   1863-64
86 Regent Street W.   1865-72
115 Westbourne Grove W.   1865

Nesbitt & Co.
50 High Road, Kilburn N.W.   1899-01

Nesbitt, George
118 High Street, Nottinghill W.   1885-95

Neville, Claude
151 Fulham Road S.W.   1876-77

New, William
3 Upp. Queens Bdgs., Brompton S.W. 1858-63
143 Brompton Road S.W.   1864-79
151 Fulham Road S.E.   1880

New British Art Co.
23 Red Lion Street W.C.   1905
84 High Holborn W.C.   1906-08-

Newcombe, Charles Thos.
135 Fenchurch Street E.C.   1860-73
109 Regent Street W.   1863-67
Coleherne Court, Earls Court. S.W.   1865
129 Fenchurch Street E.C.   1874

Newcombe, Samuel Prout
23 Poultry E.C.   1860-66

New Photographic Co.
445 Strand W.C.   1902

New Photographic Studio
20 Upper Baker Street N.W.   1882

New York Photo Co.
538 Kingsland Road N.E.   1904-06

New York Studio
James Hurry, proprietor
57 Oxford Street W.   1880

Neye, Edward Christian
12 Old Bethnal Green Road E.   1884-92

Nias, Edward
6 Kensington High Street W.   1877

Niblett, Henry A.
14 Albany Street N.W.   1867-68

Niblett, Miss Mary E.
9 Park Terrace, Regents Park N.W.   1894-95

Nicholas Brothers
90 Westbourne Grove W.   1866

Nicholas, William
214 Seven Sisters Road N.   1904-08-

Nicholls, Frederick
211 High Street, Shoreditch E.C.   1863-64
231 High Street, Shoreditch E.C.   1865

Nicholson, Edward
398 Harrow Road W.   1899-01

Nicholson, Jeffray
125 Hammersmith Road W.   1904-06

Nield, James & George
13F Dalston Lane N.E.   1901-04

Nightingale, George
149 High Street, Nottinghill W.   1875-76

Noble, George Capon
20 Upper Baker Street N.W.   1883
170 Fleet Street E.C.   1890

Noel, Cyprian A.
63 High Street, Camden Town N.W.   1863-64
130 High Street, Camden Town N.W.   1865

Norman & Norton
122 Regent Street W.   1881-82

Norris, Edward
1 Hanway St, Tottenham Ct. Rd. W.   1873

Northcote, Francis
529 Kingsland Road E.   1872

North London Photographic & Fine Art Repository Co.
356A Holloway Road N.   1876-78

Norton, John (senior)
309 Cambridge Road N.   1873
330 Mile End Rd. E.   1874-79

Norton, Nathaniel
273 Goswell Road E.   1869
394 Kingsland Road N.E.   1869-70
291 Goswell Road E.C.   1870
105 Bishopsgate St, without E.C.   1871-83
197 Junction Road N.   1899-08-

Norton, William Henry
145 Fleet Street   1853

Novelty Photo Co.
135 High Road, Kilburn N.W.   1907

Novelty Portrait Co.
133 Oxford Street W.   1894-95

Novra, Henry
97A Regent Street W.   1868
97 Regent Street W.   1869-74

Nye, Thomas
116 Walworth Road S.E.   1896-05

Nye, Thomas, & Co.
116 Walworth Road S.E.   1905-07

O

Oakshott, William & Charles
Upper Street, Islington N.   1855-57

Ogg, Herbert
53 Regent Street W.   1865

Oldham, Mrs Nora
9 Regent Street S.W.   1897

Oliver, Henry
34 Pearson St, Kingsland Rd. N.E.   1907-08-

Oliver, James, & Co.
154 Fleet Street E.C.   1905-08-

Oliver, J. Macnee
49 Brecknock Road N.   1903-04

M. B. Olley

Olley, Charles Richard
110 Southgate Rd, Kingsland Rd. N.   1903-08-
194 New Kent Road S.E.   1907-08-

O'Neil, Henry
6 Garway Road, Westbourne Grove   1854

O'Neill, James Alleyn
69 New Bond Street W.   1898-99
2 Orchard Street W.   1901-08-

O'Neill, John Robert
420 Strand   1855

Ongeane, William
2 Blackfriars Road S.E.   1881-84

Ordish, Thomas
56 Brompton Row S.W.   1859-62
13 Paternoster Row E.C.   1860-62

Oriel, Charles F.
307 Essex Road N.   1883-87

O'Rourke, Francis
13E Dalston Lane N.E.   1907

Orsich, Charles
45 Ludgate Hill E.C.	1863
131 Fleet Street E.C.	1866
352 Strand W.C.	1878-79

P

Pacey, Thomas
2 Kensington Park Road W.	1878-80

Pacifico, Jacob
255 Whitechapel Road E.	1858
45 Cannon Street Road E.	1864

Packer, Thomas
21 Blackburn Street	1854

Page, John Walter
32 Thornton Street, Horslydwn S.E.	1881
23 Thornton Street, Horslydwn S.E.	1882

Paine, Alfred
31 High Holborn W.C.	1876-85

Paine, H.
Hopkins Bdgs, Islington	10 December 1846

Paine, William
6 Hopkins Buildings, Islington N.	1849-50
5 Trinity Row, Islington N.	1855-57
211 Upper Street, Islington N.	1858

Palmer & Atkinson
4 Vctoria Pl, West India Dock Rd. E.	1870

Palmer, Charles John
18 Chippenham Terr., Harrow Rd. W.	1883-87
398 Harrow Road W.	1888-93

Palmer, Mrs Fanny
4 Vctoria Pl, West India Dock Rd. E.	1871-72

Pantascopic Co, The
Edward Harding Pattison, secretary
3 Red Lion Square W.C.	1865-69

Parascho, Nicholas Constantine
28 Milson Road, West Kensington W.	1899-00

Paris Institute of Photography
Jonathan Chaplin, secretary
11 Argyll Street, Regent Street W.	1856

Parisian Photograph Co.
27 Ludgate Street E.C.	1865

Parisian Photographic Co., The
Chas Orish & Co., proprietors;
Geo Burnley & Co.;
James Lenigar Brock, manager, 1866
1 Orchard Street, Portman Square W.	1864-69
27 Ludgate Street, St Pauls E.C.	1865

Parisian School of Photography
Chas. Orsich, proprietor, 1866
131 Fleet Street E.C.	1866, 1871-88

Noted as being established in 1861.

Park & Barratt
130 Fleet Street E.C.	1906
89 Fleet Street E.C.	1907-08-

Parker & Co.
288 High Holborn W.C.	1892-01

Parker & Collings
7 Weston Place, Kings Cross	1857

Parker & Sibley
97 Guildford Street W.C.	1865

Parker & Spicer
97 Guildford Street W.C.	1864

Parker, William Edward
7 Carlton Terrace, Harrow Road W.	1887-89

Parker, William George
7 Weston Place, Kings Cross N.W.	1858
100 Fleet Street E.C.	1866-67
45 High Holborn W.C.	1868-74
40 High Holborn W.C.	1874-82
17 Warwick Ct, High Holborn W.C.	1874-82

Parker, William George & Co.
40 High Holborn W.C.	1883-90
17 Warwick Ct, High Holborn W.C.	1883-90
288 High Holborn W.C.	1891-08-
100 Southampton Row W.C.	1902-08-

Parmintar, George
4 Rutland Terrace, Abbey Rd. N.W.   1867-68

Parnell, Robert James
42 Smith Street, Chelsea S.W.   1864-65

Parris, William A.
22A Mortimer St, Cavendish Square   1856-57

Parsons, Edwin, & Co.
45 Brompton Road S.W.   1869

Parsons, John Robert
26 Edwards St, Portman Square W.   1866-69
95 Wigmore Street W.   1870-77

Pascal & Co.
7 Windmill Pl, Camberwell Road S.   1864

Passingham, Edmund
16 Mincing Lane E.C.   1892-93
34 South Audley Street W.   1894-95

Patent Casket Portrait Co.
Henry Swan, manager
40 Charing Cross S.W.   1865

Patent Photo-Galvanographic Co.
Wm. Hry. Bosley, general manager, 1857;
Paul Pretsch, general manager, 1858
8 Holloway Pl, Holloway Road N.   1857-58

Paternoster, Thomas
28 Charlotte Street W.   1894-08-

Paterson & Co.
115 Strand W.C.   1889-92

Payer, Anthony
46 Mile End Road E.   1881

Payne, William
6 Whitefriars Street E.C.   1900

Pearce, Arthur
109 Regent Street W.   1876

Pearce, Arthur
110 Westbourne Grove W.   1883

Pearce, James
75 Blackfriars Road S.E.   1887

Pearce, Samuel, & Son
471 East India Dock Road E.   1886

Pearse, James
312 Walworth Road S.   1867

Peck, Samuel B.
8 Eastwood Terrace, Hornsey Rd. N.   1866-68

Pegram, Thomas
9 Cumberland Mkt, Regents Pk. N.W.   1859

Peirce Brothers
33 Mark Lane E.C.   1900

Peirce, Walter
432 Strand W.C.   1906

Penati, John
198 High Street, Shoreditch E.   1873-76
202 Shoreditch High Street E.   1877
203 Shoreditch High Street E.   1878-87

Percie, T., Edwards & Co.
231 & 232 Strand W.C.   1806-08-

Percival, Anthony
88 Edgware Road W.   1891-08-
1 College Cres, Belsize Park N.W.   1902-06

Perkoff, Isaac
186 Commercial Road east E.   1897-08-

Perkoff, Marks
21 Whitechapel Road E.   1892-99
41 Whitechapel Road E.   1900-05
73 Whitechapel Road E.   1906

Perkoff, Marks, & Son
186 Commercial Road east E.   1894-96
21 Whitechapel Road E.   1895-96

Permanent Portrait Co.
Zaccheus Joel Hunter, proprietor
236 Regent Street W.   1883-84

Permanent Printing Co.
Charles Ranson, manager
9A Hereford Square, Brompton S.W.   1873

Peroni, Luigi
105 Park Street, Camden Town N.W.   1904-05

Perriman, James
3 Greenland Pl, Camden Town N.W. 1872-84
1 Greenland Pl, Camden Town N.W. 1885-88
160 High Street, Camden Town N.W. 1891

Perring, Henry John
190 Bethnal Green Road E. 1872-74

Perry, John
72 Piccadilly W. 1862-64

Petit, John
7 Percy Street W. 1908

Pettingall, Joseph
213 Bethnal Green Road E. 1904-08

Peyton, Miss Mina
338A Oxford Street W. 1855
Miss Peyton traded under the name Mina's and
was operating from 1854-1855.

Philipe, Philip
31 High Holborn W.C. 1889-94

Philipps, Philip
31 High Holborn W.C. 1888

Phillips, Charles
7 Lower Sloane Street S.W. 1884

Phillips, Fredk S. D.
1B Norfolk Terr., Westbourne Gr W. 1886
304 Regent Street W. 1886-96

Phillips, M. H.
1 High Rw, Silver St, Kensington W. 1869-70

Photo Art Co.
9 Southampton St, Bloomsbury W.C. 1903
162 Clerkenwell Road E.C. 1906-07
16 Duncan Terrace, Islington N. 1908-

Photochrom Co. Ltd.
121 Cheapside E.C. 1898-05
35 & 36 Hosier Lane E.C. 1904-07
61 St Pauls Churchyard E.C. 1906-07

Photogrammic Co.
130 Strand W.C. 1895

Photographic & Fine Art Co.
122 Newgate Street E.C. 1907-08

Photographic Art Co.
92 Queens Road, Bayswater W. 1889-91

Photographic Artists' Association Ltd.
223 Pentonville Road N. 1898

Photographic Association
16 Brook Street W. 1897-99
14 & 15 Conduit Street W. 1905-08-

Photographic Association Ltd.
John S. Harvey, secretary
16 Brook Street W. 1900-04

Photographic Co.
Fredk Jackson, manager
32 King William Street, City E.C. 1858

Photographic Co. Ltd.
Stephen Bicknell, secretary
14 Brook Street W. 1889

Photographic Copying Co.
Henry Kennett Dixon, manager
102 Fleet Street E.C. 1865

Photographic Copying Offices
Henry Kennett Dixon, manager
223 Strand W.C. 1864

**Photographic House Agency &
Investment Co. Ltd.**
James Pousty, manager
97 Fleet Street E.C. 1871-79

Photographic Portrait Co.
James Elliott, manager;
Hen. Gregoire, manager, 1867
64A New Bond Street W. 1864-67

Photographic Society
Wm Crookes, secretary
1 New Coventry St, Piccadilly W. 1858-59
9 Conduit Street 1869-75

Photo-Lithographic Institute
Wm Henry Warner, manager
492 Oxford Street W.C. 1873

Photo-Printing Co.
24 Langham Street W.   1900

Picard, Mark Anthony
193 Piccadilly   1857

Pickering, Alfred
263 Camberwell Road S.   1864-92

Pickford, Frederick Wm.
60 Bow Road E.   1906-08-

Pike, Charles
214 Old Kent Road S.E.   1876-83
118 Praed Street W.   1883-84

Pike, William
9 Elgin Crescent W.   1907

Pimm & Raymond
68 Euston Road N.W.   1868-69

Pimm, William
68 Euston Road N.W.   1863-71

Pimms, William
16 York Place, Kennington Road S.   1858

Pinn, William
177 City Road E.C.   1875

Piper, Rees William
160 Walworth Road S.E.   1881-91

Piper, William
146 Walworth Road S.E.   1873-75

Piper, William
14 Crown Street, Walworth Road S.   1862-66

Pipere, Mrs Ann
10 Hemmings Row W.C.   1875-86

Pipere, Frederick
37 Chandos St, Covent Garden W.C.   1871-73
10 Hemmings Row W.C.   1871-74

Pitcher, Walter Broadway
27 Church Lane, Islington N.   1908

Pitcher, William
146 Euston Road N.W.   1904-05

Pitt, James
215 Bethnal Green Road E.   1872-73
213 Bethnal Green Road E.   1874-83
Pitt first appeared at 4 Bethnal Green Road in 1858 which was re-numbered to number 215 in 1866. His photographs show a founding date of 1857.

Pitt, James, & Son
213 Bethnal Green Road E.   1884-03

Platt, Edmund George
85 Hyde Road, Hoxton N.   1872-75

Plowright, Edward
224 East India Dock E.   1884-92

Plumer, Charles J.
3 Coventry Street, Piccadilly W.   1864

Plumridge, William Hy., & Co.
158 Regent Street W.   1869-72

Podger, Charles K.
8 Elizabeth Street, Walworth S.E.   1890
38 Elizabeth Street, Walworth S.E.   1891-92

Pollett, Thomas
7 Wellington Terrace, Bayswater W.   1857-58
5 Kensington Terrace, Nottinghill W.   1859
36 High Street, Nottinghill W.   1860-71
15 Leonard Place, Kensington Rd. W.   1866-69

Pollok, Hermann
37 Stamford Road N.   1908-

Polsky Brothers
136 Whitechapel Road E.   1903-08-

Polybank & Co.
72 Piccadilly W.   1868

Pool, Henry
3 Robinhood Lane, Poplar E.   1879

Poole, Harry
775 Commercial Road east E.   1875-78

Poole, Harry, & Sons
785 Commercial Road east E.   1879-80

Poole, Henry
202 Shoreditch High Street E.C.   1872-73

Pootinger, Charles
24 Cannon Street, west, St Pauls   1856

Porcher & Co.
4 Tottenham Court Road W.   1895-99

Portbury, William
72 Piccadilly W.   1863-67
7 Westbourne Grove W.   1868-81

Portbury, William, & Co.
7 Westbourne Grove W.   1882-86

Porter Brothers
33 South End Rd, Hampstead N.W.   1904

Porter, George
9 Pleasant Row, Pentonville   1857
222 Pentonville Road N.   1858-60
216 Pentonville Road N.   1861

Portrait Artists Association
249.5 High Holborn W.C.   1908

Potter, Richard
9 Claro Terrace, Richmond Rd. S.W.   1890

Potter, Robert
31 Clinger Street, Hoxton N.   1854-56

Pottinger, Charles Richmond
41 Ludgate Hill   1854-57
Crystal Palace, Sydenham   1855-56

Poulton, Samuel
147 Strand W.C.   1859-60
352 Strand W.C.   1861-64

Praetorius, Charles
7 Gloucester Grove west S.W.   1873-76
14 Clareville Grove S.W.   1877-95

Pragnell, Miss Kate
164 Sloane Street S.W.   1894-01
39 Brompton Square S.W.   1902-08-

Pratt, Alfred Thomas
440 Old Kent Road S.E.   1887-89

Press Picture Agency
11 Tothill Street S.W.   1904-08-

Preston, Walter
60 Camberwell Road S.E.   1881-88

Prestwich Brothers
49 King William Street E.C.   1893-95

Prestwich, William Henry
1 St Mary Abbotts Terr., Ksngtn W.   1871-76
155 City Road E.C.   1873-93
30 St Mary Abbotts Terr., Ksngtn   1877
98 Cheapside E.C.   1880-84
62 Brunswick Place, City Rd. N.   1885

Price, Lake
43 Piccadilly W.   1860

Price, Thomas
64A New Bond Street W.   1863

Priestman, John William
31 Poplar High Street E.   1870-75
29 Poplar High Street E.   1880
142 East India Dock Road E.   1882-84

Prince, William Banks
307A High Holborn W.C.   1869-70

Prince, William Morden
4 Newland Terr., Kensington Rd. W.   1885

Printing Arts Co. Ltd.
119,121 & 123 Shaftesbury Avenue   1900-02

Prior, David
12 Middle Row, Knightsbridge S.W.   1881

Prior, Frederick Charles
98 Bridge Road, Lambeth S.   1863-64
258 Westminster Bridge Road S.   1865-68

Pritchard, Edward Henry
77 Cornhill E.C.   1871

Procktor, Edwin William
74 Edgware Road W.   1870
16 & 74 Edgware Road W.   1871-73
16 Edgware Road W.   1874-80
90 Edgware Road W.   1874-90

Prout & Mills
22 Newman Street, Oxford St W.   1871

Prout, Edgar
13 Murray St, Camden Square N.W.   1870-88
76 St Pauls Rd, Camden Town N.W.   1889-00

Prout, Victor Albert
15 Baker Street W.   1863-65

Pryer, Charles
93 Edgware Road, Marylebone   1857

Pullen, William
5 Francis Terr., Hampstead Rd. N.W.   1863
4 Chalk Farm Road. N.W.   1864-69

Pulman, Charles
324 Portobello Road W.   1894

Pulman, Charles Octavius
321 Portobello Road W.   1893
112 Pentonville Road N.   1895-00

Purnell, J.
21 Albion Grove west, Barnsbury N.   1862-65

Purssell, John Roger
162 Regent Street W.   1862-63

Pyemont, Charles
148 Holborn Bars E.C.   1857-58

Pyne, Charles & John
369 Strand W.C.   1860

Pyne, James Baker (junior)
32 Leighton Gr, Kentish Town N.W.   1858-60
40 Roxburgh Terr., Haverstock Hill   1861-63
167 Prince of Wales Road N.W.   1864-77
109 Regent Street W.   1878

Q

Quertier, Miss Mary Stuart
125 Hammersmith Road W.   1908

Quinn, Charles William
78 Newgate Street   1855-56
51 Oxford Street W.   1860-61

Quinn, Charles Wm., & Co.
78 Newgate Street E.C.   1857-59
44 Regents Circus   1857

Quinton, John
113 Fleet Street E.C.   1858-63

R

Raivid, Herman
83 Gracechurch Street E.C.   1908-
145 Whitechapel Road E.   1908-

Randolph, Thomas
5 Cobourgh Place   1857
39 Queens Rd, Bayswater   1857

Rands, Harry
35 Buckingham Palace Road S.W.   1880-82

Rands, Harry, & Co.
309 Euston Road N.W.   1874-83

Ransom, Harry
122 Newington Butts S.E.   1890-95

Ransom, William
21 Poplar High Street E.   1870-73

HENRY T. REED

PHOTOGRAPHER
16 Tottenham Court Road
LONDON

COPIES MAY BE HAD BY QUOTING NAME OR NUMBER
NEGATIVES KEPT ONE YEAR ONLY

271 Poplar High Street E. 1874-76
197 Poplar High Street E. 1878
5 St Leonards Road E. 1882

Rawles, William
122 Regent Street W. 1860
101A Park Street N.W. 1868-71

Ray, George
170 Holloway Road N. 1890-93

Rayner, George
83 Newington Causeway S.E. 1866-67

Redman & Alexander
77 Cornhill E.C. 1858-61

Redman and Co.
108 Fleet Street 11 June 1846

Redman, Theodore Smith
77 Cornhill E.C. 1854-68

Reed, Henry Thomas
16 Tottenham Court Road W. 1873-04
443 Strand W.C. 1899-07

Reeks, Gambier
529 Fulham Road S.W. 1900-08-

Rees & Julien
61 Cheapside E.C. 1864-65

Rees, David
187 Roman Road E. 1890

Reeve, Thomas
20 Lower Phillimore Pl, Kensington 1867-75

Reeves, —
Charing Cross 31 May 1849

Reeves, Percy
Barnsbury Street N. 1902-04

Reeves, Thomas
498 Oxford Street 1854-56

Reeves, Thomas
101A Park St, Camden Town N.W. 1872-81

Regent Portrait Co.
122 Regent Street W. 1894-97

Rejlander, Oscar Gustav
(Gallery) 5 Haymarket W. 1862
7 St. George's Terrace,
[129] Malden Road. N.W. 1862-1869
1 Albert Mansions,
Victoria Street S.W. 10 April 1869-1875
Primarily an artist and art photographer Rejlander moved from Wolverhampton to London in April/May 1862. He is best known for his *Two Ways of Life* study but he advertised portrait taking which probably helped pay for his studio. His collection of around 400 original negatives were acquired from his widow by the Fry Manufacturing Company (A. E. Hayman) of 5 Chandos Street, Charing Cross, W.C. The company proposed holding an exhibition of the works and publishing them as prints, enlargements and lantern slides. (*Photographic News* 2 January 1891, p. 15).

Rembrandt Portrait Studio
Jas. H. L. Hyatt, manager
70 Mortimer Street W. 1901

Resta & Co.
101 Shaftesbury Avenue W. 1905-06

Resta, Enrico
4 Coburg Place, Bayswater Rd. W. 1889-96
158 Regent Street W. 1898-03

Reta, Samuel Stanley
1 Harrow Road W. 1907-08-

Reynolds & Newlyn
240 Oxford Street 1867

Reynolds, Arthur
238A Seven Sisters Road N. 1899-01

Reynolds, John
6 Stamford Road, Kingsland N. 1858

Reynolds, St Claire
194 & 196 Brompton Road S.W. 1903

Reynolds, William
Mare Street, Hackney N.E. 1856-59

Richardson, Alvin M.
135 Regent Street W. 1886

Richardson, Thomas
287 Walworth Road S.E. 1892
286 Albany Road S.E. 1893-00
342 Albany Road S.E. 1901-08-

Richards, Thomas Percival
7 King Street, Cheapside E.C. 1895-00

Richey & Foskey
7 Conduit Street, Regent Street W. 1858

Richmond, Samuel
258 Burdett Road E. 1896-97
246 Burdett Road E. 1898-07

Riddington, Thomas F.
15 Finsbury Place E.C. 1859

Ridington, T. F., & Co.
High Rd, Tottenham 1881

Ridley, William Dobson
130 Fleet Street E.C. 1891-95

Rigge, Henry
35 New Bond Street W. 1862-64

Riley, James
187 Roman Road E. 1891

Riley, John William
271 Edgware Road W. 1908

Ritchie & Co.
435 Fulham Road S.W. 1895-97
143 Brompton Road S.W. 1898-02

Robbins, Edward W.
12 Pall Mall east S.W. 1868

Roberts, George Wm.
88 Prince of Wales Road N.W. 1886
96 Prince of Wales Road N.W. 1887-99

Roberts, Walter Wm.
77 Cornhill E.C. 1869

Roberts, William
9 Charing Cross S.W. 1863

Robertson, John
35 King William Street, City 1850

Robertson, William, (junior)
38 & 39 Queens Rd. west, Chls. S.W. 1857-58

Robey, T. F., & Co.
119 Pall Mall S.W. 1896

Robins & Wheeler
12 Pall Mall east S.W. 1867

Robinson, James, & Sons
172A Regent Street W. 1884-90

Robinson, Harry
56 Holloway Road N. 1888-89

Robinson, Mrs Isabella Esther, & Co.
104 Bishopsgate Street, without E.C. 1907

Robinson, Thomas
203 Shoreditch High Street E. 1888

Robinson, William Holding
467 Commercial Road east E. 1900

Rodd, Claud Edward Hogarth
5 Metre Court, Fleet Street E.C. 1890

Rodese, Charles
51 Richmond Road, Barnsbury N. 1871-75

Rodger, Thomas Rodger
4 Coburg Place, Bayswater W. 1884

Roemer, Henry
58 Brick Lane E. 1907-08-

Rogers & Nelson
215 Regent Street W. 1874

Rogers, Charles E.
30 Bonamy St, Rotherhithe New Rd. 1896-00

Rogers, Henry
140 Jamaica Road S.E. 1881

Rogers, John
47 Kentish Town Road N.W. 1874
61 Regents Park Road N.W. 1876-86

Rolph & Salsbury
77 Cornhill E.C.   1872

Rolph, Thomas Owen
40 Gracechurch Street E.C.   1864-67

Romney Studio Ltd.
122 Regent Street W.   1899-00

Romney, James
99 Regent Street W.   1904-06

Rooker, James E.
17 Conduit Street, Paddington W.   1864-65

Rose & Coop
135 Regent Street W.   1898-05
36 Beak Street, Regent Street W.   1899

Rosenschein, Daniel
37 Stamford Road N.   1907

Rosney, Leon
5 Duke St, Tooley Street   1856-58

Rosney, Durand & Bequet
5 Duke St, Tooley Street   1854-55

Ross, Thomas
56 Albany St, Regents Park N.W.   1863

Ross, William
343 Edgware Road W.   1887

Rotary Photographic Co.
10 & 11 Austinfriars E.C.   1899
24 Edmund Place E.C.   1899

Rottman, Guy
11 Levells Court E.C.   1892

Rouch, George
162 Regent Street W.   1860

Rourke, James Michael
52 Cheapside E.C.   1889
51 Threadneadle Street E.C.   1889

Roux, Maurice D.
18 Bridge St, Westminster S.W.   1857-62

Rowland, Walter & Co.
45 Westbourne Grove W.   1868-70

Royal & Britannic Photographic Association
123 Regent Street W.   1857-61
125 Regent Street W.   1862-63
In 1861 Mrs Caroline Beerski was the photographic artist at the Association's studio. She was assisted by her son Charles and her daughter Sophia.

Royal Exchange Photographic Co.
Thos Barrow, manager
9 Cornhill E.C.   1881

Royal Exchange Portrait Co.
John Martin, manager;
James Cotton Leake, manager, 1868;
Gilmore Reid & Co., manager, 1873;
Sallnow & Co., proprietors
9 Cornhill E.C.   1864-77

Royal Masonic Photograph Studio
Charles Orsich, proprietor
420 Strand W.C.   1877

Rozee, Edward
42 Poole Road, South Hackney N.E.   1904-08-

Rudowsky, Carl Albin
3 Guildhall Chambers E.C.   1881-82

Ruffell, John
44 Cranbourn Street W.C.   1904-05

Russell & Sons
199 Brompton Road S.W.   1884-85

Russell, Edward
369 Edgware Road W.   1872-75
276 Holloway Road N.   1878-80
298 Holloway Road N.   1881-86

Russell, Edward John
238 Upper Street N.   1894-95

Russell, James
49A Brecknock Road N.   1885

Russell, James, & Sons
29 Union Rd, Tufnell Park N.W.   1883-85
199 Brompton Road S.W.   1884-88

49 Brecknock Road N. 1886-99
17 Baker Street W. 1889-08-

Russell, Mrs S.
4 Monmouth Road, Bayswater W. 1860-65

Rust, Thomas
26 Westbourne Grove, Bayswater W. 1866

S

St. George, Sydney
Barnsbury Hill, Barnsbury Street N. 1878-85
176 Upper Street N. 1886-98

St. George, William
232 Upper Street N. 1876-77

St. George, William Gregory
62 Leighton Road N.W. 1865

St. James Photographic Co.
72 Piccadilly W. 1883-84

St. James Photographic Institution
Ferdinand Mercer Ball, proprietor;
James Grant Macandrew, propr., 1861
44 Regent Street W. 1858-67

St. James Studio Ltd.
45 Old Bond Street W. 1907

St. Pauls Photograph Gallery
Charles Wolf, proprietor
75 St Pauls Churchyard E.C. 1865-69

St. Pauls Portrait Co.
Thos. Ordish & Co.
21 Paternoster Row E.C. 1864
63 St Pauls Churchyard E.C. 1864

Sager, Samuel
111 New Rd, Whitechapel E. 1898-00

Sale & Beach
135 Fulham Road S.W. 1908-

Salmon & Batchan
30 New Bond Street W. 1902

Salmon, James
105 Mansfield Rd, Hvrstck Hl N.W. 1899-00

Salmon, Saml. Herbert Rider
135 Regent Street W. 1887-90

Saloman, Edgar
242 St Pauls Road, Islington N. 1902-08-

Salomon & Cunanan
266 Upper Street N. 1888

Salsbury, Miss Maria
77 Cornhill E.C. 1873-74

Salter, Henry, (junior)
168 Strand W.C. 1863-64

Salter, Henry & Frederick
168 Strand W.C. 1859-62

Sanders, Alfred
146 Camden Rd, Camden Town N.W. 1866-75

Sands, Edward
3 Postern Row, Tower Hill E.C. 1867-69

Sands, Robert
3 Postern Row, Tower Hill E.C. 1856-61
79 Minories E. 1858-61

Sands, Edward & William
3 Postern Row, Tower Hill E.C. 1870

Sands, Robert, & Son
3 Postern Row, Tower Hill E.C. 1875-85

Sanger, George
207 City Road E.C. 1867

Saqui, Isaac
3 Palatine Pl, Commercial Rd. E. 1860-63

Sargood, James
21 Cumberland Row, Walworth Road 1862-65
262 Westminster Bridge Road S. 1865-68
334 Kennington Park Road S.E. 1874

Sargood, Joseph
100 Bridge Street, Lambeth S. 1857-64

Sargood, Joseph, & Son
59B Westbourne Grove W. 1864

45 Westbourne Grove W.   1865-67

Satchfield, George Mackie
12 Hannibal Road E.   1875-87

Saul, Philip James
1A Chichester Rd, Kilburn Park N.W. 1903-05

Saunders & Smith
243 Old Kent Road S.E.   1875

Saunders, John
209 Westbourne Grove W.   1896-00

Saunders, Samuel
313 City Road E.C.   1879

Saunders, Samuel Walwyn
Blue Anchor Road S.E.   1874

Saunders, Walter
106 Grove Road, Bow E.   1896-08-

Savory, John
58 Edgware Road W.   1857-63

Sawyer & Bird
87 Regent Street W.   1872-73

Sawyer, Lyddell, & Dunn, Ernest
153 Maida Vale W.   1906-08-

Sawyer & Lankester
230 Regent Street W.   1899

Sawyer, Bird & Foxlee
87 Regent Street W.   1874

Sawyer, Lyddell
230 Regent Street W.   1896-02
153 Maida Vale W.   1903-05

Sayer, Charles
220 Mile End Road E.   1869-80

Scannell, Joseph Patrick
153 Fleet Street E.C.   1891-97
51 Tottenham Court Road W.   1898-08-
165 Gt. Portland Street W.   1906
5 New Oxford Street W.C.   1908

Schnadhorst & Heilbronn
433 Strand W.C.   1864-66

Schnadhorst, Edward
433 Strand W.C.   1863
Advertised as being 'late Hughes'.

Schnack, Carl Albert
116 Albany Street N.W.   1904-05

Schuth, William
170 Fleet Street E.C.   1892-06
1A Tottenham Court Road W.   1897-03
16 Piccadilly W.   1902-08-

Scott, Augustus
349 Kingsland Road E.   1879
4 Oxford Street W.   1886-94
108 Oxford Street W.   1892-95
20 Oxford Street W.   1896-04
18 & 20 Oxford Street W.   1905-08

Scott, John, & Co.
432 Oxford Street   1856

Scott's Studios Ltd.
37 King Street, Covent Garden W.C. 1905-07
105 Park Street, Camden Town N.W.   1908-

Scott, Walter Samuel
309 Regent Street   1855-57

Scriven, Alfred M.
125 Newgate Street   1854-56

Sealey & Co.
138 Brompton Road S.W.   1875

Searle Brothers
191 Brompton Road S.W.   1882-08-

Secretan, George William
210A Tufnell Park Road. N.   1899-08-
Advertised as being 'From Morg, New York'.

Seeley, Edward
4 Nottinghill Terrace W.   1874-76

Selfe, Robert
4 Surrey Place, Newington Butts S.   1857-61

Senn, Tom
184 Fleet Street E.C.   1885-86

Serne, Leonard
46 Malden Road N.W.   1907

Shakespeare, Charles
162 Kings Road, Chelsea S.W.   1871-86

Shapland, Robert
20 Blackfriars Road S.E.   1901

Sharp & Beard
28 Old Bond Street W.   1858-59

Sharp & Melville
28 Old Bond Street W.   1857

Sharp, C.
5 Duke St, Tooley Street   12 Oct. 1846-1848

Sharp, Edward
221 Westminster Bridge Rd. S.E.   1886-08-
111 Strand W.C.   1889-91
10 Upper Street N.   1893-08-

Sharp, James
16 & 17 Poultry E.C.   1893

Sharpe, Charles William
188 Regent Street W.   1867-68

Sharpe, Herbert
188 Regent Street W.   1869

Shaw, Edmund
181 Walworth Road S.E.   1869

Shaw, Henry
274 Commercial Road. east E.   1905-08-

Shaw, Henry
243 Kentish Town Road N.W.   1904

Shaw, James
10 Westbourne Gardens W.   1859-60

Shaw, James Jesse
103 St Johns Wood Terrace N.W.   1867-73

Shaw, John
256 Oxford Street W.   1872-73

Shaw, John
10 Westbourne Gardens W.   1857-58

Shayler, Albert
176 St John Street Road E.C.   1871-72

Shayler, Edward
82 St John Street Road E.C.   1855-67
173 Upper Street, Islington N.   1864
229 Upper Street, Islington N.   1865-67
176 St John Street Road E.C.   1868-70

Shearman, Henry
4 Queens Terr., Cmmrcial Rd. east E. 1862-67
3 Regents Street, Commercial Rd. E.   1868-74

Shearman, Henry, & Son
343 Mile End Road E.   1875-78

Sheehan & Garbanati
385 Oxford Street   1854

Shepherd, John Alfred
20A Clipstone Street W.   1889

Sherley, James Thomas
5 Cottenham Road N.   1870-71

Shillibeer, James
419 Oxford Street   1854

Sibley, Henry
299 Euston Road N.W.   1890-91

Sibley, Henry John
181 Kentish Town Road N.W.   1885
181 & 343 Kentish Town Rd. N.W.   1886-89
181 Kentish Town Road N.W.   1890-08-

Same Studio

Sidney & Co.
189 Earls Court Road S.W.   1884-85

Silcox, Henry William
Uxbridge Road, Bayswater W.   1862-70

Silvester, Alfred
118 New Bond Street W.   1864

Silvy, Camille, & Co.
38 Porchester Terr., Bayswater W. 1860-61
38 & 38B Porchester Terrace W.   1862-69

Having taken over the business of Caldesi and Montecchi in 1859 Silvy established his own studio in Porchester Terrace. He was almost certainly the first *carte de visite* photographer in London. Within two-and-a-half years he had taken seven thousand portraits. Silvy's reputation both at the time and subsequently was very high with commentators praising his artistic nature and operative skill. His last portraits were made in July 1868 and the business was sold to the theatre photographer Adolphe Beau. David Lee and Mark Haworth-Booth (see bibliography) describe Silvy's work.

The National Portrait Gallery in London holds Silvy's daybooks (one volume from July 1863- May 1864 is missing) which record sitters, negatives numbers together with the date and details of their order. Most have an uncut proof print tipped in. They cover the period August 1859-July 1868. The Victoria and Albert Museum, London, hold a collection of Silvy contact proofs.

Simkins, William
3 Princes Sq, Kensington Pk Rd. S.E. 1869-82

Simmons, Arthur
258 Westminster Bridge Road S.E.   1883-07
191 Newington Butts S.E.   1889-92
238 Westminster Bridge Road S.E.   1898-08-

Simmons, Saul Morris
374 Essex Road N.   1898

Simonds, Henry Parrish
6 Chas. Place, Hertford Road N.   1854-60

Simons, Mrs Caroline
29 Euston Road N.W.   1872-78

Simons, Victor
29 Euston Road N.W.   1879

Simpson, Thomas
68 Euston Road N.W.   1872-73

Sims, Edward
4 Sussex Terr., Westbourne Gro. W.   1859
59 Westbourne Grove, Bayswater W.   1859

Sims, Thomas
44 Upper Albany St, Regents Park   1854-55

7 Conduit Street, Regent Street W.   1856-59
Thomas Sims (1826-1910) was an early photographer setting up in business 1847 at Weston-super-Mare. He worked with the daguerreotype process and in 1847 began experimenting with Talbot's calotype process. In 1852 he exhibited examples of his work at the first British photographic exhibition organised by the Society of Arts in London.

Sims moved to London in 1853 where he opened two photographic studios. Shortly afterwards he became involved in a legal dispute with Talbot who held that his calotype patent covered all photographic processes - including the collodion process then being used by Sims. Sims refused to pay Talbot for a license and an injunction was served forcing him to close his studios. Following the conclusion of the *Talbot v. Laroche* case against Talbot Sims re-opened his studio and remained in business in London until 1868. He then moved to Tunbridge Wells where he remained active as a professional photographer until his death in 1910.

A collection of Sims' work is held by the Tunbridge Wells museum.

Sims, Thomas, & Co.
76 Westbourne Grove W.   1865-68

Sims, Thomas & Edward
13A Westbourne Grove W.   1860-61
23 Westbourne Grove W.   1863-64

Sinclair & Co.
214 Marylebone Road N.W.   1883

Sinclair, William
38 Walworth Road S.   1867

Sinclair, William Henry
70 Euston Road N.W.   1863-78
410 Euston Road N.W.   1868-86
412 Euston Road N.W.   1871-86
142 Pentonville Road N.   1871-74
68 Euston Road N.W.   1874-75
116 Euston Road N.W.   1879-87

Skaife, Thomas
47 Baker Street W. 1861-63
1 Park Terrace, Regents Park N.W. 1864

Skillman, Charles Henry
9 Claro Terrace, Richmond Rd. S.W. 1897-02

Skillman, Charles Hy., & Co.
9 Claro Terrace, Richmond Rd. S.W. 1903

Skingle, Jabez
172 Blackfriars Road S.E. 1881-85
98 Fleet Street E.C. 1881-82

Skinner, Mrs Emily
131 Fleet Street E.C. 1868-69

Slader, Ernest & William
143 Gallery Wall Road S.E. 1896-97

Slater, William Ebenezer
Jamaica Level S.E. 1872-76
84 Jamaica Level S.E. 1877-79
282 Albany Road S.E. 1884-91

Small, James Charles
32 Edgware Rd, Marylebone 1857

Smallcombe, James Charles
32 Edgware Road W. 1858
33 Baker Street 1862-69

Smeeton, John
529 Kingsland Road N.E. 1869-71

Smerdon, Ernest Edward
15 Cliffords Inn E.C. 1905

Smith, A. E. & E. W.
109 Cheapside E.C. 1884

Smith, Alfred
7 Hornsey Road N. 1871

Smith, Arthur Edgar
109 Cheapside E.C. 1885-87
90 & 91 Queens Street E.C. 1888-95
17 Farringdon Avenue E.C. 1896-04
8 Farringdon Avenue E.C. 1905-08-

Smith, Bell
17 Regent Street S.W. 1863-64

Smith, Benjamin James
21 Balmes Road N. 1871-72

Smith, Edward
3 Cheapside E.C. 1881-99

Smith, Edward
258 Westminster Bridge Road S.E. 1877-78

Smith, Edwin Dalton
27A Old Bond Street W. 1860-61

Smith, George
430 Oxford Street W. 1866

Smith, George Henry
58 Edgware Road W. 1867

Smith, Harry Edward
28 Halsey Street, Chelsea S.W. 1889
83 Church Street, Chelsea S.W. 1890-93

Smith, James
35 Balls Pond Road N. 1889

Smith, James
2 Blackfriars Road S.E. 1885

Smith, James
151 Fulham Road S.W. 1871-72

Smith, James
4 Westbourne Gardens, Bayswater W. 1866
70 Norfolk Terrace, Bayswater W. 1867-70

Smith, James
250 Westminster Bridge Road S.E. 1871

Smith, John Caswell
305 Oxford Street W. 1895-03

Smith, Josiah
6 Bartholemew Terr., City Rd. E.C. 1859-60
300 City Road E.C. 1862-67

Smith, Mrs Mary Ann Harriet
258 Westminster Bridge Road S.E. 1879

Smith, Mrs Mercy
4 Albion Pl, Upper Kensington Lane 1855

Smith, Stephen John
310 High Road Kilburn N.W. 1901-08-

Smith, Thomas James
34 Upper Street, Islington N.   1876-78

Smith, William Henry
2 Crogsland Road N.W.   1873-77

Smorthwaite, Mrs Emma
174 Regent Street W.   1877-94

Smorthwaite, William
52 Cheapside E.C.   1877-80

Smuin, Stephen
22 Bishops Road, Bayswater W.   1881

Smye, Frederick, & Co.
222 Old Kent Road S.E.   1877-79

Smye, George, & Co.
26 Hatfield Street, Blackfriars S.E.   1876
222 Old Kent Road S.E.   1876

Smyth, Austin
15 Lower Belgravia Place, Pimlico   1859

Snell, Robert, (junior)
7 Glebe Terrace, Islington N.   1854-59
High Street, Kingsland N.E.   1862-67

Soar, Henry
85 Grove Road E.   1894-03

Society of Photo-Etchers
Arthur Vokins, secretary
23 Baker Street W.   1896

Soho Bazaar School of Photography
406 Oxford Street W.   1881
4, 5, 6 & 7 Soho Square W.   1881-83
77 Oxford Street W.   1882-83

Soper & Stedman Ltd.
147 Strand W.C.   1896-98

Southwell Brothers
16 & 22 Baker Street W.   1863-64
22 Baker Street W.   1865-76
64A New Bond Street W.   1868-69

In the 1880s London's Baker Street was considered 'a photographic resort'. The *Photographic News* (10 April 1884, p. 232)

ascribed the origins of this to Southwell Brothers which "it may be remembered, kept three studios going all day long. From seventy yo one hundred pounds daily were the average takings of the big Baker Street firm". W. F. Southwell died in 1883 he was described "as managing what was...perhaps the highest class photographic establishment".

Southwell, William
16 Baker Street, Portman Square W.   1858-62

Spalding, Charles Hunter
311 Kentish Town Road N.W.   1898-07

Speaight, Frederick & Richard
178 Regent Street W.   1897-03
157 New Bond Street W.   1904

Speaight Ltd.
157 New Bond Street W.   1905-08-

Spencer, John Alexander
4, 5, 6 & 7 Gold Hawk Terr, New Rd.   1865-73

Spencer, Read & Co.
4 Agar Street, Strand W.C.   1859-61

Spicer, William Isaac
47 Baker Street, Portman Square W.   1866-68

Spindlbauer, Henry
107 Great Eastern Street E.C.   1905-08
181 City Road E.C.   1907

Spratt, John
237 Blackfriars Road   1856-57

Springthorpe, George & John
10 Upper Street N.   1886

Sprinz, Philip
443 Strand W.C.   1889

Spry, George
48 High Holborn W.C.   1879
352 Strand W.C.   1880-92

Stacy, Daniel Sargeant
62 Upper Street, Islington N.   1873-92

Staff, William Arthur			**Steele, Hubert, & Co.**	
36 Chandos St, Covent Garden W.C.	1885		322 Upper Street N.	1893

Staff, William Arthur
36 Chandos St, Covent Garden W.C.   1885

Standard Photo Co.
432 Strand W.C.   1899

Standard Photo and Engineering Co.
432 Strand W.C.   1900-02

Stanesby, Joshua
114 Strand W.C.   1864-65
1 Grove Place, Holloway Road N.   1875-78

Stanesby, Joshua & Alex
13 Tachbrook Street   1855-57

Stanley Brothers
124 Brompton Road S.W.   1871-74

Stanley, Gerald
4 Featherstone Buildings W.C.   1868

Stanley, Herbert, & Co.
95 Gloucester Road S.W.   1892-04
130 Ladbroke Grove W.   1905-07

Stanton, James
78 St Ervans Road, Nottinghill W.   1881-83

Staples, Frederick James
279 High St, Camden Town. N.W.   1884-07
147 Seven Sisters Road N.   1908-

Starie, William
34 Newington Causeway S.E.   1880-85

Star Photographic Co.
536 Oxford Street W.   1893-08-

Star Photo Printing Co.
278 City Road E.C.   1908-

Stead, Richard
4 Kings Rd. Terrace, Chelsea S.W.   1858
162 Kings Road, Chelsea S.W.   1859-67

Stedman, Frederick Wm.
180 Tottenham Court Road W.   1907

Steele, Charles Benj.
396 New Cross Road S.E.   1899-02

Steele, Hubert, & Co.
322 Upper Street N.   1893

Stembridge, Ernest
202 Kingsland Road E.   1886

Stenning, Miss Jessie
18 Yoemans Row, Brmptn Rd. S.W. 1906-08-

Stent, William Henry
170 Holloway Road N.   1888-89

Stephanie, Maud Madame
25 Harrington Rd, S. Knsngtn S.W.   1907-08

Stevens, Richard
184 Fleet Street E.C.   1860

Stewart Brothers
Somerset Terr., Kensington Rd. W.   1883

Stewart, James
35 New Bond Street W.   1861

Stewart, Richard
96 St Leonards Road E.   1884-00

Stiles, Henry & Richard
6 Kensington High Street W.   1880-81
8 Kensington High Street W.   1882-88
34 Kensington High Street W.   1889-01
3 Campden Hill Rd. Kensington W.   1902-08-

Stilliard, Edward, & Co.
9 Claro Terrace, Richmond Rd. S.W. 1905-07

Stilliard, Horace, & Co.
9 Claro Terrace, Richmond Rd. S.W.   1908

Stock, Henry Stephen
39 Dean Street, Soho W.   1867-68

Stocks, Arthur, & Co.
27 Shoe Lane E.C.   1897

Stone, Harry
64 High Street, Nottinghill W.   1900

Stone, Robert
189 Earls Court Road S.W.   1886

Stoneham, Edmund John
79 Cheapside E.C.   1881-92

Stoneham, Frank & Edmund
79 Cheapside E.C. 1893-08

Stortz & Son
51 Tottenham Court Road W. 1896

Stovin & Thorp
White Lodge, Keppel Street S.W. 1862

Stovin, Charles
White Lodge, Keppel Street S.W. 1861-63

Strangman, Walter Herbert
135 Regent Street W. 1885

Stroud, Harry
270 Lower Road S.E. 1906-08-

Strudwick, William
Wardrobe Chambers, Qn Victoria St. 1882

Stuart Brothers
47 Brompton Road S.W. 1865-93
Established 1854.

Stuart, Francis Godolphin Osbourne
75 St Pauls Churchyard E.C. 1881-82

Stuart, George
11 Red Lion Passage, Holborn W.C. 1857-59

Stuart, Richard
222 Bethnal Green Road N.E. 1869
437 Bethnal Green Road E. 1870-71
435 Bethnal Green Road E. 1872-74

Stuart, Rt.
16 Mid Queens Bdgs Bromptn S.W. 1857-58
9 Queens Buildings Brompton S.W. 1862-63
47 Brompton Road S.W. 1864

Stuart, William & John
47 & 49 Brompton Road S.W. 1894-08-

Stuart, William Slade
162 Sloane Street S.W. 1906

Stubbington, Clay
360 Rotherhithe New Road S.E. 1887

Stubbs, Richard
84 Kings Road, Chelsea S.W. 1868-70

Sulman, Frederick
187 Roman Road E. 1886

Sulman, John K.
9 Market Terrace, Holloway Road N. 1883

Sun Photographic Co.
Charles Fredk Smith, manager
4 Ludgate Hill E.C. 1868-69

Surl, Miss Alice
334A Essex Road N. 1901-02

Surl, A., & Co.
334A Essex Road N. 1903

Suss, Louis
58 Brick Lane E. 1900-02

Suss, Louis & Joseph
58 Brick Lane E. 1903-05
25 Whitechapel Road E. 1905-08-

Sutch Brothers
143 Brompton Road S.W. 1881-86

Sutch, George Holton
232 Euston Road N.W. 1874

Sutton, Edward
27 Rochester Square N.W. 1866-74

Sutton, Edwin
204 Regent Street W. 1857-74

Swan Electric Engraving Co.
116 Charing Cross Road W.C. 1893

Swan, Samuel
30 Sloane Square, Chelsea S.W. 1869

Swann, George
3 4 &5 Benyon Cts, Hertford Rd. N. 1872

Swatridge, Thomas Sydenham
35 Balls Pond Road. N. 1872-78
3 Alfred Terrace, Holloway Rd. N. 1885

Symmons & Co.
59 & 60 Chancery Lane W.C. 1897-98

Symons, John Damerell
28 Old Bond Street W. 1862-63

| 162 Regent Street W. | 1864-65 |
| 131 Fleet Street | 1865 |

Syndicate of Pictorial Portraiture Ltd.
| 20 Yoemans Rw, Brompton Rd. S.W. | 1900-02 |

Syrus, Napoleon
| 235 Balls Pond Road N. | 1870-90 |
| 128 Strand W.C. | 1877 |

Szarkowski, Alex
| 48 High Holborn W.C. | 1878 |
| 304 Kings Road, Chelsea S.W. | 1878 |

T

Taber Bas-Relief Photographic Syndicate Ltd.
J. Mullinder, manager, 1898;
J. A. Carse, 1899
38 Dover Street W.	1898-99
141 New Bond Street W.	1900-01
115 Newgate Street E.C.	1902-08-
27 Station Buildings, Acton St N.E.	1908

Tamesis Ltd.
| 3 Denman St, Golden Square W. | 1905 |

Tanner, William
| 7 Clarence Place, Camberwell Rd. S. | 1858 |

Tapping, Alfred
| 6 Westminster Bridge Road S. | 1865-81 |

Tardeo Camera Co.
| 17 Shaftesbury Avenue W.C. | 1904 |

Tate & Prosser
| 35 Holloway Road N. | 1865 |

Tate, William Henry Gilbert
| 45 Cheapside E.C. | 1871-76 |

Tayler, Charles, & Co.
| 2 Aldgate High Street E. | 1884 |

Tayler, Charles Bartlett
| 158 Strand W.C. | 1869-75 |

Tayler, Henry
| 168 New North Road N.W. | 1890 |

Taylor & Bastain
| 335 Kentish Town Road N.W. | 1884-90 |

Taylor & Harrison
| Jamaica Level S.E. | 1872-73 |

Taylor, Andrew & George
11 Cannon Street west E.C.	1866
67 Cannon Street E.C.	1867-71
2 Crwn Bdgs, Queen Victoria St E.C.	1873-75
129 Fenchurch Street E.C.	1875-02
70 Queen Victoria Street E.C.	1874-06
153 Regent Street W.	1877-08-
62 & 64 Ludgate Hill E.C.	1881-04
25 Southwark Bridge Road S.E.	1881-89
78 Queen Victoria Street E.C.	1882-06

The company's Forest Hill works were described in the *P.N.* 19 November 1880, pp. 553-554.

Taylor & Sainsbury
| 158 Strand W.C. | 1867-68 |

Taylor, B., & Co.
| 317 East India Dock Road E. | 1907 |

Taylor, Charles
| 73 Cross Street, Islington N. | 1867-76 |

Taylor, Edward
1 Buckingham Palace Road S.W.	1886-87
85 Chalk Farm Road N.W.	1888-90

Taylor, Frank
281 Lower Road S.E.	1897-00

Taylor, Frederick Lawson
443 Strand W.C.	1908-

Taylor, George
67 Cannon Street E.C.	1872

Taylor, Henry James
335 Kentish Town Road N.W.	1891-92
243 Kentish Town Road N.W.	1897-03

Taylor, J. & G.
1 Buckingham Palace Road S.W.	1903
72 Leadenhall Street E.C.	1903-06
15 Newgate Street E.C.	1903

Taylor, J. Cruickshank, & Son
90 Newgate Street E.C.	1891-02

Taylor, Mrs Rose
79 Oxford Street W.	1882-83

Taylor, Rowland
369 Edgware Road W.	1876-84
26 Westbourne Grove W.	1878

Taylor, Sydney
130 Kentish Town Road N.W.	1908

Taylor, Thomas
405 Oxford Street W.	1868-81
22 Tottenham Court Road W.	1880
62 Upper St, Islington N.	1895-97

Taylor, William Sidney
3 High Street, Deptford S.E.	1907

Tear, Adolphus
42 High Street, Nottinghill Gate W.	1902-08-

Telfer, William
194 Regent Street W.	1856-64
104 Regent Street W.	1865

Terry, Hyman
15 Charlotte Street, Whitechapel E.	1879

Thackrah, John
5 Coburg Place, Bayswater W.	1858-59

Theobald, Edward Miall
17 Upper Street, Islington N.	1884-85

Theobalds, James, & Co.
20 Upper Baker Street N.W.	1878-79

Thiele, Reinhold, & Co.
65 & 66 Chancery Lane W.C.	1897-08-

Thomas & Co.
7 Sloane Street, Chelsea S.W.	1904-05

Thomas, Edward
216 Pentonville Road N.	1867

Thomas, Frederick
399A Oxford Street W.	1863-64

Thomas, Isaac
6 York Terrace, Commercial Rd. E.	1862

Thomas, Jacob
1 Regents Canal Dock E.	1858-62
6 York Terrace, Commercial Rd. E.	1863-67

Thomas, Lewis James
32 Bow Street W.C.	1883

Thomas, Lewis, James & John
32 Bow Street W.C.	1884-87

Thomas, Richard Williams
121 Cheapside E.C.	1884-93
41 Cheapside E.C.	1894-08-

Thomas, Thomas
North Road N.	1858-59
29 South Road N.	1858-59

Thompson & Co.
56 Seven Sisters Road N.	1903

Thompson & Stangbye
22 Seven Sisters Road N.	1902

Thompson & Wagstaff
12 Pall Mall east	1855
112 Pall Mall east	1856

Thompson, George
7 Trinity Row, Islington High St. N.   1858
213 Upper Street, Islington N.   1859-65

Thompson, George, Roberts & Co.
289 New Cross Road S.E.   1873-74

Thompson, Robert
86 Whitechapel Road E.   1863

Thompson, Robert Winter
137 Edgware Road   1860-68
266 Euston Road   1860-64
297 Oxford Street W.   1860-71
312 Oxford Street W.   1860-63
430 Oxford Street W.   1860-64
292 High Holborn W.C.   1861-62
431 Oxford Street W.   1865
274A Oxford Street W.   1867
264A Oxford Street W.   1868-71
314 Edgware Road   1869-74
30 Edgware Road   1871-72

Thompson, Winter
6 Upper Queens Buildings S.W.   1863
151 Brompton Road S.W.   1864

Thomson & Tate
45 Cheapside E.C.   1870

Thomson, James
443 Brompton Road S.W.   1895-96
143 Brompton Road S.W.   1897

Thomson, John
78 Buckingham Palace Road S.W.   1882-84
70A Grosvenor Street W.   1885-04

Thomson, John, & John Newlands
141 New Bond Street W.   1905-08

Thomson, Wm. Dalrymple
30 Cornhill E.C.   1864-66
45 Cheapside E.C.   1867-69
Removed to the City of London Portrait
Company at 45 Cheapside.

Thorne & Saunders
343 Kentish Town Road N.W.   1885

Thorne & Waterson
343 Kentish Town Road N.W.   1884

Thorne, Herbert
343 Kentish Town Road N.W.   1880

Thorne, Herbert James
70 Mortimer Street W.   1883

Thwaites, Henry
101 East India Dock Road E.   1873-74
467 Commercial Road east E.   1880-99

Thwaites, Henry
3 Suffolk Pl, Commercial Road E.   1873-74
607 Commercial Road east E.   1875-76

Tilling & Co.
152 Fleet Street E.C.   1896-00

Timms, Charles Alfred
41 Newington Causeway S.E.   1858-63
233 Walworth Road S.   1867-68

Timms, J. F., & Son
38 Brecknock Rd, Camden Road N.   1882-89
121 Cheapside E.C.   1882-81

Timms, John Frederick
31 High Holborn W.C.   1857-73
38 Brecknock Rd, Camden Road N.   1874-81
121 Cheapside E.C.   1874-81
A *carte* showing the High Holborn address
noted the fact that the company was "late of
Langham Place, Regent Street, W".

Tippin, Albert
132 Camberwell Road S.E.   1884
80 Kennington Road S.E.   1885

Towers, Dudley
26 New Street, Dorset Square N.W.   1900-01
67 Fairfax Road, Hampstead N.W.   1905-08-

Trafalgar Photographic Co.
James Denham Wise, manager
37 Chandos St, Covent Garden W.C. 1874-75

Transfield, Thomas
228 Westminster Bridge Road S.E.   1870

Treble, Charles Fredk.
10 Stockbridge Terr., Pimlico S.W.   1889
170 Victoria Street S.W.   1890-08-

Treeby, William
70 Lillie Road S.W.   1904
25 Great Western Road W.   1907-08

Trew, Harold T.
67 Highgate Road N.W.   1880-82

Triptree, Charles
5 Deans Row, Walworth Road S.   1865
7 Deans Row, Walworth Road S.   1866

Triptree, Chas (junior)
5 Manor Road, Walworth S.E.   1872-73
342 Walworth Road S.E.   1875-79
60 Camberwell Road S.E.   1880

Triptree, Charles (senior)
188 Walworth Road S.E.   1872-74

Triptree, Charles, & Sons
188 Walworth Road S.   1867-71

Truckle & Brisco
118 New Bond Street W.   1873-74

Truckle, Miss Blanche
60 Camberwell Road S.E.   1889-91

Truckle, George
118 New Bond Street W.   1875-86

Tuck, William Henry, & Co.
204 Regent Street W.   1877-78

Tucker & Austin
90 Newgate Street E.C.   1875

Tucker, Robert
56 Offord Road, Barnsbury Road N.   1879-82

Tucker, Robert
18 Wilton Road, Dalston N.E.   1899-00

Tuhten, Augustus
31 Edgware Road W.   1906

Tulley, James
58 Fleet Street   1856-57

Tungate, Thomas John
35 Queen Street, Edgware Road W.   1874-77

Turgill, Louis
106 New Oxford Street W.C.   1906-08-

Turnbull & Sons
49 King William Street E.C.   1889-92

Turnbull, John
18 Gerald Street, Soho W.   1864

Turner & Drinkwater
17 Upper Street N.   1894-96

Turner & Everitt
17 Upper Street, Islington N.   1863-67
3 Cheapside E.C.   1865-66

Turner & Killick
17 Upper Street, Islington N.   1881-87

Turner, Alfred
140 Upper Kennington Lane S.E.   1886

Turner, Charles
88 Waterloo Road   1857

Turner, George
140 Upper Kennington Lane S.E.   1891-00

Turner, George Hogarth
43 Davis Street W.   1878

Turner, Harry Cecil
299 Euston Road N.W.   1880
60 Pentonville Road N.   1881-82
14 Pentonville Road N.   1883-94
26 Pentonville Road N.   1895-99

Turner, Henry
6 Bedford Place, Commercial Rd. E.   1870-74
245 Commercial Road east E.   1875-83

Turner, Henry Francis
422 Mile End Road E.   1900-02

Turner, Henry George
34 Newington Butts S.E.   1907
61 Newington Butts S.E.   1908-

Turner, Mrs Hettie
231 Edgware Road W.   1907-08-

Turner, John
15 Finsbury Place   1857

Turner, John
7 Garnault Place, Clerkenwell E.C.   1856-72

Turner, Thomas Charles
10 Barnsbury Park N.   1875-90
3 Cheapside E.C.   1875-76
17 Upper Street N. —   1867-90

Turner, T. C., & Co.
10 Barnsbury Park N.   1891-00
17 Upper Street N. —   1891-08-

Turner, William
140 Upper Kennington Lane S.E.   1887-90

Turner, William
7 Clarence Place, Camberwell Rd. S.   1859-63
193 Camberwell Road S.   1864-67

Turney, Barnett
58 Kings Cross Road W.C.   1876-80

Turney, Henry
150 Campbell Road, Bow E.   1877

Turvey, Barnett
34 Kings Cross Road W.C.   1871-76

Tyler, Walter Clement
115 Waterloo Road S.E.   1885-86

Typographic Etching Co.
St Dunstans Court, Fleet Street E.C.   1884-86
23 Farringdon Street E.C.   1884-88
160 Fleet Street E.C.   1887
3 Ludgate Crcs Bdgs, Farringdon St.   1889-91

Tyssen, Miss Alice
443 Strand W.C.   1890

Tytler, F.
127 Queens Road, Bayswater W.   1881

U ,

Underwood, Louis
16 Villiers Street, Strand W.C.   1895-99

Unger, Soloman
119 Duckett Street, Stepney E.   1906-07

United Association of Photography
William Morgan Brown, secretary
213 Regent Street W.   1865-67
3 Red Lion Square W.C.   1866

Universal Photographic Co.
Edward Fox, manager
121 Cheapside E.C.   1864-72

Universal Printing Co. Ltd.
280 High Holborn W.C.   1884-85
Tichborne Court W.C.   1884-85

Upton & Connolly
59 Paddington W.   1896

Upton, Alfred Adolphus
59 Paddington Street W.   1894-95

Upton, Arthur
322 Upper Street N.   1882

Uzulay, Isaac
14 Oxford Street W.   1875-76

V

Vaissier, Maurice
31 Edgware Road W.   1864-66

Valentine & Sons
1 Dyers Buildings, Holborn E.C.   1889-90

Valerie & Co.
132 Camberwell Road S.E.   1895
187 Camberwell Road S.E.   1896

Valerie, Arthur
1 Conduit Street W.   1908-

Valerie, Edward
39 Kings Road, Chelsea S.W.   1903-04

Valerie, Mrs Emma
39 Kings Road, Chelsea S.W.   1901-02

Vandeleur & Co.
100 Westbourne Grove W.   1886-87

Vandene, John
3 Nottinghill Terrace W.   1888

Van Der Weyde
182 Regent Street W.   1878-02
Van der Weyde's studios were described as
being the first to be fitted with electric light for
the purpose of photography and the first to use
a gas engine for generating electricty. The
studio was described in the *P.N.* 17 December
1880. According to Van der Weyde in the
Photographic News (24 February 1882) he set
up his electric studio in September 1877.

Vandyck, Heiman
107 Clarendon Road W.   1881-87
20 Ladbroke Grove Road W.   1884-94
130 Ladbroke Grove W.   1895-04
46 Archer Street W.   1897

Vandyk, Carl
125 Gloucester Road S.W.   1882-08-
37 Buckingham Palace Road S.W.   1902-08-

Van Hilda, John
3 Addison Studios, Blythe Road W.   1904

Van Meegan, Hans
72 Seven Sisters Road N.   1904

Varley Brothers
88A Oakley Street, Chelsea S.W.   1863-68

Varley, Frederick Charles
317 Kings Road, Chelsea S.W.   1871-80

Varley, Mrs Gertrude Emma
57 Beaufort Street W.   1882-91

Vaughan, Samuel Frederick
140 Jamaica Road S.E.   1888-93

Vernon, Alfred Henry
417 Kingsland Road E.   1882-83

Vernon, Fred
28 Jubilee Street E.   1906-07
312 Kingsland Road N.E.   1907

Vernon, Frederick
2 Gibralter Walk, Bethnl Green Rd. E.   1904

Vernon, Henry
529 Kingsland Road E.   1873

Verre & Co.
30 Essex Street, Strand W.C.   1902-03
88, 89 & 90 Chancery Lane W.C.   1903

Vesey, John Alfred
81 Lupus Street, Pimlico S.W.   1873-80

Vickers, Thomas Henry
285 New Cross Road S.E.   1885-87

Vickery, James
309 Euston Road N.W.   1873

Vickery, William
85 Pleasant Place, Kingsland Rd. N.E.   1862

Villiers, Charles
16 Villiers Street, Strand W.C.   1890

Villiers, Edward
16 Villiers Street, Strand W.C.   1882-94

Villiers Photo Co.
398 Harrow Road W.   1902-04

Vincent, Clifford
408 Edgware Road W.   1907

Vincent Clifford Ltd.
408 Edgware Road W.   1907-08-

Viner, Frederick
107 Southwark Park Road S.E.   1883-84
110 Southwark Park Road S.E.   1885-04
109 Cheapside E.C.   1890
40 Walworth Road S.E.   1895-03

Viner, William Robert
14 High Holborn W.C.   1864

Vinicombe, Joseph Emanuel
448 New Cross Road S.E.   1883

Vivian, Mark
53 Kensington High Street W.   1892

Voigtlander & Evans
3 Lowndes Terrace   1853

Volz, Peter Anthony
95 Grand Junction Terr., Edgware Rd   1857

Voy, Harold
190A Broadhrst Gdns, Hmpstd N.W.   1899-02
177 West End Lane, Kilburn N.W.   1903-05

W

Wade, George
Grove Road, Bow Road E.   1873-76
12 Grove Road, Bow Road E.   1877-99

Wade, George
27 Bridge Street, Lambeth S.   1864
5 Mount Place, Whitechapel Road E. 1864-65
189 Westminster Bridge Road S.   1865

Wager, George
376 Oxford Street W.   1868-71

Wagner, Charles
420 Mile End Road E.   1871

Wagstaff, William
12 Pall Mall east   1857

Wakefield & Kemp
17 Assembly Row, Mile End Rd. E.   1864
108 Mile End Road E.   1865-66

Walde, Brown
45 St Georges Place S.W.   1901

Walden, Alfred, & Co.
22 Mortimer St W.   1907

Walery Limited
164 Regent Street W.   1891-98

Walery, Stanislas O.
5 Conduit Street, Regent Street W.   1884-86
164 Regent Street W.   1887-90

Walery practised in Paris before moving to London to open a studio in Conduit Street in May 1883.

Walker & Boutall
16 Cliffords Inn E.C.   1888-00

Walker & Co.
36 Elizabeth Street, Eaton Square W.   1887
189 Earls Court Road S.W.   1888

Walker & Cockerell
16 Cliffords Inn E.C.   1901-04

Walker & Sons
64 Margaret Street W.   1865-66

Walker, C. A., & Co.
176 Upper Street N.   1904

Walker, Cecil
62 New Bond Street W.   1865

Walker, Charles
235 Balls Pond Road N.   1866-69
73 Balls Pond Road N.   1872-93

Walker, Charles Bristow
369 Strand W.C.   1862-63
Pembridge Villas, Bayswater W.   1864-65
91 Upper Street, Islington N.   1879-83

Walker, Charles
14 Stockbridge Terrace, Pimlico S.W.   1868

Walker, Cuthbert Archibald, & Co.
20 Blackfriars Road S.E.   1900

Walker, Emery
16 Cliffords Inn E.C.   1905-08-

Walker, James Robert
291 Goswell Road E.C.   1871-85
283 Goswell Road E.C.   1886-89

Walker, John
14 Stockbridge Terrace, Pimlico S.W.   1867

Walker, Samuel
4 Prospect Place N.E.   1867-79

Walker, Samuel, & Son
4 Prospect Place, Cambridge Road E.   1880
18 Bishops Road, Cambridge Rd. E.   1881-84

Walker, Samuel Alex.
64 Margaret Street W.   1863-78
230 Regent Street W.   1879-95
Walker took over Mayland's negatives on the latter's move out of London. According to the *Photographic News* (2 June 1882, p. 319) much of Walker's work was undertaken at the sitter's own home, rather than at his studio. Walker advertised as specialising in portraits of the clergy.

Walker, William, & Sons
64 Margaret St, Cavendish Sq. W.   1867
The National Portrait Gallery have holdings of Walker's work.

Wall, Alfred Hy.
35 Westbourne Grove W.   1863

Wallace & Co.
101 East India Dock Road E.   1891

Wallace Brothers
329 Kentish Town Road N.W.   1879

Wallace, William Fredk.
88 Burdett Road, Mile End E.   1882-87

Wallis, Mrs Enid
100 Westbourne Grove W.   1899-00

Wallis, George
34 Upper Street N.   1894
16 & 295 Edgware Road W.   1895-97
16 Edgware Road W.   1898-00

Wallis, Henry
100 Westbourne Grove W.   1901

Walsham, Alfred Ernest
45 Chancery Lane W.C.   1908-

Waltenberg, Theodore
339 Bethnal Green Road E.   1887-91
449 Bethnal Green Road E.   1891
419 Bethnal Green Road E.   1892-08-

Walter & Shead
443 West Strand W.C.   1891-92

Walter, Harry
413 West Strand W.C.   1893

Ward, Alfred
421 Kings Road, Chelsea S.W.   1891-08

Ward, Henry
289 Walworth Road S.   1867
287 Walworth Road S.   1868-79

Ward, John
78 Euston Road N.W.   1866-71

Ward, John
7 Palace Row, New Road   1856-57
135 Tottenham Court Road   1856-58
1A Clayton Place, Kennington Road   1857
266 Euston Road N.W.   1858-59

Ward, Secundus
1 Adelaide Street, Strand W.C.   1903-04
147 Strand W.C.   1906-08-

Wardall Brothers
12 Tottenham Court Road W.   1903

Warde, George
33A High Street, Nottinghill W.   1859
100A High Street, Nottinghill W.   1860-64

Wardhurst, Stephen
94 Clarendon Road W.   1869

Warner, John
72 Fleet Street E.C.   1862

Warren, George Christopher
81 Farringdon Street E.C.   1904-08-

Warren, William R.
2 Clarence Place, Cambridge Road   1857

Warwick, Thomas
32 Sloane Street, Chelsea S.W.   1859-63

Washbourne, Thomas
34 Cheyne Walk, Chelsea S.W.   1872

Waterman, Thomas Lambert
189 Earls Court Road S.W.   1883

Waterworth, Edward
206 High Street, Shoreditch N.E.   1865

Waterworth, Edward D.
3 Sarah Place, Old Street Road E.C.   1866-69

Watkins and Haigh
213 Regent Street W.   1874
1 Torriano Avenue N.W.   1874

Watkins Brothers
34 Parliament Street S.W.   1867-71

Watkins, Charles
54 Chancery Lane W.C.   1870-77

Watkins, Charles
1 Torriano Avenue N.W.   1880-82
Wakin's died in July 1882 at his home inCamden Town. He was especially known for his theatrical portraits. The *P.N.* reported that his negative of the Prince of Wales in Masonic costume was sold to Marion and Co. for £180.

Watkins, Charles
34 Parliament Street S.W.   1876

Watkins, Herbert
215 Regent Street W.   1858-73
1 Torriano Ave, Camden Road N.W.   1866-78
158 Regent Street W.   1896

Watkins, John
34 Parliament Street S.W.   1856-75

Watson, George
23 Freeschool Street, Hrsleydn S.E.   1871

Watson, John
118 New Bond Street   1860
88 New Bond Street   1861

Watson, John, & Co.
118 New Bond Street   1856
17 Regent Street W.   1857-59

Watson, W., & Co.
3 Lower Nottinghill Terrace W.   1895

Watson, William
103 St Johns Wood Terrace N.W.   1874

Waverley Supply Stores Ltd.
68 Aldersgate Street E.C.   1899-05

Webel, Max Franz W.
449 Southwark Park Road S.E.   1886-90

Webster Brothers
4 Porchester Row W.   1877-01
25 The Pavement, Clapham S.W.   1887-91
Clapham S.W.   1892-96

Webster, Henry
2 Albert Terr., Bishops Rd. W.   1865-76

Webster, Joseph, & Son
4 Porchester Road, Bayswater W.   1902-08-

Weddige, Raphael
357 Cambridge Road E.   1901

Welch, Joseph S.
355 Albany Road, Camberwell S.   1865-75

Wellington, Miss Mary
13E Dalston Lane N.E.   1905

Wells, Charles
149 High Street, Nottinghill W.   1877-82
6 Queens Road, Bayswater W.   1880-82
307 Essex Road N.   1882
118 Praed Street W.   1882

Wells, Francis Ross, & Co.
61 Regents Park Road N.W.   1887

Wells, Frank
5 New Oxford Street W.C. — 1897-05
190 Ebury Street S.W. — 1907-08-

Wensel, John Louis
125 Regent Street W. — 1866-67

Wesson, Ernest, & Co.
85 Mortimer Street W. — 1901

Wesson, Gear & Co
101 Great Portland Street W. — 1899

Westbourne Grove Photo Co.
108 Westbourne Grove W. — 1885

West End Photographic Co.
Fredk. James, manager
226 Oxford Street W. — 1866-81
516 Oxford Street W. — 1882-05

West, Francis, & Co.
41 Strand W.C. — 1854-57

West, Henry
41 Strand W.C. — 1858-64

West London Photographic Co.
Miss Annie Davis, manager, 1868;
Geo. Barat, manager, 1875
194 Oxford Street W. — 1866
267 Fulham Road S.W. — 1868-69
43 Norfolk Terrace W. — 1875-78

Weston, Arthur
84 Newgate Street E.C. — 1887-96
52 & 53 Newgate Street E.C. — 1897-00
16 Poultry E.C. — 1901-08-

Weston, J., & Son
27 Sloane Street S.W. — 1906-08-

Weston, Lambert, & Son
27 New Bond Street W. — 1905-08-

Whaite, Edward Gay
471 East India Dock Road E. — 1887
485 East India Dock Road E. — 1888-93
13 Prince of Wales Road N.W. — 1895-97

Whatley, Frederick
3 Strewan Place, Kings Road S.W. — 1865-71
103 Church Street, Chelsea S.W. — 1873-74

Wheeler, Charles
56 Holloway Road N. — 1885-87

Wheeler, Percival
124 High Road, Kilburn N.W. — 1907-08-

Whelpdale, Andrew
44 Regent Street W. — 1855-56

Whiffin, William
199 East India Dock Road E. — 1884-88

Whitchelo, Augustus George
1A George St, Euston Square N.W. — 1858

White, George
240 Oxford Street W. — 1863-66
2 Kensington Park Road W. — 1869-70

White, Harry
41 London Road S.E. — 1881-84

White, Herbert
435 Fulham Road S.W. — 1900-02

White, Herbert, & Son
439 Fulham Road S.W. — 1903

White, Thomas
83 Newington Causeway S.E. — 1882-87

White, William James
161 High Road, Kilburn N.W. — 1899
278 High Road, Kilburn N.W. — 1900-01

White, William, & Co.
435 Fulham Road S.W. — 1892-93

Whiteley, William
147-159 Queens Road W. — 1887-08-
26 Westbourne Grove W. — 1901-08
31-51 & 61 Westbourne Grove W. — 1887-96
31-55 & 61 Westbourne Grove W. — 1888-08-
49-53 Kensington Gardens Square — 1904-08-

Whitfield, George Carpe
17 Regent Street W. — 1856-57

Wichel, George
108 Westbourne Grove W.   1878-79

Wickmer, Charles
169 Hampstead Road N.W.   1905-08-

Wicksteed & Palmer
109 Cheapside E.C.   1900-08-

Wiedhofft, Frederick
338 New Cross Road S.E.   1897-08-
106 Holland Park Avenue W.   1899-08-

Wigley, Miss Jane Nina
Anderson Street, Chelsea   2 July 1847
108 Fleet Street   11 May 1848-55
Jane Wigley was an artist and purchased her daguerreotype license from Richard Beard in 1845 which allowed her to practise in Newcastle-upon-Tyne, Gateshead and the surrounding area. She closed her Newcastle gallery on 5 June 1847 and opened a London establishment at 10 Anderson Street, Kings Road, Chelsea, later moving to 108 Fleet Street. By March 1852 she had begun using the new collodion process. She continued to use the process until March 1854 when she reverted solely to daguerreotype portraiture. Miss Wigley left the photographic profession early in 1855.

Wigram, Miss Enid
13A Pembridge Place W.   1900-05

Wilcockson, Mrs Sarah
103 Seven Sisters Road N.   1908

Wilcockson, William
103 Seven Sisters Road N.   1899-07

Wilcockson, William Richard
508 Holloway Road N.   1891-08-

Wilcox, George
5 Hand Court, Holborn W.C.   1894-95

Wilkins, Henry
110 Westbourne Grove W.   1895-96

Wilkins, Louis
64 High Street, Nottinghill W.   1894-99
110 Westbourne Grove W.   1897-99

Wilkins, Walter
13E Dalston Lane N.E.   1908

Wilkins, William, & Co.
429 Mile End Road E.   1869-70

Willcox, Alfred
110 Westbourne Grove W.   1891-94

Williams & Co.
6 Queens Road, Bayswater W.   1885-86

Williams & Mayland
236 Regent Street W.   1871-80
Mayland was partner to T. R. Williams and carried on the business after the latter's death. The *Photographic News,* (5 March 1880) on a visit to the studio reported the patronage of the Duke of Connaught and Princess of Wales and the fact that the studion had been built for daguerreotype use (by Williams).

Williams, Edward V.
3 Elizabeth Road, Westminster Road   1854

Williams, Edwin
27 Clapham Road Place   1854

Williams, Ernest
22 Chaple St, Edgware Road N.W.   1907-08
82 Seven Sisters Road N.   1908-

Williams, Fras George
72 Leadenhall Street E.C.   1881

Williams, George
1 Phoebe Place, Holloway Road N.   1864-65
Peartree Cottage, Holloway Road N.   1866-70
385 Holloway Road N.   1871-73
358 Holloway Road N.   1874-86

Williams, George
343 Harrow Road W.   1908

Williams, John
299 Euston Road N.W.   1873

Williams, Mrs Mary
50 Gray Street, Blackfriars Rd. S.E.   1888-91

Williams, Thomas Richard
236 Regent Street W.   1855-70
35 West Square Southwark   1855-57
Williams was born in 1825 and died on 5 April 1872. He began his career in the studio of Claudet as one his first assistants and appears to have set up his own photographic business in 1850 in Regent Street. He undertook photography at the Crystal Palace for P. H. Delamotte - although the exact relationship is unclear and took stereo-daguerreotypes of the re- opening of the exhibition by Queen Victoria at Sydenham in 1854. He published several series of still-life stereo subjects. According to the *Photographic Journal* (15 January 1872, p. 115) "in some branches of the photographic art he stood unrivalled".

Williams, William
5 Bridge Street Lambeth   1855

Williams, William Charles
1 Oxford Street W.   1856-60

Williamson, James
3 Lower Nottinghill Terrace W.   1890

Williamson, James
26 Westbourne Grove W.   1886-87

Williamson, James Lenville
118 Broadhurst Gardens N.W.   1908

Wills, John
107 Talbot Road N.   1878

Willson, Reginald Fellows
118 New Bond Street W.   1899-01
141 New Bond Street W.   1902-03
57 Bedford Gardens Kensington W.   1905-06
4 Sloane Street S.W.   1907-08-

Willson, Richard Roberts
48 Penrose Street S.E.   1878-83
11 Walworth Road S.E.   1884-95

Wilson & Beadell
69 New Bond Street W.   1866-71

Wilson & Rees
210 Strand   1857

Wilson & Sons
95 Harrow Road W.   1907-08-

Wilson, Albert H.
6 Pratt Street, Lambeth S.E.   1882-84

Wilson, Alexander
33 Chippenham Terr., Harrow Rd. W. 1879-82

Wilson, Augustus Wm.
77 De Beauvoir Road N.   1871-94
25 Liverpool Street E.C.   1896
13F Dalston Lane N.E.   1899

Wilson, Augustus Wm., & Co.
13F Dalston Lane N.E.   1900

Wilson, George Washington, & Co. Ltd.
8 Catherine Street, Strand W.C.   1895-96

Wilson, James
125 Hammersmith Road W.   1907

Wilson, Richard Robert
48 Penrose Street S.E.   1879

Wilson, Miss S. R.
1 Buckingham Palace Road S.W.   1898-00

Wilson, William
346 New Cross Road S.E.   1892-94
95 Harrow Road W.   1894-06

Wilton, William Arthur
5 Symonds Inn   1855-56

Wiltons Limited
62 Cheapside E.C.   1895

Window & Bridge
63A Baker St, Portman Square W.   1864-67

Window & Grove
63A Baker Street, Portman Sq. W.   1873-89
63 Baker Street, Portman Square W.   1890-08-

58 Westbourne Grove W.   1908-

The studio was one of the first to settle in Baker Street which became a focus for other photographic studios. F. R. Window was the originator of the cabinet-size portait

Window, Frederick Richard
63A Baker Street W.   1863-72

Window, Adolphus
48 Piccadilly W.   1863-68
9 Albany Court Yard E.C.   1864-68

Winn & Co.
369 Kingsland Road E.   1874-77

Winn, Benjamin
369 Kingsland Road E.   1873

Winningale, William
246 Whitechapel Road E.   1869

Winser, Douglas Fitz P.
91 Regent Street W.   1864-65

Winter, Thomas Henry
12 Ridinghouse St, Langham Pl. W.   1857-67

Winterbon, Charles
75 Westbourne Grove W.   1891

Witt, Alfred Paul de
103 St Johns Wood Terrace N.W.   1875-80

Witton & Warton
152 Fleet Street E.C.   1891-92

Wood & Co.
190 Brompton Road S.W.   1872-78

Wood & Lee
326 Oxford Street W.   1861

Wood Brothers
6 Kensington High Street W.   1874-76

Wood, Cecil William
56 Brompton Row S.W.   1852-63
190 Brompton Road S.W.   1864-71

Wood, Edward
21 Tabernacle Walk E.C.   1872

Wood, Frederick
408 Edgware Road W.   1897-98
347 Edgware Road W.   1899-08-

Wood, Frederick William
22 Bishops Road W.   1895-08-
Also listed on *cartes* with head studios at 347 & 349 Edgware Road. Wood himself was "from Elliott and Fry".

Wood, William
38 Brecknock Road N.   1891-92

Wood, William John
28 Grove Road E.   1889
106 Grove Road E.   1890-95

Woodbury Permanent Photographic Printing Co.
Chas. Ranson, manager;
Thos. Wm. Fry, secretary, 1877
9A Hereford Sq, Old Brompton S.W.   1874-75
157 Great Portland Street W.   1876-81
178 Regent Street W.   1876-78

The *Photographic News* (25 March 1880) visited the Woodbury company's premises at Kent Gardens, Ealing. It reported that 30,000 cartes could be printed in a day and described the production methods in use. A limited company, Woodbury, Treadaway & Co., was formed in 1883 to work Woodbury's stannotype process. The Woodbury Company and it's business was acquired by Eyre and Spottiswoode, the printing company in 1891.

Woodhouse, William
3 Sarah Place, Old Street Road E.C.   1857-59

Woods, George
219 Fulham Road S.W.   1869-72

Woodward, Frederick
143 Strand   1854-55

Woolfe, Karl
43 Well Street, South Hackney S.E.   1908-

Woolfe, Kresovsky
58 Brick Lane N.E.   1899
411 Mare Street, Hackney N.E.   1903

Woolfe, John Henry
34 Upper Street N.   1908-
109 Whitechapel Road E.   1908-

Wooley & Dow
44 Baker Street, Portman Square W.   1876

Worden, Thomas
39 Spring Street, Paddington W.   1874

Worger, Thomas, (junior)
3 Chester Mews, Grosvenor Pl. S.W.   1857-58

Worger, Thomas E.
21 Lower Eaton Street, Pimlico S.W.   1859-60

Worrall, Philip
82 Kings Road, Camden Town N.W.   1904

Worth, John
29 London Road, Southwark S.   1863
5 Deans Row, Walworth Road S.   1864
218 Walworth Road S.   1867-71

Wright, Charles
235 High Holborn W.C.   1857-81

Wright, Edward
213 Salmons Lane, Limehouse E.   1873-74

Wright, George P.
12 Pall Mall east S.W.   1864-66

Wright, Miss Marie Elizabeth
279 City Road E.C.   1890-95

Wright, Thomas
134 East India Dock Road E.   1868-73
199 East India Dock Road E.   1869-83

Wright, William
189 & 190 Bethnal Green Road E.   —1880-85
98 Cheapside E.C.   ←1885-96
188 Bethnal Green Road E.   ⌐1886-93
190 Bethnal Green Road E.   1886-93
10 Upper Street N.   1887-92
81 Whitechapel High Street E.   ⌐1887-96

422 Mile End Road E.   1890-99
83 Bishopsgate without E.C.   1892-08-
189 Bethnal Green Road N.E.   1894-97
93 Whitechapel High Street E.   1897-00

Wyatt, Charles Christopher
9 North Audley Street W.   1864-86

Wyatt, William
4 Oval Cottages, Hackney Road N.E.   1861-64
3 The Oval, Hackney Road E.   1870-72

Wynn and Co.
76 Cornhill   14 September 1846
62 Piccadilly   14 September 1846

Wynne, Courteney
267 Fulham Road S.W.   1870-87

Y

York, Frederick
3 Alfred Row, Shepherds Bush W.   1871-75

York, Frederick
87 Lancaster Road W.   1873-76

York, William
4 & 5A Tottenham Court Road W.   1885-88

Young & Sons
59 & 60 Cornhill E.C.   1883

Young, Albert
17 Regent Street W.   1886

Young, Edward
258 Westminster Bridge Road S.E.   1882

Z

Zastrow & Borough
43 Piccadilly W.   1859

APPENDIX 1. New additions

The following names or additonal addresses have been reported since the publication of the first edition as being photographers through their appearance on *cartes de visite* backs. The companies *or* the addresses given here do not appear in the *London Post Office Directories* which suggests they were working for a short period, not working as a photographer as their main profession or, in most cases, were working beyond the area or time period covered by the Post Office directories. They are included here for completeness sake and further research is needed to determine their exact status and period of working.

Some entries represent new addresses for photographers listed in the main part of this directory.

A

Abbot, W. E.
51 Oxford Street, Westminster
Abney House Studio
104 Stoke Newington Road, Shacklewell
Adams & Co.
Myddelton Hall, Upper Street, Islington
Adkins & Co.
46 Stamford Hill, Stoke Newington
Albemarle Photo Co.
62 Piccadilly, Westminster
Albert, E.
68 Westbourne Grove, Bayswater
Albion Art Studio
39 Lauriston Road, South Hackney
Aldridge, G.
6 Verulam Terrace, The Grove, Hammersmith
Alexandra Studio
45 Westbourne Grove, Bayswater
Allen & Baxter
627 Romford Road, Manor Park
Allen & Son
50 The Grove, Stratford

Alliance Photo Co.
405 Oxford Street, Westminster
87 Farringdon Road, City
American Photographic Co.
172 Blackfriars Road
160 Walworth Road S.E.
Andrew, T.
96 Commerical Street, Spitalsfield
Army & Navy Stores
15 Regent Street, Westminster
Art Studio
3 Cheapisde, City
Artiste
108 Oxford Street, Westminster
Artistic Photo Co.
73 Oxford Street, Westminster
Artistic Portrait Studio
167 Kennington Park Road, Kennington
Artists Association
238 Tottenham Court Road, Westminster
Ascoli
Commerce Road, Wood Green
Ash, William
57 Clapham Road, Oval
Ashby, G.
26 Elizabeth St., Eaton Square, Belgravia
Ashford Brothers & Co.
76 New Gate Street, City
Astley & Peacock
Whips Cross, Walthamstow
Atkins, T.
7 Westow Hill, Upper Norwood
Austen, W.
5 Buxton Place, Lambeth Road, Lambeth
Austen & Co.
232 Mare Street, Hackney
Austen & Co.
142 Trinity Road, Upper Tooting
Austen & Co., E.
196 Coldharbour Lane, Camberwell
Avery, Edward C.
26 Junction Road, Upper Holloway

Avery, John J.
12 Shacklewell Lane, Kingsland
770 Harrow Road, Kensal Green
209 Kings Cross Road, Kings Cross
7 Archway Road, Upper Holloway
338 New Cross Road, New Cross

B

Bailey, William
10 Nashville Place, Hanwell
Bowen, John
161 High Road, Kilburn N.W.
Bridge, E. L.
94 High Road, Chiswick
Bridge, F. A.
9 Norfolk Road, Dalston Lane, Dalston
Britannia Photo Co.
Rye Lane, Peckham
British Continental Photo Co.
48 High Holborn, Holborn
British & Foreign Copying Co.
102 Fleet Street, City
Britton, G. H.
10 High Street, Forest Hill
Brock, Walter Bino
30 Clapham Road, Oval
Brooker, T. L.
80 South Street, Greenwich
Brookes, F.
79 Oxford Street, Westminster
Brookes & Co., A.
369 Kingsland Road, Haggerston
Brooks, F.
187 High Street, Borough
Brooks, W.
Forest Lane, Forest Gate
Brooks & Co., A.
10 New Street, Westminster
Brown, G.
26 Harold Street, Camberwell
Brown, James
132 Camberwell Road, Camberwell
Brown, T.
52 High Street, Eltham

Brown, Walter
19 High Street, Stoke Newington
Burder, J.
521 High Road, Tottenham
Burnham, F. C.
18 Atlantic Road, Brixton
421 Brixton Road, Brixton
Busbridge, H. W.
Vanbrugh Park, Blackheath

C

Calvert, A.
192 Barking Road, Canning Town
Canden Photo Studio
56 High Street, Camden Town
Carlton Studio
7 Carlton Terr., Westbourne Park
Carpenter, E.
25 London Street, Greenwich
Carpenter & Co.
120 mile End Road, Stepney
Carrick, T.
32 Regent Street, Westminster
Carter, George E.
20 Lower Phillimore Place, Kensington
Casbon & Kittel
6 Alexandra Road, Hornsey
Cassinello, G.
49 Dartmouth Road, Forest Hill
Cassinello, J.
11 Church Street, Woolwich
Cattle, G.
2 Highbury Road, Wimbledon
Central Photographic Rooms
76 Cannon Street, City
35 Westbourne Grove, Bayswater
Chambers, Alfred P.
211 Clapham Road, Stockwell
Chambers, C.
23 Victoria Road, Pimlico
Chapman, A. J.
27 Topsfield Parade, Crouch End
Chapple, Arthur
9 Lansdowne Terr., Acre Lane, Brixton

Cheapside Portrait Company
61 Cheapside, City
Christmas, L. L.
104 Stoke Newington Rd., Shacklewell
Church, Atlas
196 Goldhawk Road, Shepherds Bush
Citizens Photo Art Studios
84 Newgate Street, City
City of London Photo Company
2 Queen Street, Cheapside, City
45 Cheapside, City
City of London Institute of Photography
24 Cornhill, City
City Portrait Company
19 St. Martins Le Grand, City
City Studio
83 Gracechurch Street, City
Clackett, F.
141 Sydenham Road, Sydenham
Clark, F. W.
284 Romford Road, Forest Gate
19 Alice Road, Stratford
Clark, Mackinnon
Campden House, Wimbledon
Clarke, I.
HIgh Street, Peckham
Clarke, William
7 Gayton Road, Hampstead
Clarke & Clarke
63 St. Johns Hill, Clapham
Cleare, G. Risdale
45 King Edward Road, South Hackney
97 Lower Clapton Rd., Lower Clapton
Cleaver
21 Old Town, Clapham
Clements, A. C.
3 Amersham Road, New Cross
Clements, A. E.
159 Upper Fore St., Edmonton
Clerke, J. B.
4 Russell Villas, Seven Sisters Rd., Stamford
Hill
Clerke & Co.
4 Russell Villas, Seven Sisters Rd., Stamford
Hill

Climar Photo Co.
20 Cheapside, City
Cobb, Harold
234 High Street, Tottenham
Cobb, William
77-78 Wellington Street, Woolwich
Cobb & Bridge
77-78 Wellington Street, Woolwich
Cobb & Challis
77-78 Wellington Street, Woolwich
Cobb & Keir
29 Plumstead Road, Woolwich
Cocking, Edwin
Queens Road, Peckham
Cocking, H. Garrett
Lee Bridge Studio, Lee
57 Queens Road, Peckham
Cocking, R. C.
60 High Street, Peckham
High Street, Denmark Hill
Cohe, A. F.
63 Wellington Street, Woolwich
Colas, L. F.
57 Cheapside, City
Collier, Gwyn
Albert Gate, Belgravia
195 Brixton Road, Brixton
57 Clapham Road, Oval
Collier, J. T.
136 Uxbridge Road, Shepherds Bush
Collis, Charles
68 Cornhill, City
Collis, G. L.
68 Cornhill, City
Colson & Co., Natrowsky
27 & 29 New Broad Street, City
204 Regent Street, Westminster
Combe & Co.
88 Cheapside, City
Cooper, Smyth
Wawman Terrace, Balham
122 High Road, Balham
Cooper, T.
7 Henry St., Vassall Rd., Brixton
Cox, Henry
12 Dalston Terrace, Dalston

Cribb-Wallis, H.
100 Westbourne Grove, Bayswater
Cronchey, W. F.
34 Gunter Grove, Chelsea
Cross, C.
2 Grove Place, Brixton Rd., Brixton
Crouch
204 Regent Street, Westminster
Cruickshank, Taylor J.
90 Newgate Street, City
Crystaltype Company's Studio
Adj. Bruce Grove Station, Tottenham
Currie & Bridges
16 Edgware Road, Westminster
Curtis
50 London Road, Forest Hill
Curtis & Co., J. H.
30 Albany Rd., Old Kent Road
9 Manor Park Place, Romford Rd., Manor Park
1 Harold Road, Upton Park
Curzon Studios
115 The Grove, Stratford
224 High Road, Kilburn
Dalby Art Gallery
Oscar House, Lewisham
82-83 Wellington Street, Woolwich

D

Dale, Antonia J.
Station Terrace, New Southgate
Damer, W. J.
170 Sumner Road, Peckham
Darnell, W.
105 King Street west, Hammersmith
Davies, G. B.
22 Wellington Street, Woolwich
Davies, A. W.
Orchard House, Tottenham
Davies, William
48 Rochester Row, Pimlico
Day
46 Albemarle Street, Westminster

De Witt, Paul
103 St. Johns Wood Terr., St. Johns Wood
Dean, Clare
Norfolk Rd., Dalston Lane, Dalston
Debenham, W. E.
Massingham House, Haverstock Hill, Belsize Pk.
Deposit Photographic Studio
77 Cornhill, City
Dobay, Victor
179 High Street, Stoke Newington
Dollhopff, J. von
8 Dorset Terr., Clapham rd., Stockwell
Dore
52 Regent Street, Westminster
Dorrett, Harry Gordon
119 St. John's Hill, Clapham Jnctn. 1896-1898
Dowle
34 Barking Road, Canning Town
Downing, Miss M.
356a Holloway Road
Dron, A. W.
Dyne Road, Brondersbury
Dugdale, J.
10 Munster Terr., Fulham Road, Fulham
Dunn, G.
266 Romford Road, Forest Gate
Dupre, F.
440 Old Kent Road, Bermondsey
Durban, W. Lang
29 Grand Parade, Harringay
Dyball, R. H.
3 Lower Terrace, Nottinghill

E

Eason & Co., A.
16 Dalston Lane, Dalston
Eastbourne Photo Co.
2 The Pavement, Clapham Common
Eden, Charles
High Street, Ealing
Edwards, B. J.
6 The Grove, Hackney

Edwards & Co.
102 Leytonstone Road, Leytonstone
Stratford
Forest Gate
Bow
East Ham
Electric Art Studio
207 Old Street, City
Eleve de Nadar
7 Gloucester Grove, South Kensington
Elmes, Sidney W.
3 Balham Place, Balham
Emberson
54 Broadway, Wimbledon
England, William
St. James Square, Nottinghill

The *Photographic News* (9 April 1880, pp. 171-173.) visited the premises of England whom they described as "probably the largest Continental publisher of European views. The premises were actually England's home with the darkroom at the back of the building. England travelled Switzerland, the Tyrol and Italy during the summer mostly using a 10 x 8 inch camera for stereoscopic or whole-plae negatives. The report describes his technique and processing details.

He, or his son, began commercial manufacture of albumenised and sensitised papers in mid-1882.

Essex Studios
75 Essex Road, Islington
Evans, J. P.
60 Clarence Road, Hackney
Evans, M. E.
36 Elizabeth Street, Belgravia
Everitt, Henry
17 Upper Street, Islington
Ewings & James
220 Wandsworth Road, Wndsworth

F

Fairbairn & Bennett
29 Guildford Road, Greenwich

Farley, Herbert A.
2 Fitzjohns Parade, Hampstead
Farley, C. J.
74 Wellington Street, Woolwich
Farringdon, A. V.
The Studio, East Sheen
Farthing & Son
Merton Road, Tooting
Faulkner, Edwin T.
82 Wellington Street, Woolwich
Faulkner, Robert
46 Kensington Garden Square, Bayswater
Fawn, W. H.
Crosby House, Clapham Common
146 Rye Lane, Peckham
Field & Co., W.
9 High Street, Putney
Field, Mortimer, & Co.
670 High Road, Tottenham
Fincham, Philip H.
Myton Road, Dulwich
Fisher, Charles
Church Street, Hackney
Fisher, M. C.
214 King Street, Hammersmith
Fisher, T.
521 High Street, Tottenham
Fitt, A. T.
Cornwall Terr., Battersea Park
Fitt, George Robert
100 Regent Street, Westminster
Flint, A. & J.
321 Stanstead Road, Catford
Flint, Albert
68 Church Street, Camberwell
211 Clapham Road, Stockwell
Foat & Lattimer
12 Stamford Hill, Stamford Hill
Ford, W. C.
130 Camden Road, Camden Town
Fortescue & Co.
122 High Road, Balham
Fossey, T.
77 Hackney Road, Haggerston
Foster, J. W.
128 Lynton Road, Bermondsey

Fox & Hill
23 Crouch Hill, Crouch Hill
Francis
58 Regent Street, Westminster
Frankland, H. B.
83 Clapham Road, Stockwell
Friedman, Henry
Leytonstone
50 The Grove, Stratford
Frost, W. R.
69 Abbey Road, St. Johns Wood
Frost & Thomas
16 & 17 Poultry, City
69 Abbey Road, St. Johns Wood
Fruwirth, D.
1 & 2 Palace Road, Upper Norwood
Fryer, G.
Ealing Dene

G

Gabrielli, Enrico
Broadway, Walham Green
Garner, Myles
90 Stoke Newington Road, Shacklewell
Gauntlett Brothers
7 Cheyne Walk, Chelsea
Gay, David
74 Cheapside, City
Gearing & Co., Charles J.
68 Church Street, Camberwell
31 The Pavement, Clapham
57 Durham Road, Finsbury Park
35 Milkwood Road, Herne Hill
104 Stoke Newington Road, Stoke Newington
Gearing & Co., H.
35 Milkwood Road, Herne Hill
Gibbs, J. T.
7 Aston Villas, Lavender Hill
Gibson, Mrs
115 Upper Kennington Lane, Kennington
Gidney, C. M.
4 Mornington Pl., Holloway Down,
Leytonstone

Gill & Donald
38 Brecknock Road, Tufnell Park
Gladwin, W. W.
23 Station Road, Norwood
Globe Photographic Co.
83 Gracechurch Street, City
Goodwin, E. T. F.
63 Anerley Road, Crystal Palace
4 Hamlet Terrace, Upper Norwood
Gosby, T. C.
Albert Terr., Upper Richmond Road
Goulder, C.
9 Royal Parade, Blackheath
Gregory, E. R.
291 Friern Road, East Dulwich
Griffiths, Alfred E.
18 Carmichael Road, Norwood
Gromann & Gobeli
26 Westbourne Grove, Bayswater
Gustave
Putney

H

Hackleton Brothers
60 High Street, Peckham
Hackleton, J. H.
Lordship Lane, Dulwich
Hadlow, F.
Upper Richmond Road, Putney
Hales, G. H.
High Road, Leyton
Hallier, H.
41 High Street, Sydenham
Hammersmith Photo Co.
31 King Street west, Hammersmith
Hancock & Williams
4 Ethel Villas, Snells Park, Edmonton
Harding, H. H.
66 Evering Road, Stoke Newington
Harlesden Studio
11 High Street, Harlesden
Harman & Co., Alfred
79 High Street, Harders Rd., Peckham
2 Ewell Villas, Surbiton Hill

Alfred Harman was the founder of the Britannia Works Co. which was later to become Ilford Ltd. He began his photographic career with studios in Peckham and Surbiton before moving to Ilford, Essex, in 1879. Harman set up his first studio at Gunnersbury Villas, Albert Road (later Harders Road) in Peckham around 1864.

The Surbiton address was also where Harman lived and the studion was advertised as being open on Wednesdays and Saturdays only. It is likely that all processing and finishing was done at Peckham.

Harman was certainly involved in taking cartes de visite as well as more specialised printing for other photographers and the preparation of plates - which was to form the basis of the Britannia Works Co. business.

Harrison, Fred
1 Woodside Terr., 37 Gipsy Hill, Norwood
Harrison, Walter G.
4 Stanley Terr., Southwark Park, Rotherhithe
Hart, John
275 Leytonstone Road, Leytonstone
Hatherill, J.
104 Stoke Newington Road, Shacklewell
Hatt, W.
16 Surrey Terr., Upper Lewisham Rd., New Cross
Hawkins, C.
309 Regent Street, Westminster
Hayward, A.
53 Queens Rd., Lavender Hill, Clapham Jnt.
Hayward, Robert
Opp. the Theatre, Alexandra Palace, Finchley
Hazard, J. S.
27 Trafalgar Road, Greenwich
6 The Pavement, Clapham Common
Graham Road, Wimbledon
Heath, Alfred T.
36 Camden Street north, Camden
Heathman, W.
63 Wellington Street, Woolwich
Hellis, R. J.
10 The Terrace, Athenaeum, Kensington
Hellis & Sons
13 Silver St., Nottinghill Gate

30 Clapham Road, Oval
6 The pavement, Clapham Common
211 Queens Road, Peckham
71 Green Lanes, Highbury
7 Munster Parade, Fulham Road
688 Fulham Road, Parsons Green
Hemery & Co.
13 Hanover St, Rye Lane, Packham
Hemery & Harty
213 Regent Street, Westminster
Henry Studio
107 Great Eastern St., City
181 City Road, Angel
Henwood, Charles
1 West Place, Turnham Green
Herbert, F.
102 Uxbridge Road, Shepherds Bush
Herdman, W. G.
34 Hanover Road, Plumstead
Herman C.
72 Church St., Camberwell Green
Hester, Albert
31 Upper Clapton Rd., Clapton
Higgins, A. P.
112 Mildmay Road, Kingsland
Hilder, A. J.
267 Barking Road, Plaistow
Hill, C. & E.
5 Bank Buildings, Streatham
Hill, R.
159 Fore Street, Edmonton
Hinton
521-523 High Road, Tottenham
Hitchcock, G.
9 Prince of Wales Rd., Kentish Town
Hockley, C.
212 King Street west, Hammersmith
Holden, George
10 Avenue Road, Acton
Holland, Frederick W.
13 Homerton Terr., Homerton
Holloway, J.
1 Versailles Terrace, Anerley
Holmes, H. W.
Station Parade, Willesden Green

Hood, C.
138 Camberwell Road, Camberwell
Hooper, George
68 Canonbury Park south, Canonbury
Hopgood, E.
High Street, Ealing
Horne & Thornthwaite
121-123 Newgate Street, City
Horton, W.
13 New Street, Kennington Park Road S.
Hounsell, J.
178 Great College St, Camden Town
Howell, T.
135 Tottenham Court Rd., Westminster
Hubert, J.
238 Mare Street, Hackney E.
Hudson, Frederick A.
6 Verulam Terrace, Hammersmith
Huff, James
Blackheath Road, Greenwich
Hughes, H.
59 Fenchurch Street, City
Hull, William
52 Northwold Road, Clapton
Humphreys, A., & Co.
88 Brixton Hill, Brixton
Hunnings, W. J. & H.
Tottenham
Hunt, E. S.
361 Seven Sisters Rd., South Tottenham
216 Millfields Rd., Clapton
700 High Road, Tottenham
Hunt, George
36 Brafards Rd., Peckham
Hunt, S. Wallace
361 Seven Sisters Rd., South Tottenham
Hutchinson, Hugh W.
22 Archway Road, Highgate
Hyett, A.
High Street, Southgate

J

James, George
5 Church Street, Hackney

304 Mare Street, Hackney
Jeffray, A. E.
12 Lansdowne Villas, Richmond Rd, Fulham
Jellicoe, E. P.
Goldsmith Road, New Southgate
Jennings, Constantine
3 Durham Cross, Manor Park
Jessamine Studio
53 East Hill, Wandsworth
Johnson, H., & Co.
High Street, Wood Green
Johnson, H. E.
304 Mare Street, Hackney
Johnson & Co.
8 Stoke Newington Rd., Stoke Newington
103 Seven Sisters Rd., Finsbury Park
 60 High Street, S
New
Johnstone
Joubert, F.
36 Porchester Terr., Bayswater
Jubilee Photo Co.
Mr A. James, manager
1 Buckingham Palace Rd., Pimlico S.W.

K

Keens, J.
204 Mare Street, Hackney
Keir, H. & W.
Common Road, Plumstead
Kemps Belgrave Studio
656 Romford Rd., Manor Park
Ken, A.
213 Regent Street, Westminster
Kendall, G.
82 Stratford Road, Plaistow
Kent & Nelson
86 Regent Street, Westminster
115 Westbourne Grove, Bayswater
Kerton, H., & Son
13 Jane St., Blackfriars Rd., Southwark
Killick, J. H.
Rosslyn Hill Studio, Hampstead
Kirby, T. C.
85 Hill Street, Peckham
Kirk
Hoe Street, Walthamstow

Kirkby
263 Regent Street, Westminster
Knagg, C. James
275 Romford Road, Forest Gate
Knights, J. F.
30 Clapham Road, Oval
20 Dorset Place north, Clapham Rd, Oval
2 College Place, High Rd., Lewisham

L

La Porte, M.
204 Kings Road., Chelsea
Wandsworth Common, Wandsworth
Laing, T.
Station Road, Norwood
Lainson, J.
23 Hetherington Road, Clapham
Lane, J. Talbot
28 Hanover St., Rye Lane, Peckham
Lang Sims, R.
437 Brixton Road, Brixton
Law, A. & F.
30 Victoria Road, Peckham
Lawrence, Henri L.
19 Melbourne Grove, Dulwich
Le Rose Studio
95 Green Lanes, Stoke Newington
Lee, Arthur
Fortis Green Road, Muswell Hill
118 Stroud Green Rd, Finsbury Park
Leighton, Rupert
414 Brixton Road, Brixton
Lennotype Co.
478 Fulham Road, Fulham Broadway
Lenville & Co.
60 Rosslyn Hill, Hampstead
Levermore, C. R.
10 Blackheath Road, Greenwich
Levermore & Brooker
80 South Street, Greenwich
Life Size Photo Co.
343 Edgware Road, Paddington
320 Bethnal Green Rd., Bethnal Green
78 & 80 Kennington Rd., Lambeth

Lile, J. H., & Co.
129 New North Road, Shoreditch
Lile & Lacy
129 New North Road, Shoreditch
Linn, H.
36 Taylor Street, Woolwich
Lock & Whitfield
The Broadway, Ealing
London & Paris Photo Co.
139 & 141 Brompton Rd., Chelsea
London & Provincial Photo Co.
6 Victoria Cottages, North End Rd., Fulham
London Artistic Portrait Co.
108 Oxford Street, Westminster
London Crystal Palace Photo Co.
Regent Circus, Oxford St., Westminster
London Mutual Photo Association
170 Fleet Street, City
London Photo Copying Co.
40 High Holborn, Holborn
London Portrait Studios
78a Fore Street, Edmonton
810 High Road, Tottenham
London Portrait Co.
158 Strand, Westminster
London School of Photography
Mydellton Hall
52 King William Street, City
London Suburban Photo Co.
103 Seven Sisters Rd., Finsbury Park
Long, S.
Brockley Road, Brockley
82 Wellington Street, Woolwich
Long & Faulkner
Brockley Road, Brockley
82 Wellington Street, Woolwich
Lonsdale & Co.
45 Stroud Green Road, Finsbury Park
Lord, Fred
327 High Street, Stratford
Louis, Monsieur
326 & 333 Euston Road, Regents Park
Lucas
3 St. Johns Wood Rd., Regents Park
Lupson, Augustus
6 Church Street, Stoke Newington

Lupson, Frederick
6 Church Street, Stoke Newington
Luxograph Company
9 Strand, Westminster

M

Macey, R. H.
Rosslyn Hill Studio, Hampstead
Macey, William
314 Edgware Road, Paddington
Macfarlane, Robert
187 Queens Road, Dalston
Maddison & Co.
The Shrubbery, Stamford Hill
133 Stoke Newington Road, Shacklewell
11 High Street, Stoke Newington
Maltby, W. Flower
4 Dean Terr., Forest Hill
Malthouse, F.
42 Beckenham Road, Penge
Manby
27 High Street, Wandsworth
Manders, V.
1 Hoe Street, Walthamstow
Manley, Leopold F.
20 Orchard St., Portman Sq., Westminster
Marble Arch Studios
548 Oxford Street, Westminster
Margetts, J. W.
404 Kingsland Road, Dalston Junction
Marshall, C.
21 Cambridge Road, Hammersmith
35 High Streetm, Ealing
Martin, John
Cambridge Road, Mile End
Mason, Robert H., & Co.
7 Amen Corner, City
Matheson
1 Kelvin Grove, Sydenham
Mathews, F.
103 Hill Street, Peckham
Mathews, Edwin
35 Northampton St., Essex Rd., Islington

Maull, G.
8 Montpeliar Vale, Blackheath
Maull & Co.
68 Cheapside, City
55 Gracechurch Street, City
May, W. D.
69 Wellington Street, Woolwich
Mayer Brothers
Fulham Road, West Brompton
Mayhew, J.
58 Edgware Road, Westminster
McLanachan, J. L.
2 The Mall, Ealing
McLeod, A.
29 Stockwell Street, Greenwich
Mendellsohn, Hargreaves
155 City Road, E.C.

Formerly worked with Prestwich of London.

Mertens, H. W.
35 Clapham Park Road, Clapham
Miles, W.
7 Hawthorn Road, Hornsey
Mill, W. G.
7 Clifton Terr., Lancefield St., Queens Pk. W.
Millard, J.
322 Upper Street, Islington
Millard, Messrs
93 Upper Street, Islington
Millen Brothers
3 Queen Street, City
Railton Road, Brixton
Mills, Frederick
45 St. Georges Place, Knightsbridge
Mitchell, G.
137 High Street, Lewisham
Mitchell, Percy
High Street, Sydenham
Mitchell & Co.
142 Trinity Road, Upper Tooting
37 Cheapside, City
Moll, Peter
208 Battersea Park Rd., Battersea
Moore, S. J.
26 The Broadway, Crouch End
Moore's A1 Portrait Rooms
9 St. Annes Place, Stepney

Morgan, S.
63 Wellington Street, Woolwich
Morgan, W. T.
Circus, Greenwich
Morgan & Kidd
Circus, Greenwich
Morgan & Laing
Circus, Greenwich
Morris, Mrs H.
8 Lordship Terr., Battersea Rise
Morris, S. W.
Upper Fore Street, Edmonton
Morton, H.
1 Collins Street, Blackheath
Mote, S. C.
3 Amersham Road, New Cross
Mowels, S. A.
142 Sloane Street, Belgravia
Mozart
138 Anerley Road, Anerley
Muir, S. J.
78 Uxbridge Road, Ealing
272 Regent Circus, Oxford Street
Muller, C. L.
225 Hackney Road, Haggerston
Mullins & Route
136 Goldhawk Road, Shepherds Bush
Mumby, C.
22a Mortimer Street, Westminster
Musitano, G.
31 South St., 37 South St., Greenwich

N

Navana Ltd.
518 Oxford Street, Westminster
Neve, Charles.
63 St. Pauls Churchyard, City
45 Cheapside, City
New School of Photography
29 Euston Road, Kings Cross
Nicholls, G. E.
Fore Street, Edmonton
Nickels, Edouard
Well Street, Hackney

Norris & Co.
5 Church Road, Norwood
Norsworthy, William J.
130 Copenhagen St., Kings Cross
North Kensington Photo Studio
20 Ladbroke Grove Rd., Nottinghill
North London School of Photography
35 Balls Pond Rd., Kingsland
Northampton Photo Studio
75 Essex Road, Islington
Norton & Iris
78 Bishopsgate St. without, City

O

Old Bond Street Photo Gallery
28 Old Bond Street, Westminster
Opalette Company
211 Clapham Road, Stockwell
Organ, George R.
215 The Grove, Hammersmith
Osborn, C.
10 Beauclerc Road, Hammersmith
Owen, A.
50 Wood Street, Walthamstow
Owen, George H.
Circus, Greemwich
Oxford Photographic Institute
30 Oxford Street, Westminster
Oxford Photographic Studio
14 Oxford Street, Westminster

P

Pacey, T.
22 Bishops Rd., Westbourne Grove
Palmer, Fred T.
258 Brixton Hill, Brixton
Palmer, Harold
258 Brixton Hill, Brixton
Palmer & Bennetto
258 Brixton Hill, Brixton
Parisian Photo Establishment
45 Ludgate Hill, City

Parisian School of Photography
246 Old Kent Road, S.E.
78 Chalk Farm Road, Camden Town
Paton, W. G., and Co.
40 High Holborn W.C.   1888
Paul, Aubrey
1 Thames Place, Putney
Pearce, Ernest
46 Stamford Hill, Stoke Newington
Pearce & Smith
46 Stamford Hill, Stoke Newington
Penge Photo Co.
Penge
Penton Studio
82 Pentonville Road, Pentonville
Perkoff, I
18 Lea Bridge Road, Clapton
Permanent Photograph Co.
4 Brunswick Place, Blackheath
111 Grove Lane, Denmark Hill, Camberwell
149 High Street, Nottinghill
Peroni
16 Upper Tollington Park, Finsbury Park
Perry, J.
64 Shakespeare Road, Herne Hill
Photo Cameo Portrait Co.
23 Poultry, City
Pimlico Phoot Copying Co.
64 Shakespeare Road, Herne Hill
Plumer, C. J.
47 Baker Street, Westminster
Plumridge & Barnes
158 Regent Street, Westminster
Polytechnic School of Photography
309-311 Regent Street, Westminster
Poole, S. J.
116 Upper Richmond Rd., Putney
Porter, E. C.
2 The Mall, 6 The Esplanade, Ealing
Porter, Harold
51 High Road, Willesden Green
Potter, F. J.
4 Brunswick Place, Blackheath
Prestwich, W. H.
744 High Road, Tottenham

Prestwich Brothers
49 King William Street, City
Pritchett, E. H.
142 Queens Road, Peckham
Proctor
4 Oakfield Road, Anerley
Prout, E., & Co.
109 Regent Street, Westminster
Pym, W. H. Douglas
Belle Vue Studio, Streatham

R

Rands, Harry
2 The Pavement, Clapham Common
63 St. Pauls Churchyard, City
Ranford, A. V.
136 High Street, Lee
Rayner, J.
45 Newington Causeway, Elephant & Castle
Redding & Gyles
3 Argyll Place, Westminster
Reed, H. T.
11 High Street, Harlesden
Rees, David
170 Merton Road, Wimbledon
Rees, David
298 Clapham Road, Stockwell
5 Atkinson Place, Brixton Rd., Brixton
4 Carlton Grove, Brixton Rd., Brixton
Rees & Co.
298 Clapham Road, Stockwell
Rees, Brother, & Sons
298 Clapham Road, Stockwell
Rees, Pitcher, & Co.
298 Clapham Road, Stockwell
Reeves, J. E.
50 Hermit Road, Canning Town
Reeves, T. S.
101 Park Street, Camden Town
Regent Photographic Co.
122 Regent Street, Westminster
Reliance Copying & Colouring
5 Bishopsgate Street within, City

Rogers & Locke
215 Regent Street, Westminster
Rolfe, H. L.
1 Sussex Place, Bridge Rd., Hammersmith
Rolfes Portrait Studio
4 Haymarket, Westminster
Ross, W.
63 Hindon Street, Pimlico
Ross, W. Downe
30 Acre Lane, Brixton
Rousseau
28 Hanover Street, Westminster
Rousseau & Dendy
28 Hanover Street, Peckham
Russell, Edward G.
56 High Street, Camden Town
Russell & Co.
163 Hoe Street, Walthamstow
Russell, James, & Sons
28 Wimbledon Hill, 2 Hill Rd, Wimbledon
Russell & Taylor
369 Edgware Road, Paddington

S

Salmon, S. H. R.
10 The Terrace, East Putney
Salomon, Edgar
146 Stoke Newington Rd., Shacklewell
Sanderson
21 Blakcfriars Road, Waterloo
Sargent, F.
Derby House, Brixton
Schreiber & Dutton
101 Wellington Street, Woolwich
Schultz, Ludw   *c 1463*
London Road, Greenwich
Scott, Charles Stuart
53 Leytonstone Road, Stratford
Scott & Smith
36 Poultry, City
Scottish Union Photo Company
83 Newman Street, Westminster
Seavy, Charles
164 Camberwell New Road, Camberwell

Noted as being "Late H. Wilton, 144 Camberwell New Road, London SE".
Secourable, F. H.
57 Queens Road, Peckham
Shacklewell Photo Company
12 Shacklewell Lane, Shacklewell
Sheppard, Brickel
Lewisham High Road, New Cross
Shewards
810 High Road, Tottenham
Sibley & Co.
4 Oakfield Road, Anerley
Silvester, Alf, & Thomas, Richard
118 New Bond Street, Westminster
Sims, Samuel
King Street, Greenwich
Sims, R. L., & Co.
163 Hoe Street, Walthamstow
Sims, T.
23 Westbourne Grove, Bayswater
Sinclair & Co. (*)
70 Euston Road, Kings Cross N.W.
410, 412 Euston Road, Regent's Park N.W.
142 Pentonville Road, Islington N.
Skillman, C. H.
22 Uxbridge Road, Shepherds Bush
Smith, Buchanan
Blackheath Park, Blackheath
Smith, G. H.
8 Sutton Place, Hackney
60 Clarence Road, Lower Clapton
Smith, Josiah
22 St. Johns Villas, Holloway
10 Upper Street, Islington
Smith, Richard
16 Bennett Street, Stamford St, Southwark
Smyth, Sydney
George Street, Euston Road, Euston
Smythe, Adrian
26 High Street, Putney
South London Photo Company
15 Empress Terr., Brayards Rd., Peckham
South West London Photo Company
13 Cedars Row, Lavender Hill, Clapham Junction

Southwell, F.
448 Battersea Park Road, Battersea
11 High Street, Wandsworth
Spagliardi, L.
111 Grove Lane, Camberwell
Spencer, E. D.
Penn House, East Hill, Clapham Junction
187 High Street, Borough
Spencer, Ernest
7 Station terrace, New Southgate
Sprinz
21 Arundel Square, Barnsbury
Standard Portrait Studio
300 Euston Road, Euston
Star, John, & Co.
Cambridge Villa, 108 Seven Sisters Rd.
60 High Street, Stoke Newington
Star Portrait Co.
449 Battersea Park rd., Battersea
Starling & Bergman
Bowater Place, Blackheath
Stembridge, Ernest
185 City Road, Finsbury
Stent
8 Bruce Place, 250 High Rd., Tottenham
Stiles, H. & R.
125 Hammersmith Rd., Hammersmith
Stiles, Henry
4 Munden Terrace, Hammersmith
Stone, W. G.
290 The Grove, Stratford
Storey, E. A.
87 Newington Green Road, Kingsland
Stuart, F. G. O.
4 Hamlet Terrace, Norwood
Stuart, R.
89 Park Street, Camden Town
Stuarts Photo Studios
159 High Road, Balham
Stubbs, T.
Weston Street, Pentonville
Sulman & Co.
804 Holloway Road, Upper Holloway
Sunderland, James
75 St. Pauls Churchyard, City

Sutchfield, G. M.
Hannibal Road, Stepney
Swanlund, A.
High Road, North Finchley
Swanwick, F.
High Road, Tottenham
Syrus
209 Kings Cross Road, Kings Cross

T

Tayler, C. B.
Brixton Rise, Brixton
Taylor, A. & G.
Forest Lodge, London Rd., Forest Hill
Tyalor & Harrison
4 Stanley Terrace, Bermondsey
Taylor & Rich
232 Seven Sisters Road, Finsbury Park
Taylor Brothers (*)
48 High Holborn
286 The Parade, Kilburn
Tear, R. H.
Kingston Road, Wimbledon
Teffer, E.
12 Churchfield Road, Acton
Tempany & Co.
162 Bishopsgate Street without, City
Temple Photo Company
170 Fleet Street, City
Thomas, W. F.
11 South Street, Greenwich
Thompson, J. E.
31 King Street, Hammersmith
Thorpe, H. C.
Church Street, Edmonton
Threadwell, C.
288 High Street, Stratford
Tomlin
12 Arthur Road, Holloway
Toulmin & Gale
7 New Bond Street, Westminster
Tower Bridge Photo Company
45 Union Road, Rotherhithe
Tower Bridge Approach, Tower Bridge

Tower Hamlets Portrait Salon
144 Whitechapel Road, Whitechapel
Townshend, C.
415 Strand, Westminster
Treble, Charles F.
373 Brixton Road, Brixton
270 Lavender Hill, Clapham Junction
20 Queen Parade, Clapham Junction
Treble & Son
371a Brixton Road, Brixton
Trew & Co.
238 Seven Sisters Road, Finsbury Park
Truckle, G.
Campden house, Wimbledon
Tune & Co.
High rd., Near Park Lane, Tottenham
Tune, Charles
Tottenham High Road

Tune's studio was opened some time after 1871
and was run until Tune's death in 1887. His wife
continued with the studio for a period. He
started as a photographer in Birmingham from
the mid-1850s until 1868 when he left for
Boulogne in France.

Turnbull
294 Holloway Road, Holloway
Turner, W.
1 Clarence Place, High St., Camberwell
134 Wansworth Road, Vauxhall
Tutt & Co.
234 High Road, Tottenham

U

Universal Photo Company
16 Furnival Street, Holborn
25 The Pavement, Clapham Common
Upjohn, R.
135 Edgware Road, Paddington

V

Vandyk, C.
41 Maxilla Gardens, Nottinghill

Vernon, A. H.
146 Stoke Newington Rd., Shacklewell
Victoria Photo Co.
295 Edgware Road, Paddington
Villiers
391 Hackney Road, Bethnal Green
Voy
8 Eton Terr., Church Rd., Willesden

W

Wakefield
1 High Street, Ealing
Walker, C. B.
6 Oak Villas, Lullington Rd., Upper Norwood
Walker, Geo. P.
162 Sandringham Rd., Hackney
Walker, J. R.
25 Meredith Street, Clerkenwell
Walker & Co.
176 Upper Street, Islington
Wallich, Dr.
Trevor House, 2 Warwick Gdns., Kensington
Walter, R.
322 Upper Street, Islington
Walton, H.
Palace Parade, Fulham Palace Rd., Fulham
Ward, Mr H. & Mrs
346 Battersea Park Road, Battersea
54 Brixton Rd., 19 Spencer Place, Brixton
421 Kings Road, Chelsea
287 Walworth Rd, 5 Beckford Rw., Walworth
131 High Street, Willesden Green
Warer & Co.
64 Powis Street, Woolwich
Plumstead
Waring, F. W.
41 Trafalgar Road, Greemwich
Warlich, F. H.
111 Grove Lane, Denmark Hill, Camberwell
Watson, W.
11 Spencer Road, Holloway
Watson, William
Church End, Finchley

Wayland, Henry
Rembrandt House, Blackheath
Streatham
Webber, ALfred J.
High Road, Lower Clapton
Webber, Charles E.
887 High Road, Leytonstone
Webber, Henry
Kirkdale House, High Rd., Leytonstone
Weber, A., & Co.
23 Station Road, South Norwood
Wellings, J.
Rye Lane, Peckham
Werner, M.
6 Edgware Road, Westminster
West, W.
9 railway Terrace, Forest Gate
West End Photographic Co. (*)
Maurice Batiste & Son
369 Edgware Road W.
516 Oxford Street W.
West London Photo Studio
204 Kings Road, Chelsea
West London Photo Co.
Near Railway Station, Brixton
54 Daling Road, Hammersmith
Westbourne Studio
Kensington Gardens Square, Bayswater
Whitcher, J.
Broadway, Stratford
White, A. E.
27 Riversdale Road, Highbury
White & Co.
31 The Pavement, Clapham
Wiedhofft, F.
358 Romford Road, Forest Gate
Wilkinson, R. E.
57 Queens Road, Peckham
Wilkinson Brothers
High Street, Ealing
Willett & Corles
Parsonage Row, High St., Newington Butts
Williams, A.
26 Broadway, Crouch End
Williams, A.
Muswell Hill

Williams, A.
Hornsey
Williams, H, & Son
222-224 Grays Inn Road, Clerkenwell
Wilmott, Joseph
30 High Street, Norwood
Windser, Douglas F. P.
91 Regent Street, Westminster
Windsor
52 King William Street, City
Windsor, R.
213 The Grove, Hammersmith
Wing, Adolphus
91 Churchill Road, Kentish Town
Winter & Parsons
80 Craven Park Road, Harlesden
Wood, R. J.
272 Brockley Road, Brockley
Woodbridge, Arthur
587 Seven Sisters Road, South Tottenham
Wright, W.
21 Broadway, Stratford
232 Mare Street, Hackney
71 Green Lanes, Shacklewell
Wright, W. Edward
2 Linden Villas, Field Road, Forest Gate
65 Woodgrange Road, Forest Gate
223 Hoe Street, Walthamstow
1 Sebert Road, Forest Gate
254 High Road, Leyton
Pembroke Road, Seven Kings
Wright, C., & Co.
153 King Street, Hammersmith
Wykeham Studio
98 Balham High Road, Balham

X, Y

XL Photographic Co.
34 Pentonville Road, Pentonville
Yendall, J.
246 Regent Street, Westminster
Yeulett, Victor C., & Co.
188 Norwood Road, Norwood

APPENDIX 2: Photographer Listings

RPS HISTORICAL GROUP

The Royal Photographic Society's Historical Group is undertaking a research project documenting photographers in towns and cities across the United Kingdom. This book forms a contribution to that project. To date nearly thirty listings have been published by the group and further titles will appear when the necessary research has been completed and funds are available to permit publication. Any serious photographic researcher is strongly advised to contact the group at the address below. The group publishes the quarterly *PhotoHistorian* and supplements and holds monthly meetings from September to June in London.

Photographer listings published to date are noted below. To obtain copies or an up to date list of those available contact the group's Publications Secretary, at the Historical Group, Royal Photographic Society, 46 Milsom Street, Bath BA1 5DN. England.

Abingdon 1863-1909,
Altrincham & Sale 1860-1939
Bath 1841-1910
Birmingham 1842-1914
Brighton 1841-1901
Cardiff 1855-1920
Cheltenham 1841-1914
Colchester and North Essex 1845-1937
Devon 1842-1939
Dorset 1855-1920
Doncaster 1842-1938
Dyfed 1857-1920
Eastbourne 1877-1910
Glasgow 1842-1908
Gloucester 1857-1914
Hastings, St Leonards & Bexhill 1852-1910
Herefordshire 1856-1913
Kingston-upon-Hull & Beverley 1845-1910
Kingston-upon-Thames 1854-1911
Leeds 1842-1900

Leicester 1844-1910
Lincolnshire 1844-1910
Liverpool 1851-1900
Manchester 1840-1900
Nottingham 1841-1900
Oxford 1842-1910
Sheffield and Rotherham 1842-1900
Shropshire 1842-1913
Staffordshire (north) 1850-1940
Watford 1862-1913
Wigan 1853-1925
Worcestershire 1851-1920
York 1844-1913

INDEPENDENT PUBLICATIONS

A world bibliography of directories of photographers compiled by Richard Rudisill appeared in Peter E. Palmquist (1991), *Photographers: A Sourcebook for Historical Research.* Carl Mautz Publishing, Brownsville, CA.

Cornwall and Scilly 1839-1870. Charles Thomas (1988), *Views and Likenesses. Early Photographers and their Work in Cornwall and the Isle of Scilly 1839-1870.* Royal Institution of Cornwall, Truro.
Essex 1845-1937. David and John Appleby (1992), *The Magic Boxes. Professional Photographers and their Studios in North Essex 1845-1937.* Essex Record Office, Chelmsford.
Hertfordshire Photographers 1839-1939. Bill Smith and Michael Pritchard (1985). Privately published, Stevenage.
Ireland. Edward Chandler (1991) 'Early Irish Pioneers 1839-1850' in *The PhotoHistorian* No. 92 Spring 1991, pp. 20-28. A. D. Morrison-Low (1990). 'A Brief Survey of Nineteenth Century Photography in Ireland' in Pritchard, Michael (editor). *Technology and Art. The Birth and Early Years of Photography. RPS Historical Group, Bath.*

Isle of Wight. Raymond V. Turley (1992) 'Some Isle of Wight Photographers 1850-1940' in *The PhotoHistorian* No. 97 Summer 1992, pp. 40-45.

Manchester 1901-1939. Available from Manchester Photography Archive, Cavendish House, Cavendish Street, Manchester. M15 6BG.

Paisley, Scotland. Don McCoo (1986), *Paisley Photographers 1850-1900*, Foulis Archive Press, Paisley.

Scottish Photography including references to individual photographers, in Sara Stevenson and A. D. Morrison-Low (1990), *Scottish Photography: A Bibliography 1839-1939*. Salvia Books and Scottish Society for the History of Photography, 1990.

Wiltshire. Martin Norgate. *et.al.* (1985), *Photographers in Wiltshire*. Wiltshire Library and Museum Service, Trowbridge.

York 1844-1879. Hugh Murray (1986), *Photographs and Photographers of York. The Early Years 1844-1879.* York Architectural and York Archaelogical Society, York.

PICTURE LIBRARY/MUSEUM CONTACT ADDRESSES

The following picture libraries/museums have substantial holdings of work or archive material relating to London studios which have been referenced in the text. Other institutions such as the Museum of London also have major holdings of general London photographs.

Barnados, Archivist, Tanners Lane, Barkingside, Ilford, Essex IG6 1QG. Tel: 081-550 8822.

Hulton Deutsch Collection, Curator, Unique House, 21-31 Woodfield Road, London W9 2BA. Tel: 071-266 2660.

National Monuments Record, Kemble Drive, Swindon SN2 2GZ. Tel: 0793 414600.

National Portrait Gallery, Heinz Archive and Gallery, St Martin's Place, London WC2H 0HE. Tel: 071-306 0055.

Victoria and Albert Musem, Photographs Collection, South Kensington, London SW7 2RL. Tel: 071-938 8500.

Zoological Society of London, Librarian, Regent's Park, London NW1 4RY. Tel: 071-722 3333.